START
PULLING
YOUR
CHAIN!

START
PULLING
YOUR
CHAIN!

LEADING RESPONSIVE
SUPPLY CHAIN TRANSFORMATION

DONALD J. BOWERSOX AND
NICHOLAS J. LAHOWCHIC

OGI Enterprises LLC
Port St. Lucie, Florida

Published by OGI Enterprises LLC
Port St. Lucie, Florida

Publisher's Cataloging-in-Publication Data
Bowersox, Donald J.

Start pulling your chain : leading responsive supply chain transformation / Donald J. Bowersox and Nicholas J. LaHowchic. – Port St. Lucie, FL : OGI Enterprises, LLC, 2007.

p. ; cm.

ISBN: 978-0-9800896-0-8

1. Leadership. 2. Organizational effectiveness. 3. Business logistics. 4. Organizational change. I. LaHowchic, Nicholas J. II. Title.

HD57.7.B69 2007
658.4092—dc22   2007940719

Project coordination by Jenkins Group, Inc
www.BookPublishing.com

Printed in the United States of America
12 11 10 09 08 • 5 4 3 2 1

Dedications

To my wife and best friend, Terry, who has spent countless hours of our retirement with me working in my office on this manuscript. She is, in every way a great colleague and supporter, who has provided significant intellectual content and encouragement for my contributions to this book.

—Don Bowersox

And

To my life partner, Diane, who has always been my greatest supporter and who has been wonderful counsel sharing her talents and time during the writing, production, and distribution of our book.

—Nick LaHowchic

Acknowledgments

Having had the joy of working with Nick on his first book, I would quickly agree to do it all over again. Nick is a strong and creative leader with an unyielding passion for supply chain management. It has now been more than 40 years since the National Council of Physical Distribution (NCPDM), the predecessor organization to the Council of Supply Chain Management Professionals (CSCMP), was founded. I was a young man when I had the opportunity to be included as part of the founder group. The founders' foresight and enthusiasm for what has become supply chain management has guided my career. During four-plus decades, I had the honor to work with many business leaders who unselfishly devoted their time and resources toward making NCPDM, then CLM, and now CSCMP become a major force in both industry and academia. At Michigan State University, I had the honor to work with a strong faculty and administration that were willing to acknowledge the fledgling disciplines of logistics and supply chain management and to enable research that, over the years, has made a significant difference. Of course, it all started much earlier with a strong and supportive family. When one looks back over a career, it becomes crystal clear that far too many persons contributed to making this book a reality to be able to individually acknowledge each. My gratitude and thanks go out to all.

—Don Bowersox

I have to give my appreciation to Don for asking me to collaborate on this book. I have spent more than half my life striving to carry out the practice of its subject matter. Our journey to complete this book was new to me, but it was such a pleasure to work with him, and I would be happy to do it again in the future. Besides being a great friend for many years, Don continues to enlighten my thinking in supply chain management and business in general. My career has allowed me to experience numerous functional responsibilities within first-rate companies in a number of industries. Throughout all that time, I was fortunate to meet, work with, work for, and become friends with many people who helped me learn and understand—and, at times, who also sponsored my work and passion. These included many of the people I became responsible for and who, in each business encounter, believed in our visions and had faith in our plans and the tenacity of our convictions to achieve many of what we might have thought were dreams. And, when we might have fallen short, they had the humility to understand what we needed to do differently in our next encounter. I too have been a member of CSCMP for many years and have cherished how it helped me to become a better leader and how, through its venue, it accelerated my academic and business learning experiences. I also have to acknowledge the many business associates I have learned from in each industry, association, and company, without whom my journey would not have been as complete and rewarding. Last, I am eternally grateful for the support of my family, Diane, Tara and Nicole who always are my biggest supporters. To all above, I owe my greatest appreciation.

—Nick LaHowchic

As coauthors, we acknowledge that a great deal of support is necessary to make a book reality. In particular, Ralph Drayer was willing to work with us at an early state of manuscript planning and development. Ralph also was willing to contribute "A Preface of a Practitioner," which is included in the front of this book. Many who have made supply chain a reality were quoted throughout the book and their contributions footnoted. We appreciate the contribution of our book producer, the Jenkins Group, and, specifically, Bob Robbins, Leah Nicholson, and Nikki Stahl. Devon Ritter served as our editor and did an outstanding job helping with the clarity of our presentation. We appreciate the contribution of Darren Cranford, who created original art to accompany the introduction of each part of the manuscript. Our thanks go to David Frayer and his team at Michigan State University Executive Development Programs for assistance in the development of book illustrations. Finally, we wish to acknowledge the marketing contribution and logistical support of Rick Blasgen and all his associates who make CSCMP the leading global supply chain management professional association.

With so much able assistance, it is difficult to offer excuses for any shortcomings that appear. However, any faults are solely our responsibility.

Donald J. Bowersox
Nicholas J. LaHowchic

Contents

Preface of a Practitioner

Transformation . . . easier said than done but mission critical in today's highly connected digital economy. Successful companies in the twenty-first century will be those that exploit Web-based information technology and drive the use of collaboration to more strategically transform their supply chains, delivering differentiated capability, value, and competitive advantage in the process.

When viewed in context with today's consumer-driven marketplace and the light speed changes in consumer preferences, behaviors, and shopping options, the need and opportunity for advantage through supply chain transformation should be compelling.

The model for creating value has changed. Today, companies have highly desegregated value chains, where the majority of operational efficiencies and revenue enhancement opportunities can come only from greater visibility, integration, and synchronization among companies in a value network. Real-time responsiveness and collaboration outside the physical walls of the enterprise are the new arenas for value creation. These are in turn powering revolutionary new value propositions that delight customers while delivering exceptional economics and sustainable differentiation to the innovator.

The book you are holding describes the transformational capabilities of the responsive supply chain business model along with a comprehensive four-stage leadership transformation process map. It is a unique and valuable compilation of important learnings and best practices to help you avoid the pitfalls and accelerate the entire implementation process. As one of the early supply chain transformation pioneers who collected a few arrows in the back on the path to victory, I can attest to its value!

A foundational principle of supply chain management is that significant leverage can be obtained by working with suppliers and customers as if they were part of an integrated, seamless pipeline. Enabled with today's information technology, the dream of supply chain transparency and real-time interaction with all trading partners has become a reality capable of producing unprecedented, seamless, and continuous exchanges across the supply chain. What has been needed is an integrative framework in order to leverage and transform how twenty-first-century information technology is applied to improving essential supply chain work.

Significant efficiencies can be gained by linking the supply chain and removing unnecessary inventory, variation, and cost and reducing cycle times to create an "extended enterprise." In an extended enterprise environment, the sharing of information leads to commonality of goals, increased velocity of trade, and meshing of business processes. With this more robust collaborative commerce platform, the emphasis shifts from simply connecting partners (mostly transaction oriented) to coordinating interbusiness processes. This is key because coordination is more knowledge, and process orientation. Synchronization at this level creates more value across the chain. Case in point: the entire "lean" management concept depends on input from all links in the value chain to function successfully.

The responsive supply chain business model enables companies working together for mutual benefit to leverage each other on an operational basis so that together, they perform better than they could separately. Transformational opportunities can occur all along the value chain, from design collaboration through procurement to final distribution. This allows companies sharing information to dramatically shorten processing time, eliminate value-depleting activities, and improve quality, accuracy, and asset productivity.

Exploiting the full potential of the responsive supply chain business model demands radical changes in thinking and behavior in how business operations are conducted. There is no silver bullet. The key is good business process integration and customer focus. This requires clear consumer value identification, thinking externally, and viewing your supply chain as a strategic differentiator able to exploit the use of omnipresent, timely, and accurate data across the supply chain.

"Start pulling your chain" and welcome to the path forward in the twenty-first century!

Ralph W. Drayer
Founder and Chairman
Supply Chain Insights LLC &
Former Chief Logistics Officer
The Procter & Gamble Company
ralphdrayer@aol.com

Author Prologue

There is an old adage: "You can't push a string." As children, many of us were asked to "push" a string, only to see it buckle from the resistance of friction. It is equally or perhaps more difficult to push a chain. However, since the beginning of civilization, that is exactly what business leaders have been doing—organizing and leading talented organizations to push products along the supply chain to market. And, each time the chain buckles or kinks, we have traditionally established inventories and/or administrative resources to overcome the resistance. Twenty-first-century information technology is creating a new paradigm. It is becoming increasingly possible to establish customer connectivity and, as a result, redirect human and physical resources, thereby allowing products to be *pulled* to market. This book is about the transformation needed in today's best general business and supply chain practices to adopt and exploit the far-reaching potential of twenty-first-century information technology. It's about "pulling" the kinks out of organizational and physical supply chains.

Transformation! It seems that almost every time a business leader decides to change a function, a process, or an organization or to implement a new go-to-market strategy, the initiative is labeled "leading a transformation." Calling routine change a transformation seems to add a climate of urgency and importance. After all, transformation implies significant change. Accordingly, numerous books and articles have focused on the strategy and tactics of all types of transformations. The term "transformation" rivals "technology" and "collaboration" as the most-used word in the fledgling twenty-first-century business vocabulary.

However, from our perspective, never has senior leadership confronted a more daunting challenge or a greater opportunity. An abundance of insightful information exists throughout its supply chain, and the time is now to properly rethink how a company should be organized, behave, and direct concurrent process to successfully grow and prosper. Additionally, recent and projected economic expansion in countries throughout the world, concerning manufacturing and sale of finished goods and services or purchase of materials and components, has ushered in a truly global economy. This global state of affairs is best described as "connected"—connected in the sense that traditionally isolated areas of the world are now linked in terms of both day-to-day economic activity and near-instantaneous communication. Global connectivity is a direct result of widespread access to optic-fiber Web-based technology.

We are convinced that the first decade of the twenty-first century represents the beginning of a transition from the Industrial Age to the global connectivity of the Information Age. Global connectivity will continue to redefine and reshape business organizations and operations for the next several decades. A direct parallel exists between the social and the economic transformations that followed the Agricultural and the Industrial revolutions. True transformations are periods of significant and permanent disruption in the way we think, live, and work. We believe that traditional business organization models and leadership behavior can and must radically change to survive and prosper in this new order of global affairs. One aspect of this change that we believe to be essential is the need for comprehensive reinvention of what is considered today's best supply chain management practice.

While information technology sophistication has been making a significant impact on business structure and behavior, another, or what one might call a parallel, development has also been occurring. In approximately the last half of the twentieth century, a new approach to integrated operations became visible throughout business. This new approach evolved to better accommodate a world where accepted Industrial Age practices no longer produced the expected outcomes required by more discerning and engaged consumers. This new approach, integrated supply chain management, began to emerge in the 1950s. By the late 1990s, insightful business leaders became increasingly aware of the fundamental need to address end-to-end or integrated management of customer relationships, manufacturing, procurement, and logistics as a single integrated process. Integrated supply chain management has become a widely acknowledged academic discipline. However, the successful implementation of supply chain management across industry continues to lag. Many business leaders mistakenly see supply chain management as involving a modification of or an addition to traditional business functions rather than a need for developing and implementing a new business model. Comparatively few firms have implemented a business model recognizing cross-functional real-time interdependence and shared decision making across the business operations of both the enterprise and its collaborative suppliers and customers.

The combination of real-time global Web-based information technology and supply chain management has created a synergy capable of driving a new and innovative best practice integrative culture. Information connectivity is freeing business and supply chain operatives from their traditional dependence on forecasting. However, it also requires new collaborative behavior and attitudes throughout the company and between its supply chain partners. The time pulse of supply chain operations is swinging from an anticipatory to a response-based posture. This change from anticipatory to responsive builds on the emerging capabilities of information tech-nology. The basic paradigm of supply chain operations is shifting from a push to a pull culture.

Exploiting this basic paradigm shift constitutes the dawning of a new business model. This new model offers the capability to radically redefine today's best practices throughout total companies while achieving unprecedented levels of operational efficiency, effec-tiveness, relevancy, and sustainability. We have selected to call the emerging solution "the responsive supply chain business model."

In some ways, daily supply chain work may appear unchanged. Products still must be shipped via trucks, trains, ships, pipelines, and aircraft, despite unprecedented information connectivity. Whereas it is possible to communicate almost instantly, it still takes a great deal of time to physically move and position inventory throughout the globe. A corporate leader might rightfully ask, "What needs to be changed?" Our answer is "the basic way you position your firm to meet and exceed customer expectations."

The challenge is fundamental to business success. It is the chal-lenge of positioning, organizing, and governing a supply chain to exploit digital technology to achieve maximum connectivity and responsiveness to increasingly sophisticated customers. It is all about bringing a twentieth-century enterprise to a level of operational excellence made possible by twenty-first-century information tech-nology. Few firms have completed the essential transformation jour-ney. Many are implementing incremental change but have not rein-vented the basic governance and operating posture throughout their enterprise. Others have started down various serial paths but have misgauged the degree of change necessary to achieve and sustain a new company operating culture. Others have simply failed. Thus, for most traditional firms, sustainable transformation of an entire enterprise and its supply chain collaborators remains an important challenge on their leadership and business strategy agenda.

Of significance to this book is an effort to better understand the far-reaching implications and synergy of these two fundamental changes within the context of a complete enterprise—namely, digital information technology and overall supply chain responsiveness—as they are intersecting during the first decade of the twenty-first century. A responsive supply chain is all about achieving and exploiting unprecedented levels of customer connectivity. We believe that defining and enabling organizations to exploit real-time ubiquitous global connectivity represents an opportunity and a challenge equal to or greater than those afforded by the new technologies that spawned from the Industrial Revolution. Understanding that only a limited number of senior leaders have in-depth experience in both information technology and supply chain, we wrote this book to provide insight into the great opportunity and necessity of undertaking an enterprise-wide responsive supply chain transformation.

Part One
Awareness

Scoping the Potential of Responsive Supply Chains

This book about twenty-first-century supply chain leadership is written in the context of the successes and failures business leaders have experienced as they have dealt with the rapidly emerging Information Age. The leadership challenge is all about learning how to use twenty-first-century Web-based technology to institutionalize supply chain collaboration. Thus far, the track record is less than outstanding. The supply chain provides the collaborative framework and, when combined with Web-based technology, is driving the emergence of a new business model. We have selected to refer to this new framework as the responsive supply chain business model. It is a pull model grounded in the inclusive technology of the Information

Age that seeks global competitive superiority based on responsiveness to customer demand.

We joined forces to write this book because we believe business is in transformation. The origins or seeds of most topics discussed can be observed in contemporary business practice. Typically, when faced with disruptive technology, business leaders have difficulty in planning and implementing the necessary transformation. However, transformation is essential in an increasingly digital global economy to navigate a firm's stormy passage from the Industrial Age to the Information Age. While transformation has been under way for several years, it began to assume avalanche proportions as the Internet ushered in the dawning of technology-networked business.

While many business teams have initiated transformations, most have achieved less than satisfactory results. Most leaders felt that new technology would satisfy the operational needs of their organizations. A typical mistake was to underestimate the extent of fundamental change necessary in their organizational structure and existing practices. Most failed to take full advantage of Web-based technology.

Today's business observer views firms trying to transform from old-school, domestic "brick-and-mortar" entities into agile global enterprises. While there is no transformation blueprint or cookbook available for senior leaders to follow, early vanguards have forged a creative path forward. Senior leaders can gain valuable insight by studying the experiences reported by those who have begun the journey and by learning from their mistakes.

Chapter One

Competing in the Information Age

On February 10, 2006, the last Western Union telegram had been sent. The permanent termination of a service that had continuously operated since 1861 was announced using an e-mail. Few noticed or seemed to care. Most in Generations X and Y had never sent or received a telegram.

While recently dining on the deck of a harbor-side restaurant, the authors and their spouses enjoyed a world-class Lake Michigan sunset. People of all ages gathered to enjoy the sunset because it was spectacular. Many were taking pictures and sharing instant results with their companions. In a matter of minutes, scores of pictures had been taken, shared, and most erased. Only the best of the best pictures were retained. Throughout the picture taking process, cell phones were being used alternately to complete calls and to take pictures. Of interest was a Detroit Tigers fan using his cell phone to watch, and update for those concerned, the play-by-play telecast of the Tiger-Twins game currently under way in Minnesota. Wireless connectivity (Wi-Fi) was operative, with photos being shared with others in less fortunate locations throughout the globe. At a corner table, a Blackberry or a Sidekick was serving its master by messaging a colleague at some distance away. Because of the serious nature of the person involved, the conversation could easily have been a consultation concerning a critical medical procedure under way at a local or distant hospital. A careful look at a semi-bored teenager in the corner revealed an iPod saving the moment by allowing her to listen to a favorite tune, most likely selected from a digital library containing thousands of songs.

In today's digitally connected world, it's not hard to imagine even more forms of twenty-first-century technology that could have been actively in use on the restaurant deck. For example, to the best of our knowledge, no one present was participating in a chat room, nor was anyone creating or commenting via a blog. But, someone could have been because wireless service was available. Despite the beautiful sunset, the scene was far from a Kodak moment—in fact, Kodak, a firm currently engaged in major transformation, most likely didn't manufacture or market any of the products being used on the deck. What we experienced that evening was the reality of a connected, multitasking digital world simultaneously at rest, at work, and at play. Is there any doubt that the Information Age has arrived and that the twenty-first century is rapidly becoming increasingly different from the past? Can one deny that we have, in fact, become a highly connected digital economy?

The twentieth-century change experience, for the most part, was one of living out the natural progression of the Industrial Revolution. Most agree that the origins of the Industrial Revolution can be traced to the textile industry in Great Britain in the late eighteenth century. However, it was more than 70 years before the true forces of industrialization began to change the way we thought, worked, and lived. Most middle-age and older adults grew up in a twentieth-century culture that demanded substantial justification and testing before undertaking change. Technology adoption was gradual, and change was relatively slow. Adopters of the industrial technology progression required that most new inventions prove they would result in social and economic betterment. Technology characteristic of the Industrial Revolution was generally perceived as achieving more and more desirable results (effectiveness) for less and less total effort (efficiency). Across the decades, the Industrial Revolution translated into the highest standard of living ever known to the human race. However, the twentieth century is gone!

Having a life experience limited to the past couple of decades of the twentieth century, most members of Generation Y are accustomed to continuous and radical change.[1] They were born after cell phones became common and are not surprised by the functional progression of what they consider normal communication. In short, they have never heard of crank-operated phones, party lines, and switchboard operators. Compared to those of their parents, and even more so to those of their grandparents, their change experiences have been mostly radical instead of gradual. Most change has been positive. All such changes have come at a rapid pace. As a result of positive enforcement, most of the younger generations embrace change without question. Likewise, they do not require total understanding of the origins of change or what might be the ultimate consequence such change will have on what they do or how they do it. They are confident that mistakes can be redirected into progress. Such is the mind-set of our emerging twenty-first-century business leaders. A willingness to adopt technology and, if necessary, radically change traditional practice to exploit such technology may well turn out to be our global society's saving grace.

Thomas Friedman's mind-stretching essay "The World Is Flat" captures the dynamic changes that characterize the new global era.[2]

---

[1]   Since World War II, it has become fashionable to label generations by their dominant characteristics. Those born after 1946 are referred to as "baby boomers." Their children, known as Generation X, are currently approaching their forties. The next generation, commonly referred to as Generation Y, is the technology-savvy generation that taught its parents how to use computers. Finally, the most recent generation is known as the Now Generation because of its desire for instant gratification driven by expectations from having been born in the Information Age.

[2]   Thomas L. Friedman, *The World Is Flat* (New York: Farra, Straus and Giroux, 2006).

In terms of connectivity, he views the world as having shrunk from small to tiny. He eloquently describes "Globalization 3.0," wherein people, products, and ideas flow freely across boarders and new communication technologies and business processes create a new global platform for sharing knowledge and work across time and distance. While totally agreeing with Friedman's description of the magnitude and far-reaching implications of rapidly occurring global change, those of us deeply committed to researching, teaching, and managing real-world supply chains know that existing business models and related best practices are inadequate to fully exploit twenty-first-century technology potential. Those who live in the reality of today's supply chain know that the dream of products flowing freely throughout the globe is in stark contrast to what really happens at ports, in and between warehouses, and along the highways, railways, and waterways of the world.

Friedman includes "supply-chaining" as one of the 10 key "flatteners" facilitating the convergence of political, technological, and process-orientated forces to create a new order of global affairs. Using Wal-Mart as an example, one gets the notion that successful change is more or less achieved by the application of power and determination. The Wal-Mart business model has clearly revolutionized our understanding of how logistics can be deployed to leverage corporate success. The reality is, however, that the purpose of day-to-day supply chain work has not changed much since the beginning of civilization. How the supply chain does its daily work changed significantly as a result of the Industrial Revolution and is currently on the verge of once again changing dramatically as we navigate the Information Age. As elaborated in the forthcoming pages, much is changing in terms of both currently perceived supply chain best practices and associated leadership challenges.

A demonstration often used in elementary school serves to illustrate the fundamental information-technology-driven change occurring in supply chain management. Many teachers use a string to demonstrate ease and resistance when applying energy to movement. While it is very easy to "pull" a string along a surface, it is impossible to "push" a string even an inch without it buckling or bending. The point of the demonstration is to illustrate that pulling the string overcomes friction, resulting in ease of movement. While, in reality, very few of us would try to push a string, pushing the supply chain is exactly what we have been doing since the beginning of civilization.

Traditional supply chains have been designed to operate in an anticipatory, or a push, mode. The prevailing distribution process is a time-consuming, forecast-driven, volume-orientated, functionally centric consolidation process designed to "push" products to market destinations in anticipation of future demand. The all-too-frequent result of this anticipatory push process is far too much of the wrong inventory being pushed to the wrong markets. This missed alignment of inventory often results in firms using incentives to entice consumers to buy products they have available to sell rather than providing the exact product the customers desire to purchase. A prime example is the widespread use of consumer purchase incentives to sell automobiles that were manufactured to forecast—or what might be better called make a "best guess" of—future customer purchase desires. This traditional anticipatory, or push, practice, true of both domestic and foreign suppliers, has started to change to a responsive, or inventory pull, model across most industries!

A combination of customer connectivity and more responsive supply chain operations will increasingly enable demand sensing to "pull" products to points of desired purchase. In situations where products are built to customer specification, the entire order-to-delivery cycle can be dramatically compressed to allow fast and precise customer accommodation. The information technology enabling rapid demand responsiveness and customer connectivity is becoming more and more available and economical. The time has arrived to stop pushing and start pulling your supply chain.

At the 2005 Aspen Institute Roundtable on Information Technology, 25 thought leaders discussed the broad implications of push versus pull economies. The following definitions capture the fundamental differences between push and pull.

> A "push economy"—the kind of economy that was responsible for mass production in the 20th century—is based on anticipating consumer demand and then making sure that needed resources are brought together at the right place, at the right time, for the right people. A company forecasts demand, specifies in advance the necessary inputs, regiments production procedures, and then pushes the final product into the marketplace and the culture, using standardized distribution channels and marketing.
>
> By contrast, a "pull economy"—the kind of economy that appears to be materializing in online environments—is based on open, flexible production platforms that use networking technologies to orchestrate a broad range of resources. Instead of producing standardized products for mass markets, companies use pull techniques to assemble products in customized ways to serve local or specialized needs, usually in a rapid or on-the-fly process.
>
> In the pull model, companies recognize that trying to anticipate demand is a losing proposition and that, in any case, customers have far more market power than ever before. Small niches of consumer demand, long dismissed or patronized by sellers, are a growing market force unto themselves.

They can increasingly induce sellers to develop specialized products and services to serve narrow and time specific market demands.[3]

The twenty-first-century managerial challenge is one of assessing the far-reaching implications of this basic economic shift for supply chain structure and strategy.

As the power of twenty-first-century information technology is applied to supply chain operations, most twentieth-century best practices will dramatically change. The technology is here today to support such massive change. Business managers capable of innovative change are moving into positions of senior leadership. What is lacking is an integrative framework to leverage and transform how twenty-first-century technology can be applied to improving essential supply chain work. The authors and many others believe that such a framework exists in the responsive supply chain business model.

Emerging business leaders need to develop new mental models and visions of their future business operations in order to avoid marginalizing the potential of rapidly emerging technology. They needed to develop a sustainable curiosity about how to best exploit the Information Age. For better or worse, the twenty-first century will not be business as usual.

Entering the twenty-first century, we face a new, different, and more pervasive wave of change. This change force represents the first shockwaves of the Information Age. Many additional shocks are sure to follow. Even at this early date, the Information Age is characterized by a growing presence of disruptive technology (DT). DT is a new innovation or invention appearing to have great potential but one that does not fit well into existing processes, procedures, or what

---

[3]   David Bollier Rapporteur, "When Push Comes to Pull: The New Economy and Culture of Networking Technology." A report of the Fourteenth Annual Aspen Institute Roundtable on Information Technology. The Aspen Institute: Washington, DC, 2006, p. 4.

is traditionally perceived as best practice. Harnessing the full advantages of DT typically requires significant and innovative behavioral change—something humans are not good at. To fully exploit DT, leaders often have to develop a totally new approach for solving problems—something leaders traditionally have not been good at. In other situations, DT can solve or modify an existing problem, thereby eliminating the need for continued performance of a deeply institutionalized best practice.

DT is not new or exclusive to the Information Age. DT was at the leading edge of the Industrial Revolution. Inventions such as wireless messaging, the light bulb, the cotton gin, the telephone, steam, internal combustion and jet engines, transistors, nuclear energy, silicon chips, and miniaturization were some of the major disruptions associated with the Industrial Age. This earlier disruptive experience reinforces the current point. Harvesting the full benefit of DT requires significant modification of traditional practices in terms of both behavior and measurement—maybe some currently perceived best practices need to be eliminated. For most future leaders, this means that fully exploiting DT will require that the "plug-and-play" technology mentality that emerged during the late twentieth century be abandoned. (A great deal more will be said about the plug-and-play mentality later.)

While much operational development will be needed to bring current supply chain performance to the full potential offered by twenty-first-century technology, three facts seem indisputable.

First, customers are becoming more connected to businesses from which they select to purchase merchandise and services. Along the supply chain, businesses themselves are also being linked by connective information technology. The entire supply chain is simply more connected.

Second, the technology necessary to reinvent and dramatically improve supply chain operational processes is available today. Unlike generations past, wherein technology availability was a future promise, the essentials for achieving both customer and supply chain connectivity are here today and are affordable.

Third, the systems, functions, processes, imagination, and regulatory framework of the twentieth century do not offer an adequate blueprint for leading in the rapidly emerging digital global economy. Leadership in a connected and networked world requires a new framework offering significant modification in what is considered today's best practice. To fully exploit available and emerging technology requires that today's prevailing operational structure and strategy be reinvented. Such reinvention and associated transformation consist of far more intensive change than traditional business process reengineering. What we foresee developing we call the "responsive supply chain business model."

Take, for example, how "time shrinkage" is currently affecting best practices in new product design and development across industries. In the health care industry, new medical devices now move from idea to physical prototype in hours versus weeks. Technology has enabled the replacement of traditional two-dimensional physical drawings by introducing three-dimensional digital CADCAM specifications and prototypes, thereby eliminating previously required teams of engineers, construction molds, and elaborate physical prototypes. Because of the resulting speed and case, new product conceptualization and design now happen in days versus the months required in the past.

The revolution occurring in digital imaging technology is transforming the way the fashion industry performs its commercialization process and related marketing message creation. Using calibrated digital imaging and working at remote locations throughout the globe, fashion designers can validate color and finish specifications to standardize fabric and package design. The result is a dramatic reduction in production time from as many as two months to as little as a few days.

In the opening paragraphs of this chapter, an example of technology deployment taking place during a northern Michigan sunset was used to illustrate a few of the many ways that digital technology is connecting and changing our daily living. Such technology, commonplace to the Y and Now generations, is also turning companies such as Kodak and Fuji, as well as the commercial users of their products and services, on their heads! For example, in high-fashion consumer products and in publishing industries, the process of rendering "camera-ready copy" is being totally reengineered.

What is developing is that virtually the entire method of making and using photos in product design is being replaced with a new digitally based technology that is cheaper, faster, and, most important, better. Using high-quality digital cameras, photographers can repeatedly reshoot products and rapidly finalize a customized image. Additionally, as experienced in cinema, digital photos can be quickly and easily "morphed" to further enhance their viewing image for presentation to targeted consumers. This digital photo production and associated electronic catalog management have revolutionized the speed, variety, and degree of customization available to target unique buyer segments. Catalogs and Web sites are being tailored to specific and relatively small consumer market segments. This connectivity is allowing small but profitable market segments previously neglected to be turned into profitable customers. Such technology-driven practices are becoming commonplace among companies such as Victoria's Secret, Ralph Lauren, Target, JC Penney, and Amazon.com. The above examples of customization can be achieved in real time as consumers use technology to interact with a company.

Thus, wherever we look, examples of changing ways of working, buying, and consuming abound. The early signs of the evolution from push to pull are everywhere. Firms and associated best practices are being reinvented to take advantage of this global transformation. Adapting the ways and means of the responsive supply chain business model is but one part of the digital transformation being driven by twenty-first-century information technology. However, changing the ways and means of how supply chains operate is a vast undertaking.

To fully exploit the benefits of twenty-first-century information technology in the supply chain space, a major structural and philosophical shift is required in how one conducts business operations. The traditional command-and-control structure of individual organizations, as well as the sequential processes characteristic of existing business transactions, will be hard to modify or change sufficiently to accommodate the requirements of a responsive business model. Some observers have long predicted that radical organizational and operational change will be required to exploit emerging technology and warned that such massive change may not be achievable. On the basis of examples from the Industrial Revolution, others believe that the necessary radical change will be accomplished only if existing organizational structures and institutionalized best practices are completely abolished or disintegrated.[4]

While many executives may not be fully sold on the theories of destructive change, achieving twenty-first-century responsive supply

---

[4]   Christopher Meyer and David Power, *Commentary*, "Enterprise Disintegration: The Storm before the Calm" (Lexington, MA: Temple, Baker and Sloane, 1989).

chain leadership is not viewed as an easy goal to accomplish. New mind-sets, methods, and measures must be framed to achieve goals and avoid unintended consequences. While significant change will be required to exploit emerging information technology, we believe that the seeds of new and far-reaching best practices to meet and exploit future challenges can be found among today's leading-edge firms. Building on research and practice, we develop and present a framework to help guide the required change: the responsive supply chain business model. This model offers one perspective concerning how the initial waves of DT associated with the Information Age can, say, between 2007 and 2025, be absorbed and accommodated to radically affect and improve global business performance. A composite of research, experience, and speculation is used to develop a transitional model for competing in the global digital economy.

Of course, business operations represent only one facet of society that will be disrupted by rapidly emerging digital technology. Equal, or more dramatic, changes will simultaneously affect how we practice medicine, how we educate, and how we govern, as well as every other facet of how we live our daily lives. However, on the basis of the initial impact of Information Age technology (1995–2007), it appears that the business community may be one of the most disrupted of today's institutions. The significant change required in processes as fundamental as basic business operations will serve as an ongoing example of just how out of tune some existing best practices are when confronted by the opportunities of a global digital economy.

To adequately shape a process as complex as global supply chain operations requires an in-depth understanding of what is in fact changing. For example, most products are, and will remain, physical and perishable entities subject to potential damage, pilferage, and other forms of destruction. While the content and images of information-based products, such as documents, films, and videos, can be transmitted around the globe at lighting speed, most products need to be physically transported from origin to destination. At least during the foreseeable future, such transport will be performed using twentieth-century methods of transportation, namely, trucks, trains, planes, boats, and pipelines. Such transport takes time and costs a great deal of money. A reasonable estimate is that the global logistics expenditure for 2008 will exceed $8 trillion. Given proliferation of today's practices, global transportation cost alone is projected at more than $5 trillion.[5] To support this costly and time-intensive logistical process will require maintaining approximately $4 trillion of inventory, at an annual cost of approximately $1 trillion in interest, storage, handling, insurance, obsolescence, damage, and theft. While these are projected costs, they, or similar expenditures, soon will become real costs of doing business. These costs can be favorably affected and reduced—but not totally eliminated.

Adding to the complexity of contemporary supply chains is the growing amount of counterfeiting taking place in global commerce. The World Customs Organization has estimated counterfeiting to involve in excess of $500 billion of fake goods. Taking positive steps to mitigate the growth of counterfeiting is a major twenty-first-century supply chain challenge.

Thus, the debate is framed: How can an emerging generation of new business leaders facing the challenges and opportunities of the Information Age reinvent traditional operational best practice to favorably exploit the full potential of a responsive supply chain business model? Physical products will still need to be moved from origins to final destinations in a secure, damage-free, and timely manner. Much of the work of supply chain management may be outsourced throughout the globe, but it will not go away. In fact,

[5]   Alexandre M. Rodrigues, Donald J. Bowersox, and Roger J. Calantone, "Estimation of Global Logistics Expenditures: Current Update," *The Journal of Business Logistics* 26, no. 2 (2005): pp. 1–16.

the more global the operational reach of a business, the greater the degree of supply chain reliance and complexity. It is also logical to conclude that physical movement constraints and elapse time required to transport products, components, and materials will continue to serve as operational impediments or barriers.

In order to take advantage of emerging information technology and capitalize on what in fact is happening, business leaders must face the reality that most of their firms as well as their existing supply chain processes are, to a significant degree, operationally obsolete. In early attempts to adopt digital technology, many leaders failed to fully understand the extent of operational change necessary. They felt that integrated software would facilitate the necessary work. In most cases, it did not. The managerial challenge, similar to that faced during the impact stage of the Industrial Revolution, is to reinvent existing business operations. Operational practices and rules need to be reinvented to exploit ubiquitous or omnipresent timely and accurate information. The old business model and its associated value proposition are increasingly inadequate to drive leading-edge performance while confronting head-to-head the challenges and opportunities of the Information Age. All of the required change must be conceptualized and financially supported while the firms involved in transition continue to maintain profitable operations. No sabbaticals are available to excuse business leaders from the need to simultaneously achieve enterprise financial and operational goals while leading a transformation.

While firms that manufacture and sell products face a fundamental transformation challenge in the twenty-first century, firms that provide essential services face the same reality and related challenges. At the 2007 Longitudes conference presented by UPS and Harvard Business School Publishing, Michael L. Eskew, recently retired chairman and CEO of UPS, positioned the overall transformation challenge from the perspective of all global companies and their service providers:

> Consumer pull requires one-to-one solutions and supply chains that can deliver them. The world is no longer driven by producers pushing products through their supply chain. Increasingly, power is in the hands of consumers who now pull products through the system. They pull what they want, when they want it, from whomever they choose anywhere in the world. And consumers want and expect a personal, relevant, individualized experience. This is a big shift that will only intensify.

And then Eskew went on to elaborate his vision of what this basic shift to a pull economy means for UPS and its need to transform.

> UPS is poised to deliver this kind of personal experience by being "one-to-one" with each customer. For UPS, one-to-one means serving each customer as if they are UPS's only customer, and operating as if each transaction is the only transaction and each package is the only package. UPS is focused on this "one-to-one" vision and on a strategy that seeks to help customers synchronize their global supply chains. It is UPS's aspirational view of the supply chain done right.[6]

Clearly, all companies and their service partners are participants in the essential transformation.

Transformation: Getting it and Keeping it Right

The process of leading the business transformation to operationally exploit information technology and benefit from its anticipated disruption in the responsive supply chain space is our subject. In the twenty-first century, firms will continue to seek strategies that

---

[6] *Longitudes 07: Competitiveness and the Global Supply Chain,* June 20–21, 2007, Toronto, Ontario (UPS and Harvard Business School Publishing), p. 5.

combine the benefits of specialization and integration. However, the basic value creation model in a global economy has changed. Some readers might quickly conclude that neither Web-based technology nor supply chain represents a new topic to twenty-first-century senior leadership. Both have significantly affected our business landscape for nearly a decade. What is emerging is a more comprehensive understanding of the appropriate leadership necessary to initiate and sustain a complex organizational transformation. Such a transformation constitutes a fundamental reinvention of the basic way an organization operates. The goal is to maximize the favorable impact of Web-based technology. Initially, many senior executives felt that the challenge could be met by purchasing integrated software, commonly called enterprise resource planning (ERP). While such plug-and-play practices worked in the past, harnessing the scope and power of Web-based technology proved to be more demanding. Most limited transformations failed to meet expectations. To put it bluntly, most simply failed. The unexpected reality is that most twentieth-century organizations need to be reinvented in order to take advantage of twenty-first-century Web-based technology.

Lessons concerning the resources and human capabilities required for success have been learned from the failures and partial successes of early transformations. This book develops a four-stage leadership transformation process or map proceeding from awareness, to ratcheting, to catapulting, to sustainability.

Awareness, Part One, identifies the synergistic opportunities of competing in the Information Age and digitizing. It introduces the responsive supply chain business model. The objective of Part One is to establish awareness and excitement about the opportunity and necessity of supply chain transformation.

Given awareness, Part Two elaborates the managerial challenges related to creating a technology-driven thrust by "ratcheting" the first three imperatives, namely, consumer connectivity, operational excellence, and integrative management. These three imperatives combine to drive a new and market-sensitive perspective concerning the fundamental importance of elevating and maintaining exacting day-to-day performance. Such exacting performance is considered an operational prerequisite for successful competition in the global digital economy. The analogy to "ratcheting" is used to capture the intensity and synergies generated by leading-edge performance. A firm capable of successfully ratcheting is positioned as ready to catapult to performing at the level of a responsive supply chain. The essential leadership challenge is not to get stuck with marginal improvement. The key is to catapult beyond marginal change to achieving a new business model.

By building on the momentum of ratcheting, a leading business is positioned to raise the prevailing industry performance standard. In Part Three, "catapulted" firms are viewed as supply chain orchestration leaders. They are the select firms whose demonstrated customer responsiveness leads or sets the operational standard of excellence for their respective industries. Catapulting is all about exploiting operation competency on the basis of three additional imperatives. These additional imperatives are real-time responsiveness, leveraging networks, and collaboration. It is during the catapulting phase that the potential of global leadership evolves. Firms reaching the lofty distinction of "leading edge" in the Information Age will set new standards concerning what level of performance constitutes world class.

The final three chapters, Part Four, are devoted to the challenges of endurance. Once achieved, maintaining response-based world-class performance requires vigilance concerning what firms do and how they do it. This phase of a transformation is viewed as representing the greatest leadership challenge: sustainability. Sustainability is a long-term proposition requiring continued and renewed leadership. The challenges of sustainability are not the same as those confronted in the first three stages of transformation of an enterprise. Whereas the spirit of leading essential change was the driving force during transformation, sustainability involves day-in and day-out commitment to maintaining and renewing all six transformational imperatives. Individual chapters are devoted to relational leadership, measurement and motivation, and 2025 and beyond. The general thesis is that the emerging leadership model is becoming increasingly inclusive, to involve all levels of employees. Most of the work essential for supply chain excellence occurs outside of the vision of supervision. Flat and globally extended organizations need leadership at all levels of engagement. In a similar vein, driving cross-organizational performance creates the need for new measurement metrics. The main body of the book ends with a chapter devoted to futuristic perspectives. The discussion centers on how the impact of the Information Age is likely to continue to explode on and change business best practice much faster than experienced during its Industrial Revolution predecessor. In the final chapter, the authors speculate concerning some of the initial implications of this rapid emergence.

The overall presentation concludes with a postscript "Initial Steps towards the New Information-Driven Frontier." Unlike all previous chapters, this postscript is framed as a "How to Get It Going" guide. With full realization that business operations must continue to achieve day-to-day operational goals, we designed the postscript to assist senior leadership in developing a plan for initiating responsive supply chain transformation. An appendix provides basic details concerning functional supply chain operations. This appendix provides a person new to the supply chain discipline a fundamental understanding of its operational component.

No individual chapters are devoted to technology. The reason is quite simple—all chapters are about technology. It is perceived in twenty-first-century supply chain as being as ubiquitous as air, water, and oil once were.

Penetrating Questions for C-Level Executives

Is the collaborative enterprise extension described in the responsive supply chain business model practical and needed by my firm? Do we have a handle on what it would take to increase our responsiveness? Is the "pull" concept of operational responsiveness even a viable alternative, given the complexity of our current distribution process? Does this vision fit the future of our firm? Given the challenges discussed, what are the practical limits of change? What bottom-line results will be achieved in the short and long run as a result of transformation? Do we have the relational leadership, curiosity, creativity, organization culture, and sustainability necessary to embrace such a bold journey? Do we have adequate leadership to enable such a change? Are we strategically and culturally aligned and operationally connected to our customers and suppliers to successfully operate this new model and achieve the desired results? What are the pitfalls, short and long term? How do we balance and influence critical capital and human resources to continue to meet current goals while building new capabilities needed for tomorrow's success? How do we get shareholders, Wall Street analysts, and our employees to understand that there may not be an alternative? In starting such a journey, how do we simultaneously pace the changes needed and maintain the necessary organizational mantra to reach the desired destination? What new tensions have to be addressed within and across our organization to succeed? Do we believe that the notion of networked collaboration is real and not just another fad?

The above queries represent some of the penetrating questions an inquisitive CEO might ask the directors and senior leadership team in a well-established but operationally stagnant "brick-and-motor" company. "Stagnant" in the context used here is defined as currently performing at or above industry average.

Chapter Two
Digitizing

> *"Experience teaches that men are so much governed by what they are accustomed to see and practice that the simplest and most obvious improvements in the most ordinary occupations are adopted with hesitation, reluctance and by slow graduations."*
>
> —Alexander Hamilton, 1791

The twenty-first-century model for creating business value has changed. In all likelihood, behaviors capable of maximizing value will continuously change during the next several decades as the full impact of the Information Age unfolds. At the outset, let's clearly position and understand the transformation challenge. The change necessary in a contemporary business is not a consulting project or a one-time improvement initiative. It is the challenge of continually reinventing a business to fully exploit information technology to achieve unprecedented levels of operational excellence. Such transformation requires that collaborative relationships with customers and suppliers be constantly reinvented to achieve and maintain supply-chain-wide connectivity. For short, this transformation journey is called "digitizing."

The challenge of digitizing is to refocus and energize those attributes that originally made individual business enterprises great. These brick-and-mortar businesses were designed to take advantage of Industrial-Revolution-driven technology. These established businesses have great leadership and highly capable human resources. They enjoy financial stability and are positioned to capitalize on solid product and service traditions. These firms have earned, by virtue of past performance, outstanding customer loyalty. In truth, they have only one significant weakness: they are operationally obsolete. As such, they face a growing risk of losing customer loyalty as a result of erratic overall performance.

Senior leadership at firms such as Corning, Motorola, Ford, and General Motors can testify that becoming a digital enterprise is not a destination easily achieved. The leadership challenge is one of reinventing each and every detail of how a business operates. This reinvention must be accomplished while maintaining profitable performance. Most shareholders expect profits and dividends. Change is not high on their agenda. Comprehensive change in a global enterprise is a time-consuming initiative. Fully digitizing a twentieth-century global enterprise could transcend the majority of the careers of newly minted business school graduates. For most firms, the journey may take longer to complete than the time remaining in the career of top-level executives who conceptualize and initially drive the change process. Digitizing is not a quick fix. It is the process of designing and motivating how business operations can be ratcheted and catapulted from the best practices of the Industrial Age to capture new opportunities made possible by the technology of the Information Age. Digitizing is about having the training and capability to continually reinvent how a firm plans, arranges, leads, performs, and measures essential day-in and day-out work. It is also about learning how to effectively collaborate with customers and suppliers.

The barriers to achieving the necessary change are not and will not, for the foreseeable future, be technological. Rather, the major barriers are inadequate leadership visioning and human resistance to change. It is a failure to identify, implement, and sustain behavior modification necessary to achieve leading-edge performance. Today's institutionalized methods of work were identified and perfected decades ago to solve problems that, for the most part, no longer exist. In many situations, these historically innovative methods, typically referred to as best practices, have become major barriers to achieving significant breakthroughs in new and more meaningful ways to work. Across a broad range of business operations, leaders, managers, and workers are far too often assigned and incentivized to perform work that, in final analysis, adds no real customer value. Well-meaning workers, the backbone of any company, can be observed striving to perform traditional work better and better. However, in many situations, the work involved adds no real value for consumers and shouldn't be done at all! To make matters worse, many so-called best practices are often encouraged and reinforced by financial and other incentives to perform such meaningless or sometimes counterproductive work better and faster. Finally, financial investors and Wall Street analysts, with their financial models, have traditionally encouraged and rewarded established practices, provided that overall results meet or exceed short-term sales and earning projections.

In combination, the significant forces discussed above have increased the personal risk of business leaders who confront this need to lead change. In the January 23, 2006, issue of *Business Week*, it was reported that chief executive turnover in 2005 doubled that of the previous year, with 1,322 CEO departures. From 2000 to 2005, the first six years of the new millennium, there were 5,464 CEO departures. The numbers continued to increase in 2006, and by November 2006, 1,112 CEOs were looking for new employment.[1] Who can challenge the conclusion that given the realities of change, either leading or not leading digitizing is risky business?

[1] *Business Week*, January 23, 2006, and November 13, 2006.

The Digitizing Journey

Digitizing requires conceptualizing and implementing new and innovative business operating arrangements that consistently meet and exceed customer expectations. For the individual firm, the goal is to maximize long-term success by virtue of a sustainable commitment to operational excellence. In a connected or networked society, such sustainable performance can be established only by virtue of synergistic collaborative behavior among business organizations aligned to serve customers. To exploit this challenge, business operations must be integrated across collaborating companies and extended globally. This requires establishing and maintaining collaborative relationships with multiple companies to satisfy all targeted customers and a commitment to scoping and exploiting the vastly uncharted and seemingly unlimited capabilities of emerging Web-based information technology.

Digitizing an enterprise involves continually evaluating every facet of every job across the entire supply chain by asking hard questions: Does this specific behavior or action add value for our customers? If so, what is the value proposition, and how can it be maximized? If not, how can we best eliminate the practice and redeploy currently used resources to perform and support more desirable or customer-beneficial behavior?

This reinvention or transformation represents a major part of what digitizing is all about. However, digitizing is about much more than business process reengineering. A successful transformation depends on fully understanding how to organize and lead a business to leverage the power of Web-based communications. Such a communication framework offers an uncharted alternative to the traditional one-to-one, one-to-many, or many-to-one communication models that dominated the twentieth century. The information technology of the twenty-first century provides the capability to implement and conduct business operations within the structure of a "many-to-many" collaborative communication "network." The network potential is a significant force having far-reaching implications that were missed in enterprise resource planning (ERP) design and development.

A many-to-many supply chain architecture offers the potential for all participating in the "network" to simultaneously share identical information across the entire supply chain in real time. "In real time" means, as the word "real" implies, all at once, at the same time, or simultaneously. The advent of simultaneous real-time visibility constitutes an enormous technological breakthrough having far-reaching ramification. Visibility of simultaneous events across a supply chain means that participants responsible for any organized work, regardless of geographical location, do not require the time, effort, and expense traditionally necessary to perform event-driven business communications or associated data collection and transfer.

For example, given simultaneous visibility, order entry, as well as most of the work required to manage the order-to-delivery process of a traditional business, may no longer be needed and has the potential to be eliminated. With exact inventory status being continuously shared between all participants in a network, sequential information transfer steps could be skipped or totally eliminated. It may no longer be necessary to communicate sales or inventory status in order to guide inventory replenishment. Quite frankly, the many-to-many communication model, while technically available today, is something leaders don't have the slightest idea of how to exploit, given existing business operating paradigms.[2]

---

[2] Such a shared-information-based order-to-delivery process is discussed in greater depth in Chapter Eight.

Examples of real-time systems can be observed in such emerging innovative practices as online banking, billing, and payment systems and airline travel reservation systems. All of these connected networks include consumers as at least limited participants. With airline ticketing, consumers can select between various options and book tickets without calling travel agents. This has required airlines to deal with greater complexity as well as provide more transparent pricing. However, at the same time, this connectivity has allowed airlines to deal directly with their customers. Most online systems complete transactions without face-to-face communications and without the benefit of a paper trail. The impact has been revolutionary—for example, online banking has made the branch banks and their many vice presidents near obsolete.

From a business operations perspective, the best examples of multiple-node communication networks are currently found in the downstream operations of large retailers such as Home Depot, Lowe's, Target, and Wal-Mart. These organizations own or control vast operating assets that are supported by information networks designed to facilitate integrated performance. In the manufacturing sector, somewhat similar multienterprise collaborations are emerging in supply base operating arrangements. Some examples of cross-enterprise collaboration are vendor-managed inventory (VMI) and collaborative planning and forecast replenishment (CPFR) between companies and their customers. Tier-one supplier alliances are creating networks of complementary suppliers that provide their common customers a combined- or shared-solution buying opportunity. Network services are emerging in transportation management systems (TMS) wherein firms such as LeanLogistics and Sterling Software host on-demand operating networks enabling multiple shippers and carriers to collaborate in real time. Such collaboration allows shippers and carriers to match movement of goods and services from point to point in a time-definite manner. Meanwhile, United Parcel Service, Federal Express, and other service firms are reinventing traditional for-hire transportation by launching global networks offering real-time tracking and on-demand logistics services. Yes, it seems that things are changing!

As impressive as these early collaborative efforts are, they are somewhat analogous to the Wright brothers' achievements at Kitty Hawk in comparison to modern jet aviation. These initial efforts represent a start, a first, but also a modest step forward when compared with the far-reaching ramifications of a fully functioning many-to-many network.

To fully understand the ramification of "digitizing," consider the following contrast between typical change management and digitizing. In today's business environment, business operations are, by and large, conducted the same way we play and coach sports. In sports, the things we don't change are the number of players on the field or court. Only seldom are the rules changed. Players are, for the most part, allowed to do one thing or play one position on each play. For example, the quarterback leads the play, and all other players have specific assignments. The plays are documented in a playbook, and the goal is winning.

In contrast, digitizing brings into question the fundamental commandments of "how" we compete in business. Fundamental commitments, such as how many people should be on the playing field and what each position should be able to do, become the responsibility of leaders. Once in play, the knowledge ball is everywhere. Team members take turns leading in a networked world, and the playbook is continuously referenced for context so we can adjust the plays in real time.

A digital transformation is not just creating a better playbook. It is continuous redefinition of the rules of the game as well as how we play it. To gain competitive superiority in the twenty-first century, business operations must integrate within and across enterprises bound together in a joint mission to capture ultimate consumer loyalty. In global companies, a single position's responsibilities may have specific accountabilities matrixed across two or more departments or divisions within a company. In short, the traditional organization model has become obsolete.

A digital business makeover requires a far-reaching assessment of how available technology can improve the performance of existing and future operations. Regarding any technology adoption (information or otherwise), the following three fundamental questions must be answered to the satisfaction of the supportive leadership team: How will technology adoption affect (1) consumer relevancy, (2) end-to-end operating efficiency, and (3) sustainable competitive advantage? While the second and third questions may fit most firms' strategic perspective, the first question, concerning consumer relevancy, may be troubling.

A great deal of misunderstanding exists concerning the difference between a customer and a consumer. For all firms engaged in marketing, the only transaction of ultimate importance is one resulting in end user consumption of a product or service. Thus, while product creation and distribution transactions are important to achieving smooth and profitable operations, they are secondary to transactions that result in end user consumption. Every business involved in a supply chain must be interested and engaged in knowing why, how, and when consumers purchase products and services. While basic, this truism seems to have been forgotten in many aspects of existing business operations.

Returning to the three basic questions asked above, unless the answers identify long-term opportunity, the technology implementation and necessary transformation will not justify the pain of adoption. However, if the assessment is positive, then all necessary changes such as functional alignment, reorganization, traditional operational procedures, metrics and measures, and perceptions regarding internally versus externally based performance must be fully examined. Given the comprehensive and far-reaching nature of emerging technology, it is becoming increasingly difficult to perceive an adoption plan that does not justify undertaking end-to-end operational redesign. Here we come face to face with plug-and-play mentality. Perhaps a closer look at past behavior, given the all-seeing vision of hindsight, will yield some understanding concerning why information technology adoption continues to be marginalized.

Y2K: The Shakey Start

It is very difficult to pinpoint just when the Industrial Age ended and when global society began the journey into the Information Age. Information technology has received growing attention from business leaders since shortly following the conclusion of World War II. However, most people did not become fully aware of the disruptive ramifications associated with the Information Age until some time during the late 1990s. To avoid debate, let's assume that the Information Age started to arrive in a meaningful way at some point during the last decade of the twentieth century and was fully under way as the world embraced the first few hours of the twenty-first century. We crossed the first major hurdle when it became clear that the fears of Y2K arrival and widely predicted social and economic disintegration did not in fact materialize. Despite near panic, most businesses and public sector organizations at least limped into the new millennium. Computers, as proven, could be coached (actually programmed) to recognize that a double zero didn't automatically mean that it was once again the start of the twentieth century.

During the following few years, an object of less public fanfare, the Internet, supported by the creation of browsers, search engine software, and the global proliferation of broadband optic-fiber networks, exploded on the business scene to fuel a boom-to-bust e-technology-driven market cycle. The dynamics of the e-driven market cycle attracted global attention and publicity while simultaneously serving to hide and mask the far-reaching ramifications of what was really happening. Only a handful of visionary business leaders and educators seemed to sense that the industrial world was at the threshold of an epic change—the business world was being propelled into the Information Age. Few foresaw the impact such change would soon have on established firms such as Xerox, Corning, Motorola, and IBM, to name but a few corporate icons that soon were forced to accommodate unexpected and unprecedented rates of dramatic change.

Several apparently unrelated events occurred during the first five years of the new millennium that combined to forever change global economics. Occurring simultaneously, these events clouded or obscured widespread realization that the Information Revolution was gaining momentum. During the first half-decade of the twenty-first century, the business environment experienced increased global terrorism, ignited by the first modern-time terrorist attack on U.S. homeland, followed by new global security measures that fundamentally changed rules for travel of people and products everywhere. Significant corporate accounting fraud was followed by passage and initial effort to enforce the 2002 Sarbanes-Oxley Act and finance standards reform that permanently changed accountability for business operations. Our country experienced political fraud and a turbulent national economy, as indicated by a financial market that did not fully recover pre-9/11 Dow average levels until early 2006, only to witness stock markets reach all-time highs by late-2007. Additionally, we experienced renewed military conflict in the Middle East, extensive concern for governmental invasion of personal privacy, and, to top it all off, a series of record-setting natural disasters, including a tsunami in Asia, Hurricane Katrina, and wildfires in Greece. Such was the economic and political footing from which the business sector began to face the initial leadership challenges of the Information Age.

ERP to the Rescue?

Today's digital challenge has intensified as a result of valiant attempts by business leaders to take immediate action once it became clear that permanent change was in the wind. Faced with a growing awareness that their firms were losing ground, many leaders undertook major initiatives to revamp their information technology capabilities during the late 1990s. While these leaders were driven by visions and plans, what lay ahead was a barrage of unintended consequences. The most common or widespread leadership initiative to meet twenty-first-century-perceived business requirements was the purchase and attempted installation of ERP software. ERP packages hit the market in the mid-1990s and promised to facilitate integrated financial accountability and to stimulate cross-functional work processes. All of these promises were to be achieved while also assuring Y2K compatibility. ERP was positioned and sold as the integrated replacement for internally coded functional software, commonly called "legacy" systems. In addition to licensing software for internal use, firms typically contracted with consulting organizations to help install ERP software on upgraded, but soon to be obsolete, computers then called mainframes.

These initiatives cost business multibillions of dollars. In short, business leaders did what had worked in the past—they threw financial resources at the problem. Most firms survived; some didn't. For many firms, the new term "shelf-ware" became part of their operating vocabulary. Shelf-ware being purchased licensed software sitting on a shelf and gathering dust while waiting to be used. In hindsight, the whole ERP era was plagued with at least two leadership issues and two design flaws. It soon became obvious to business leaders that ERP failed to address the far-reaching challenges inherent in the emerging Information Age.

Leadership Issues

The first leadership issue was the continued utilization of traditional work processes and practices to guide the adoption of new technology. Rather than redesigning key value-added processes to fully exploit the new technology, leaders once again followed the traditional practice of deploying new technology to assist and facilitate existing work processes. Few took the time to undertake business process redesign and related organizational changes. Most followed a plug-and-play adoption practice. This adoption practice appeared logical, achieved what appeared would be rapid implementation, and, most of all, didn't rock the boat of either labor or management or challenge the functionally based landscape. However, progress wasn't always what resulted. Many business leaders soon became aware of the full meaning of "unintended consequences."

The most typical result was initial operational discontinuity, followed by no or limited operational improvement. The expenditures to install ERP systems to satisfy prospective financial and/or numeric issues for some firms had the impact of reducing operational functionality. Many modifications did not recognize unique and value-added processes within a business and between business partners. Additionally, at times, the systems modification was not supported by required changes in activity accountability between and among functional organizations within and across firms. Some venturous firms attempted to modify the ERP source code. Many firms were soon forced to return some or all business operations to their well-tested legacy systems. The functional, or silo, approach to management, fine-tuned by the Industrial Revolution, where the new dimension was mechanical and not informational, was reinforced and continued to dominate the practice of early twenty-first-century management. Given the benefit of hindsight, it has become clear that the potential for ERP operational improvement potential was marginalized from the outset.

A second common leadership issue was the widespread failure among business leaders to organizationally position technology responsibility where it could truly benefit a widest base of enterprise information technology users. Since business initially automated payrolls, computers have been the tightly guarded servants of accounting and finance. Business leaders were content to introduce ERP, a potentially powerful integrative operational capability, using their traditional data processing organizational model. Despite the fact that operational managers—marketing, sales, logistics, manufacturing, and purchasing—had, by the late 1990s, become by far the largest users of computers and communication technology resources in a typical business enterprise, computers and information continued to be viewed as integral to financial stewardship. The enactments needed for Sarbanes compliance reinforced this practice. The result was, as one might expect, a new and better generation of integrated financials. However, the impact on business operations proved disastrous.

Many firms were faced with the failure of ERP systems to perform basic and essential functionality, such as order processing and product shipment. In an effort to sustain operations, many firms needed to develop ERP work-arounds. Some purchased supplemental planning and operational software, commonly referred to as "bolt-on systems." Bolt-on, or best-in-class, software was supposedly designed to work in concert with, or hooked on to, ERP systems. The objective of bolt-on functional software was to provide operating capabilities, such as customer relationship management (CRM), manufacturing operating systems (MOS), supply chain event management systems (EMS), transportation management systems (TMS), and warehouse management systems (WMS). The additional functionality of these key operational applications often was not adequate to replicate the full range of unique features built into legacy systems. For a host of reasons, the grand architectural scheme to integrate software didn't work as anticipated for many firms.

Five highly respected firms, Nike, Hershey, Nestle USA, Hewlett-Packard, and Whirlpool, operationally ground to a standstill as they were unable to ship customer orders shortly after they activated their new ERP systems. Hershey and Nestle USA spent in excess of $112 and $210 million, respectively, on ERP systems in order to fully resolve their Y2K compliance issues.[3] Hershey, after activating its systems, failed to ship and deliver retail orders in a timely manner, losing in excess of $150 million in sales during the ERP implementation year. The other companies spent millions of dollars on their ERP projects and had various operational shortcomings in business results that affected their annual profit and market value. The *Wall Street Journal* reported the operational chaos in a featured front-page column.[4]

---

[3]   CIO May 15, 2002; November 15, 2002; and June 15, 2004.

[4]   "Software Glitch Snags Whirlpool," *Wall Street Journal*, November 3, 1999.

Other prominent firms, such as Dow Chemical, Johnson & Johnson, and Kraft–General Foods, spent significant dollars beyond those anticipated in their ERP budgets to "glue" operations together. As noted earlier, many firms were forced to return all or part of their operations to legacy systems. Once again, business was experiencing the pains of plug and play—because more times than not, it didn't "play" and required work-around. The result for those who couldn't financially or operationally hold the course: costly shelf-ware!

Design Issues

While leadership issues occurred with respect to ERP adoption practices, there were also structural problems with the basic design logic of the software. In addition to lacking essential operational capabilities, much of the software itself contained two significant design flaws that are proving to be increasingly disruptive as firms proceed deeper into the twenty first century.

First, ERP product structure, or architecture, was designed to operate on sales or demand-driven forecast logic ("push," or what is often called "anticipatory," logic). The basic architecture functioned in a sequential manner that failed to take advantage of the real-time information becoming increasingly available as a result of emerging Web-based information technology. Such real-time information introduced the potential of developing response, or "pull," supply chains. However, the commitment to a forecast focus caused the entire enterprise to operate on anticipatory logic. The assumption that business leaders can or ever will be able to accurately forecast future sales represents a powerful leap of faith after so many decades of trying without much success. This anticipatory planning focus, while not critical to collecting information for accounting and financial stewardship, remains a critical operational concern, given

today's challenge to implement increasingly more consumer connected responsive operations. In short, the information was increasingly becoming available to implement response-based pull systems,
but the new integrated software was designed to operate in an anticipatory posture.

The second ERP design flaw, which is increasingly gaining widespread awareness and attention, is the growing recognition that software packages installed on internal mainframe computers may not
have sufficient size or flexibility to fully accommodate and exploit the
rapidly changing delivery model of emerging technology. In short,
many firms made significant investments to upgrade internally operated computer mainframes to host ERP and bolt-on applications at
the very time that software and hardware and how they are delivered
to users began to radically change. Such far-reaching developments
as open-sourced software (OSS), on-demand computing, software as
a service (SaaS), grid processing, and hosted applications that exploit
the synergism of user networks were only to a limited degree accommodated by ERP architecture. This was the start of a period during which Internet and information service providers began making
massive investments in computer processor farms to support their
Web-based architecture. The result of implementing ERP packages on internal computers, coupled with the challenges of working through assorted implementation problems, created a barrier for
firms in terms of exploiting rapidly emerging Web-based technology
across their business operations. In short, with the exception of integrated financials, digitizing didn't really get operationally started in
most firms until late in the first decade of the twenty-first century.

The far-reaching impacts of these ERP leadership and software
design flaws are elaborated throughout the chapters that follow. The
resounding point is the realization that many executives undertook

what appeared to be "heads-up" leadership initiatives to adapt their organizations to the initially perceived challenges and opportunities of the emerging Information Age. However, similar to getting lost on a cross-country journey, they made a major wrong turn when they failed to fully understand the assumptions driving ERP, the operational disruption they would face, and a dramatic change taking place in the delivery of information technology. Both the business executives and the technology experts overlooked the growing need for interoperability across the entire supply chain. The real challenge was not to purchase and implement a new generation of software in the same manner as in the past but to begin the process of digitizing their organization to exploit twenty-first-century information technology.

The Twenty-First-Century Digital Enterprise

When all is said and done, what will the organization of tomorrow look like and act like? That's a difficult question to fully answer because no existing practice or industry model exists to help provide dimension or define what will constitute future best in class. In fact, extreme competitiveness between extended supply chains is likely to dictate unique organizational arrangements and operating structures. One thing we can be sure of is that digital organizations will not be structured similar to the silo, or functional, line-and-command organizations characteristic of the twentieth century. In fact, it seems quite likely that the digitally extended enterprise that thrives on leveraging collaborative relationships may be highly transparent with respect to formal organizational structure. While not quite virtual, the twenty-first-century organization will clearly depend on relationships and information technology to extend synergistic impact and mobilize operations to successfully operate end-to-end demand-driven collaborations.

Thus far, it should be clear that digitizing an organization is neither business as usual nor the traditional exercise in change management. Involved in digitizing is a total revamping of traditional and, even more important, currently successful supply chain arrangements to fully exploit the benefits of the unfolding Information Age.

Clearly, no enterprise can rapidly or completely implement such a massive change for at least two basic reasons. First, the technology, while fully able to support the transformation, continues to emerge, thereby cascading the range and scope of transitional opportunities. Second, an organization and its human resources can absorb only limited change during a specified time if it and they are to remain productive and stable. Thus, digitizing is characterized as a state of mind that requires an ongoing commitment to undertake meaningful change. It is a journey with the most likely characterization for the next several decades being a continuous work in progress. The starting point is to understand the origins and growing potential of the responsive supply chain business model.

Chapter Three
The Responsive Supply Chain Business Model

"If the world seems a confusing place at this moment, part of the reason may be that we are living in an epochal period of transition bridging two very different types of economies and cultures."[1]

—David Bollier

The primary purpose of a business model is to provide enterprise leaders and associates with a creative framework to guide resource deployment to achieve strategic goals. A business model details a firm's value propositions and describes how the value creation and distributive processes are achieved. The most prevalent business model following the Industrial Revolution was commercialization of mass manufacturing. Following World War II, a more comprehensive understanding of marketing influenced the development of a customer-driven business model centered on increased consumer choice and satisfaction. The prevailing business model of this period became the marketing concept. Distinctive developments during this period were retail mass distribution and the maturity of manufacturer product branding. The emergence of the global business model late in the twentieth century augmented mass manufacturing and consumer choice with the attributes of timely and cost-effective worldwide manufacturing and marketing. The twenty-first-century

---

[1] David Bollier, Rapporteur, op. cit.

global digital economy is rapidly being characterized by the emergence of the responsive supply chain business model.

It is extremely important to understand that business models are additive. As new models emerge, they assume and incorporate relevant attributes of the model being augmented. The knowledge and experience gained from one model accumulate as transformations occur. Likewise, the transformation from one model to the next is not uniform across or within industries. Thus, in the early twenty-first century, firms can be observed still creating value using primarily the mass-manufacturing model. Meanwhile, other firms in the same industry may have progressed to either the marketing or the global competitive model. Finally, it should be noted that disruptive technology serves to redefine the relevancy of business models, calling forward relevant value propositions from some while replacing others with new and more meaningful frameworks.

Most firms have a value proposition that serves to define and articulate how and why the products and services they market will benefit customers, employees, and shareholders. In turn, the value propositions are encapsulated in a business strategy specifying the way products and services will be positioned for sale.

In a broad sense, two strategies have dominated the post–World War II business economy. A selected number of firms adopted a single-industry strategy. This single-industry strategy, often referred to as "pure play," is characteristic of firms in heavy industries such as chemical, automotive, and food processing. For many years, Dell Computers popularized the pure-play strategy with the commitment to doing one and only one thing well—making and direct marketing computers. Pure play can be a risky proposition because such a commitment to specialization incurs the risk of rapid duplication or technical obsolescence. The result could be failure to sustain the unique value proposition over time or increased cost to attain continued incremental market share. Dell, faced with growing competition, first diversified into printers, flat-screen televisions, and software services. In 2007, Dell expanded its business model to include retail store marketing. This fundamental expansion of distribution strategy was to increase relevancy to more diverse segments of the rapidly maturing retail technology market, instead of switching sales channels.

The dual business strategy, often called the conglomerate strategy, became popular during the late twentieth century. In essence, the value proposition of a conglomerate is to gain leverage and security by diversification. Textron, General Electric, and Johnson & Johnson are examples of firms that are actively engaged in multiple industries. The recent acquisition of Gillette by Proctor & Gamble represents movement toward increased diversification.

The question of current concern is what is the difference between a pure-play and a conglomerate strategy, with respect to adopting a responsive supply chain business model? Clearly, the principles of supply chain management are relevant to both. All firms selling and distributing products require supply chain support.

In the case of the pure-play enterprise, the principles of integrated supply chain performance are essential to achieving a firm's value proposition. In such situations, the leadership challenge is to develop integrated functionality across both internal and external supply chain operations to support a focused marketing strategy. Because of the singular focus of the enterprise, all supply chain resources can be focused on integration with key customers.

The answer becomes more complicated in a conglomerate business structure. When firms in many different industries have the same ownership, does it make sense for all to use a single supply chain operational platform? The answer—as always when dealing with strategic issues—is maybe or maybe not.

The correct strategic answer needs to be broken down into capabilities related to individual customer need, supply chain knowledge, and the operational requirements related to sustain specific operations. In situations of joint ownership, but significantly different operating requirements, the minimum collaboration between individual companies is knowledge sharing concerning best practices related to the external and internal environments. Firms such as VF Industries, which is a conglomerate consisting of highly diverse businesses, carry on extensive supply chain executive development for operational managers across their enterprises in an effort to introduce new concepts, jointly evaluate emerging leading-edge processes, and foster informal networks for cross-enterprise employees to share knowledge.

In situations where conglomerates have common customers, it is likely that those customers will demand consolidated delivery of products from separate but associated firms on the same shipment and under a single invoice. Similar opportunities for consolidation can develop among a firm's suppliers. Wal-Mart, Target, and large food retailers place a premium on integrated supply chain connectivity with "all" operating companies owned by their key suppliers.

In situations where the conglomerated firms market to distinctly different customers, such as Textron selling golf carts and jet aircrafts, decisions to share or not to share all or part of their supply chain capabilities become questions of favorable economy of scale, scope, or customer-perceived value. The development of shared services should be driven by the ability to gain otherwise not available efficiency while maintaining needed service differentiation.

However, for a growing number of firms that operate on a global basis, the potential to increase overall market reach and improve quality of intercontinental operations may drive overall corporate strategic positioning. For this growing number of global firms, supply chain management has particular relevancy.

The responsive supply chain business model is concerned with the timely delivery of necessary materials, specific products, and related services to locations throughout the world when and where demanded in a manner that maximizes value. This competency requires that the correct product assortments and associated services be delivered in a time-specific manner to customers, as well as internal enterprise locations, at the lowest total cost. The overall product manufacturing and delivery specifications must be understood before addressing total cost minimization. For example, it is quite common, because of global sourcing and tight product cycle times, for some products such as toys, electronics, and fashion apparel to have their components or finished products shipped by air transportation to meet their time-sensitive go-to-market strategy. To achieve the lowest total delivered cost for any product, required materials must be purchased and products manufactured across the global economy at lowest-cost locations. Once products are created, they must be delivered to customers worldwide in an efficient, effective, relevant, and sustainable manner. The responsive supply chain business model provides the framework within which global business strategies are developed and executed. As such, the responsive supply chain business model is an inclusive concept that seeks to manage time-relevant cost-to-cost trade-offs while integrating the value-added capabilities of customer accommodation, manufacturing, procurement, and logistics into a single value creation process. These four value creation activities of a firm are strategically combined to form the responsive supply chain business model.[2]

Supply Chain Evolution

The starting point for understanding modern supply chain structure and strategy is to gain an understanding of just how and why such entities began to emerge in modern business. As the Industrial Revolution unfolded, firms began to specialize their manufacturing and marketing efforts. While the world's industrial structure was in its infancy, most firms sought to be vertically integrated or self-sufficient, in order to assure quality and operational continuity. In an emerging economy, as was the United States in the early twentieth century, industrial giants such as U.S. Steel, Ford, DuPont, and General Motors considered self-sufficiency essential to assure profitable growth. Henry Ford described the strategic spirit of this era in his classic book *Today and Tomorrow*.[3] In Chapter Nine of his book, "Reaching back to Sources," Mr. Ford explains the essence and competitive benefit of vertical integration as he describes the strategic role of "Fordson," the award-winning manufacturing complex that served as the logistics hub of the Ford empire.

However, following the industrial challenges of World War II, the structure of manufacturing rapidly changed. Individual firms found greater success by focusing operations on being best in class at performing selected operations or processes. To a significant degree, the roots of such specialization can be traced to the massive amount of coordinated manufacturing required to support the global World War II effort. Government contracts required institutionalizing the

---

[2] The fundamentals of these four value creation activities are discussed in greater detail in the appendix.

[3] Henry Ford, *Today and Tomorrow* (New York: Doubleday, Page, and Company, 1926). Reprinted by Productivity Press (Portland, OR, 1988).

practice of specialization. Aircraft assembled by Ford at Willow Run contained engines, propellers, electronics, and a variety of other components manufactured across the United States and Canada. The seeds of industrial specialization were a consequence of global conflict.

Whereas Ford once owned and operated the Detroit, Toledo, and Ironton Railroad, it soon became clear that his organization had far more expertise in assembling and selling automobiles than it did in running a railroad. Throughout, business firms began to specialize. With specialization came a growing need to identify best available suppliers of materials, components, and services. In order to synchronize suppliers into a manageable arrangement, integrated logistical processes were required. Looking back, this was, of course, the point in time when business first began to embrace collaborative management. However, few understood or had a vision that this changing behavior represented the early origins of twenty-first-century supply chain management and its emerging business model.

Extreme Functionalism

The common business success equation was to seek specialization and scale. Specialization requires business operations to be focused on performing very well a narrow range of value-added activities. Such specialization creates the opportunity to exploit economies of scale. The classical example of scale is to generate sufficient length of manufacturing run to assure the lowest possible total cost per unit produced. The postwar world of twentieth-century manufacturing was driven by scale economies. The link of such manufacturing capability to market reality required the development of transportation capacity to move raw materials and finished products to geographical locations where and when they were forecasted to be needed.

Thus, forecasting, far from an exact science, became the critical link to successful operations.

Business structure of this era, 1945–1975, was, by and large, driven by specialization myopia. Firms thrived, and economies grew. Both in the United States and throughout the world, manufacturing capabilities became volume oriented and specialized. One unintended consequence of specialization was the development of extreme functionalism. Firms and suppliers became very focused on doing a limited number of value creation activities extremely well. In fact, to assure continuous improvement in the specialization process, firms began to focus attention on the principles of quality.

From a managerial perspective, extreme functional excellence creates a dilemma wherein the focus of a process becomes the end rather than the means. By the very nature of specialization, some of the inherent and important synergy of a unified business model is lost. All company resources should be focused on servicing customers. If an activity fails to provide value added to customers, it should be eliminated. A few examples will illustrate the dilemma.

Purchasing or procurement, under extreme functionalism, is encouraged to focus efforts on negotiating the lowest cost possible for a component. Meanwhile, manufacturing is encouraged to produce at maximum economy of scale in order to assure lowest total cost of product assembly. Finished goods distribution is typically conducted in a manner that assures lowest transportation cost. Sales and marketing strategies, in such volume-orientated arrangements, are designed to load dealers and retailers with maximum inventories. In turn, because of forecasting inaccuracy, consumers are frequently offered incentives to purchase the products resulting from such commitment to volume-orientated business strategies. This practice of offering consumers incentives to stimulate purchase of mass-manufactured products, common in automotive, apparel, and consumer product retailing, is based on a belief and practices that stem from the days of the Yankee Peddler—namely, "You can't do business from an empty wagon." At the peak of extreme functionality, every facet of most businesses was focused on achieving maximum economy of scale.

Extreme functions were each, in their own manner, highly efficient. However, three unintended consequences began to raise significant doubt concerning the long-term viability of extreme functionality: (1) customers who were not happy with product assortments available for purchase; (2) excessive stockpile of finished product, work in process, and raw material inventories; and (3) disappointing financial results despite record sales levels. In short, all of the emphasis on doing each and every job to the peak of generally recognized best practice didn't combine or add up to total enterprise success. It became clear that business needed better overall results and functional integration to support this goal.

Integration: Phase One

Throughout business, leaders began to reexamine what in fact had become accepted best practice. Despite attention to improving work methods, the results were increasingly disappointing. Business leaders and consultants had difficulty explaining why, at the end of the day, week, or month, despite inventories reaching all-time highs, out-of-stocks were excessive. It was difficult to fully understand why 80 percent of trade sales of products consumed day in and day out, such as baby food, bathroom tissue, and disposable diapers, occurred during the last week of a business quarter. How was it possible that firms manufacturing consumer products would offer purchase incentives near the end of a fiscal period, resulting in retailers buying and selling trailer loads of product to each other—sometimes without ever taking delivery?[4] Suffice it to say that extreme functionalism had created some very strange practices!

Aided by the early vanguards of data processing, firms began to reinvent their internal activities and practices. Throughout, industry attention was directed toward improving operational integration. By the 1980s, two main centers of integrated management became observable. In industries characterized by heavy manufacturing, such as appliances, industrial equipment, capital goods, and transportation, business leaders began to drive integration around a concept commonly called "materials management." In consumable goods industries such as food, beverage, personal care, electronics, furniture, and health care products, the focus of integration was more typically called "physical distribution management." Some progressive firms focused separate initiatives on both materials management and physical distribution.

While both materials management and physical distribution management focused on integration to reduce total cost, their orientations were at opposite operational ends of a typical business enterprise. Materials management focused on reducing the total cost of making things, ranging from sourcing and procuring raw materials, components, and supplies to final product assembly. In contrast, physical distribution management had similar objectives of achieving lowest total cost, but the focus was on delivering finished goods from the end of manufacturing to distributors, retailers, and, in some cases, consumers. While each of these integrative initiatives was driven by different motivations, both initiatives had the common objective of focusing on reducing the total cost of a process instead of managing

---

[4] This practice, called diversion and reconsignment, was part of a forward-buy practice common in the food industry prior to the industry-wide efficient consumer response (ECR) movement and the passage of the Sarbanes-Oxley Act.

the cost related to specific functions. Both materials management and physical distribution management reduced total cost by managing trade-offs between subprocesses. Materials management focused on the inbound channel; physical distribution was focused on the outbound channel.

To illustrate, let's look at the benefits of total cost analysis and managing trade-offs involved in physical distribution. During decades of focus on functional performance, the traditional mandate for transportation managers was to do whatever possible to drive expenditures for transportation to a minimum possible while still achieving timely performance. Thus, transportation carriers were the targets of intense negotiation to reduce rates. Additionally, shippers did whatever possible to bundle or consolidate a number of different customer orders into larger shipments. Typically, in transportation pricing, carriers offer lower rates per unit of weight as the size of the total shipment increases. The impact of such efforts to reduce transportation cost often resulted in two unplanned results. First, the delivery of a customer's order could be delayed beyond the expected arrival date if time were required to consolidate small shipments into one larger and less expensive per-pound shipment. Second, costs related to holding inventories increased as a result of efforts to minimize transportation costs. However, inventory costs were not typically the responsibility of traffic managers.

As firms began to think about servicing customers on an integrated basis, it became increasingly clear that what really mattered was the level of customer service sustained and the total cost to serve. Higher service performance had the potential to generate more customer satisfaction, which, in turn, resulted in increased sales and consequently drove top-line revenue or sales growth. A reduction in the total cost to serve as a result of the integration of order processing, inventory, warehousing, and transportation had the potential to drive bottom-line cost reduction and increased profitability.

Similar examples of reducing total cost could be detailed in the integration of manufacturing and purchasing involved in materials management. The operational improvements during the decades from 1970 to the early 1990s were remarkable. In the case of toys, apparel, and electronics industries, overseas sourcing resulted in significant cost savings while maintaining equal or improved quality. Firms enjoyed the total cost and performance benefits of integrated operations. In doing so, they were reducing both materials management and physical distribution costs. Both integrative management initiatives designed to reduce total cost were adopted as best practice. However, additional integrative management opportunity remained.

Integration: Phase Two

By the mid-1990s, aggressive firms were looking beyond the independent thrusts of materials management and physical distribution. By 1990, the term "physical distribution" was commonly referred to as logistics management. The need to integrate across the total enterprise was driven by at least three forces. First, information technology was becoming available to drive extended integration. Second, firms began to encounter conflict in day-to-day operations between materials management and logistics management operations. Third, collaborative opportunities were emerging to redefine the scope of potential integration. Issues related to information technology were discussed in Chapters One and Two. The second force, end-to-end processes, and the third force, collaboration, combined with technology to drive integration—Phase Two.

It is natural and to be expected that materials management, the back end of the business process, and logistics management, the front end of the business process, could develop conflicting plans and operating goals when viewed from the perspective of the total enterprise. Each of these integrated activities resolved trade-offs within its unique range of functional responsibilities. However, when viewed from an overall enterprise perspective, they could be potentially conflicting. This conflict has been documented by research and labeled the "great divide."[5] Simply put, the great divide is a reflection of a firm's leadership inability to synchronize separate operational ends of an enterprise. It is the inability to tackle the trade-off opportunities between the process of selling things and the process of making and/or buying things. While business observers may differ concerning their estimates of the timing of specific firms harnessing end-to-end integration, few would disagree that what had philosophically and operationally arrived was one of the value propositions driving the evolution of the responsive supply chain business model.

Lessons learned from initial efforts to achieve end-to-end integration of internal enterprise processes created general awareness that a new perspective concerning customer and supplier relationships was essential to achieve the full benefits possible—namely, collaboration. "Collaboration" has become one of the most used of all business words during the first decade of the twenty-first century. The entirety of the transformation process builds on the importance of collaborative processes. Chapter Nine, "Collaboration: Creating Legendary Relationships," is devoted to in-depth understanding of this critical process. For now, however, it is clear that the process of dependency that began when firms initially abandoned self-sufficiency and began working together was being institutionalized. The paradigm has moved from cooperation and coordination to collaboration.

---

[5]   Donald J. Bowersox, David J. Closs, and Theodore P Stank, *21st Century Logistics: Making Supply Chain Integration a Reality* (Oak Brook, IL: Council of Supply Chain Management Professionals, 1999).

Collaboration has become the major force driving the evolution of the responsive supply chain business model.

In the twenty-first century, the words "responsive supply chain management" have gained prominence in business and throughout society. The words "supply chain" were not a common part of our vocabulary as recently as the early 1990s. Today, the words "supply chain" and "supply chain management" are regularly used in consumer and trade advertising, corporate publications, educational programs, and varied other daily communications. It was clear that new terminology was needed and continues to be refined to capture the significant change being encountered regarding how we work and how we live in a global digital economy. The logic of a responsive supply chain business model offers business leaders a framework to compete in a global economy.

Integrated Supply Chain Management

In the eyes of many observers and participants, the last half of the twentieth century represented a period of major development in organization structure and integrative management. Armed with the power of emerging information technology, business and academia collaborated in developing an understanding of the new and far-reaching responsive supply chain business model. What resulted was a framework for the integrated management of four key operating areas of a typical enterprise—namely, customer relationship management (CRM), manufacturing, purchasing, and logistics. Integration and holistic management of the four operating parts is now commonly acknowledged as supply chain management.

Prior to the development of integrated supply chain management, each area of competency matured into a separate and respected professional and academic subject, with each represented by professional societies, campus recruiters, and professional journals. Yet, something was missing! That something missing was a framework for higher-level integration, namely, the responsive supply chain business model. Successful integration within one or more of the primary operational areas still neglected the opportunity to integrate across the entire scope of enterprise operations and collaboratively with other firms across the overall process of building and distributing products and associated services. While cross-enterprise internal operational integration had inherent appeal, at least four significant obstacles made the leap across the supply chain to embrace customer and supplier integration a difficult transition: (1) integrative technology, (2) organization structure, (3) firm boundaries, and (4) measurement. Each obstacle is briefly discussed.

Integrative Technology

In Chapter Two, several shortcomings inherent in the initial wave of enterprise resource planning (ERP) software were discussed. The fact of the matter was that most early ERP adopters had not implemented software capable of the cross-function integration necessary for end-to-end supply chain management. Most ERP systems provided a fairly integrated financial package, but as noted earlier, they came up short with respect to integrated operations. A failure to integrate within and across functions created a major barrier to adopting the responsive supply chain business model. New ERP releases are promising and, to a degree, are delivering more operationally integrated software. Firms are identifying new methods of integrating specialized software that drives functional integration. While the perfect technology package still does not exist, firms are slowly but surely bringing integrated software to a level capable of supporting digitizing. Across the supply chain, integration challenges are unique to each firm. Therefore, firms will have to resolve their own technology challenges if they wish to excel in the world of responsive supply chain operations.

Organization Structure

A second barrier to adopting a supply chain perspective is traditional organization structure. A single organizational model has dominated the business landscape for the past several decades. Typically referred to as line and command, the organization is structured around functionality. While human resource reporting arrangements are clear in line-and-control structures, the organization model tends to encourage internal competition. As such, the pursuit of functional excellence can easily be positioned to encourage operational practices contrary to the goals of the enterprise. Such internal competition is intensified by the fact that most incentive compensation plans are driven by functional accomplishment, such as increased sales, reduced costs, or some other functional achievement.

Compensation based on enterprise-wide performance is typically reserved for senior leadership. The reality is that functional organizations, with functional goals, will compensate functional managers for functional achievement. Challenge most managers with a compensation plan based on achieving an operational goal and they will respond with valiant efforts to meet or exceed that goal. In regard to the earlier logistics discussion, offer a traffic manager a financial incentive to reduce transportation cost and the likely outcome may well be an increase in total logistics costs in such areas as inventory, warehousing, and material handling, despite the achievement of a year-over-year reduction in transport cost. Such trade-offs exist both within and between all operational functions.

Firm Boundaries

A third obstacle to implementing a responsive supply chain business model is a general historical failure to extend managerial influence and control across organizational boundaries. The traditional free enterprise model has been the negotiation of product and service commitments as well as transfer prices at business ownership boundaries. From a marketing perspective, this means negotiation based on selling price and terms. An important foundation of supply chain management is interorganizational collaboration. To be successful, supply chain managers must facilitate collaborative performance with both customers and suppliers. Although collaboration is not new, to a significant degree, when it has occurred, it has traditionally been between functional areas and their counterparts. Those responsible for customer relationships have been collaborating with customers. The same is true for both procurement and logistics managers, who have been developing improved operating relationships with their supplier counterparts. Within manufacturing, the boundary spanning activity has focused on outsourcing, which has been extensive throughout the world.

What remains to be developed is higher-level strategic collaboration across the entire supply chain space. The early collaboration between Wal-Mart and Proctor & Gamble represented a first-generation effort. The original model was expanded to other suppliers and now involves other retailers, wholesalers, and manufacturers. It was, and continues to a significant degree to be, an example of Wal-Mart carrying the big stick rather than a truly broad based collaboration. In other words, what is typically lacking is an integrated collaborative framework reflecting total enterprise engagement with all customers and all levels of suppliers. Such a collaborative enterprise framework is the responsive supply chain business model.

Measurement

Finally, our metrics and processes of measurement are bogged down in historical practice. New operating and financial metrics are needed to gauge the success of end-to-end supply chain operations. Such metrics are not typically found in today's arsenal of operational measures. Much more will be discussed about essential metrics in Chapter Eleven.

The Responsive Supply Chain Business Model

A real-world supply chain arrangement is immediately complicated and difficult to illustrate as a result of the fact that multiple customers and suppliers are involved. The essential characteristic of the responsive supply chain business model is the commitment to integrate with selected customers in a synergistic and unique way that generates maximum value. The shear magnitude of engagements across a large number of customers and vast range of suppliers requires deep understanding and a multiplicity of integrative relationships. The picture is complicated by the fact that most of the businesses embraced in any supply chain arrangement are typically also simultaneously engaged with competitors.

It follows that no two firms will ever have identical supply chain structures. To state this reality differently, no two supply chains will ever be identical. Each supply chain has unique and distinctive DNA. It is this DNA, resulting from each firm's unique strategy and network of business relationships, that constitutes the heart and soul of a specific firm's responsive supply chain business model. The model reflects a unique multimedia communications extranet positioned to exploit both real-time ubiquitous and proprietary information among customers and suppliers.

Figure 3-1 uses a flow diagram to illustrate linkages and functionality of a responsive supply chain business model. The supply-chain-strategic structure of a firm is the backbone, or spine, that links operations from suppliers, throughout the enterprise, along its distributive network, and, finally, to markets. The destination is, of course, those who consume the products and related services. The hub is the communication capability that integrates four operating management competencies, namely, customer relationship, manufacturing, procurement, and logistics. Trade-offs between these four operating competencies combine to create supply chain capability and to drive operational performance.

Figure 3-1   Responsive Supply Chain Business Model

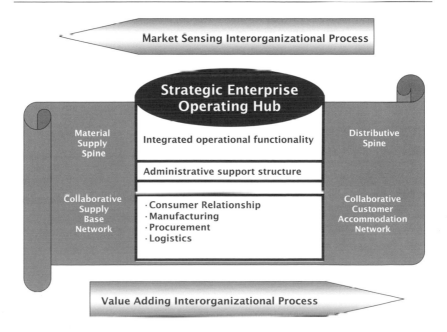

In a broader context, the strategic framework of a responsive supply chain business model represents a blend of six imperatives that are discussed in Parts Two and Three. These imperatives, or essential elements, are (1) consumer connectivity, (2) operational excellence, (3) integrative management, (4) real-time responsiveness, (5) leveraging networks, and (6) collaboration. Each of these six imperatives represents a firm's unique supply chain DNA. Though not possible for human DNA, business leaders can design their genome.

The simple fact of the matter is that most senior leaders do not have the experience or understanding to orchestrate these six imperatives into a coherent strategy. All six of the imperatives require cross-functional operational and information integration. Such integration means that technology infusions must be aligned toward achieving very specific operational goals. Here is where the transformation plan must focus on integrated leadership. Each and every facet of an organization must be aligned toward meeting and exceeding customer expectations. As noted earlier, if an activity or process is not directly linked to creating customer value, it should be eliminated.

This is not a comfortable message for senior leaders. Most executives seem, at best, to tolerate both information technology and supply chain management, but these things haven't been their passion. As one business observer stated, "Senior leaders know supply chain and related technology are important operational areas, but since they don't understand them, they delegate to the people they think can handle it."

The result of such delegation is, too often, the marginalization of the opportunity to differentiate on the basis of integrated supply chain competency. This failure results from senior leadership not fully understanding the responsive supply chain business model. While operational performance in such situations may be adequate, the opportunity to excel and differentiate on the basis of supply chain competency is lost. What, then, is the responsive supply chain business model?

The responsive supply chain business model is a customer-facing organization and operational strategy focusing the highest priority on providing exacting and sustainable customer service. The goal of the model is to achieve and maintain operational excellence at the lowest associated total cost. In companies having multiple divisions serving many identical customers, the supply chain model will typically involve integrated operations. Thus, customers who purchase products from different firms having common ownership can receive an assortment of all products purchased in a single shipment and in one transaction. For purposes of strategic advantage, high-level performance, and operational economy, the responsive model will typically feature centralized and integrated operations. For firms having a highly diverse customer base, the most attractive variation of the supply chain model may be a centralized organization that provides shared expertise and services for individual operating units. Thus, depending on the business structure and go-to-market challenges, the most appropriate responsive supply chain business model may be operational, shared services, or a staff support organization. Whichever the appropriate structure is, two facts will be consistent.

First, responsive supply chain strategy and implementation will be based on integrated cross-functional performance guided by leading-edge technology. In the twenty-first century, information technology will be deployed to render operations as responsive as possible by allowing customized products and related services to be rapidly pulled to market by customers. This fundamental shift from push (Industrial Age) to pull (Information Age) is what transformation is all about. It is what creates the key capability—responsiveness. Even at this early stage of maturity, the capability of pulling is affecting a broad array of overall twentieth-century institutions.[6] The change-over required to reinvent supply chain operations from an antici-patory toward a responsive posture is the transformation challenge. A fundamental leadership responsibility is to determine the degree of responsiveness that a collaborative supply chain can sustain over time. The "responsiveness" of the resulting supply chain is enhanced by real-time and networked information connectivity.

Second, the resultant responsive supply chain will be a constantly changing collaborative structure. The structure should be viewed as dynamic and flexible, maximizing the contribution of all types of suppliers and customers. The shape and form of linked operation-al capabilities will constantly change to maximize consumer value. Those firms capable of consistently meeting and exceeding customer expectations will be twenty-first-century winners.

These and related aspects of the responsive supply chain business model comprehension are, at best, in their infancy. A clearer picture of the ultimate potential of digitizing the supply chain will continue to emerge over the next few decades. However, even at this early stage of understanding the synergistic potential, it is clear that the range of future opportunities will exceed what even the most cre-ative leader can imagine. The dynamic interaction of collaborative, virtual, and disposable supply chain arrangements will yield bold, new, exciting, and hard-to-duplicate strategies. The chapters that fol-low seek to establish a foundation to help leaders explore the many dimensions and capabilities inherent in the responsive supply chain business model. The combination of Chapters One, Two, and Three provided a foundation to help understand the untapped potential of

---

[6]   John Hagel and John Seely Brown, *The Push-Pull Economy: The Only Sustainable Edge! Why Business Strategy Depends on Productive Friction and Dynamic Specializations* (Harvard Business School Press, 2005) and From Push to Pull: Emerging Models For Resource Mobilization, (The McKinsey Quarterly, 3rd Q, 2005).

the responsive supply chain business model. Digital transformation of twenty-first-century business operations is clearly not going to be business as usual. In Part Two, the process of ratcheting is developed as the foundation for supply chain mobilization. Ratcheting, the second stage to supply chain leadership, involves the imperatives of consumer connectivity, operational excellence, and integrative management.

Part Two
Ratcheting

Supply Chain Mobilization

A ratchet is a mechanical device that leverages momentum by driving and accelerating energy movement in a single direction. The purpose of a ratchet is to cause an increase or a decrease of a specified momentum by a steady increment. Thus, the process of ratcheting means to continuously reach a new level of achievement. The term "ratchet effect" is commonly used in disciplines as varied as medicine, political science, military science, and mathematics. Adopting the analogy helps illustrate the fundamental importance of a firm's integrated and sustained commitment to achieve higher and higher levels of operational excellence. The challenge is to progressively ratchet from industry average to become among a small group of firms that are operationally superior and, finally, to achieve leading-edge status.

Leading-edge status does not happen overnight. Industry leading-edge performance is the earned acknowledgement of continued commitment to performing basic business operations better and better.

This commitment to detail and excellence in every facet of operations requires industry leaders to constantly seek new and better ways to perform essential operational tasks. These new ways and means result from adopting and exploiting new technology and, then, more important, a willingness to change traditional operational practices and work processes to maximize the impact of such technology. In other words: adapt organization structure and practice "ratcheting" information technology. Twenty-first-century ratcheting is not business as usual.

We have selected to use the ratcheting analogy to describe the second stage of supply chain transformation. Following awareness, ratcheting highlights the fundamental importance of achieving the first three key imperatives of implementing a responsive supply chain business model. The first imperative is consumer connectivity. Many firms have unintentionally distanced their executive leadership from the realities of those who consume their products. All firms, regardless of position in a channel of distribution, must be concerned with the process of consumption. Understanding what drives consumption requires extensive connectivity.

The second imperative is operational excellence. It is clear that the drive for excellence requires some revolutionary change in traditional perceptions of what levels of performance are essential to win in the global digital economy. Operational excellence is not measured by averages. Every customer contact is a unique event having specific ramifications for future success. Regardless of the inconvenience, customers need to be fully serviced—each one and one at a time.

The third imperative is integrative management. What the best of the best are doing to counter extreme functionalism is detailed. Eight core processes critical to integrated management are presented. The discussion concludes with the presentation of a hypothetical organizational structure that is truly revolutionary.

Chapter Four
Consumer Connectivity

> *"Our customers are the only reason our job exists. If we don't figure out how to enable a supply chain with attributes that delight customers, we will have failed."* [1]
>
> —Stu Reed

onnecting with consumers and customers is important to business success. However, how a business organization responds to the challenges and opportunities involved in engaging these two important constituents is remarkably different. In this chapter, we will examine the importance of these two groups from a variety of viewpoints. The fundamental objective is to develop and reinforce understanding that a firm's responsive supply chain business model will increasingly be driven by connecting with both customers and consumers. As a business leader, the best perspective for approaching this chapter is to force yourself to read and evaluate the content as an outsider viewing your company.

The content argument starts and ends with the proposition that value—a primary end purpose of all business organization—is created only when a product or product-related service is consumed. During the distribution process, a given product may be bought and sold numerous times. As a part of such buying and selling, a product may be logistically moved many times to many different locations—

---
[1] Stu Reed, President, Motorola Mobile Devices Business.

even around the world. Sometimes, during the manufacturing process, products are transported to far-away destinations in order for
value adding activities to be accomplished and then moved back
close to where they originally started. This is true for many products
in the technology, electronic, health care, and apparel industries. All
such business activity is driven by economics, availability, capability,
and risk. Each sale and resale results in profit or loss for the individual firms responsible for the process. However, the important point
is that no sustainable value is created until the finished product is
consumed. In some situations, such consumption may occur within
hours after the product is manufactured or assembled. In fact, in res-
taurants, consumption typically occurs within minutes of a meal having been manufactured. In other situations, the lapse time between
production and consumption may be weeks, months, or even years.
Product life cycles, in the case of fashion-based products, such as
some apparel, electronics, or other similar items sold during holidays,
may be as short as a few weeks.

For executives schooled in the dynamics of twentieth-century
competition, this effort to differentiate between consumers and customers may, at first, seem trivial. For those working in the twenty-
first century, understanding the growing power and connectivity of
consumers to directly affect business operations is the first imperative of success. Firms capable of directly connecting with consumers
are best positioned to excel in the global digital economy. By "connecting," we mean gaining and maintaining consumer patronage and
loyalty. By "connecting," we also mean not just satisfying a consumer's
need but satisfying some part of a consumer's aspirations. By "connecting," we mean having the full range of information technology
in place to directly dialogue with consumers.

Differentiating Between Consumers and Customers

The starting point is to understand what differentiates a consumer and a customer. It is important that this distinction between a consumer and a customer be firmly in mind as we discuss concepts introduced in subsequent chapters. A consumer is an individual or purchasing unit that buys a product or product service for consumption. All of us around the world are consumers in most every facet of our daily lives. The ability to purchase for consumption varies significantly among individuals between and within countries and regions. But, one way or another, we all consume.

Customers, on the other hand, buy products and/or product services for both resale and commercial use. When engaged in commercial consumption, the objective is to perpetuate a firm's value creating process by using the purchased material, component, or intellectual ingredient to manufacture or assemble and market an even more valuable product or product service. However, no sustainable value is created until the product or service is finally consumed. Thus, all material and products purchased for industrial use represent dependant demand. "Dependent" means that the demand for such intermediate products or services is based on ultimate consumer purchase and consumption of a finished product or service.

Of course, all of the sequencing discussed above is well documented by economists and business school faculty. For decades, channel dynamics have been the subject of academic research and publication. What is changing in the global digital economy is the speed of the value creation process, the connectivity, and the direct relationship between supply chain participants. In a digital world, the lines of distinction among suppliers, manufacturers, wholesalers, retailers, and consumers have blurred. The new economy involves different participants who are connected in new and different ways.

Traditionally, dominant enterprises and non-value-adding activities are being dropped from the new value creation process. "Industrial marketing" and "business-to-business marketing" have given way to collaborative relationships.

Manufacturers and assemblers are increasingly being held responsible for product performance until final consumption. The massive challenges of reverse logistics were, for all measurable comparisons, nonexistent a few decades ago. Manufacturers and assemblers now depend on highly tuned networks of wholesalers, retailers, and service providers to orchestrate the flow of products and services to and from consumers. The supply chains supporting this process are networks of managed relationships based on clearly stated agreements between all participating businesses. These businesses are increasingly viewing their commercial relationships as a collaborative network.

At the end of the distributive process stands a consumer who enjoys full veto power. In the twenty-first century, the connected consumer has high expectations. Consumers who prefer specific brands or shop in selected stores could care less about traditional customer service connectivity between the businesses involved. Their expectations are very simple. Consumers of specific brands expect items to be available when and where they have been told they will be available. Such expectations are true regardless of price. Increasingly, consumers view product performance and availability claims as commitments. They also expect the buying experience to be a valued hassle-free and comfortable experience, whether it is face to face in a store, over the telephone, or using Web-based technology. The consumer may also redefine the value of the buying experience. Think about it. Do you go into Starbucks just for the coffee? Has the location now become a place to visit with others, read the paper, do some work, listen to and or buy music, hold meetings, and, for some, connect with others?

Perhaps more important, the connected consumer is increasingly willing to play an active role as a participant in the business process. Many retail experiences are engaging the consumer to be a part of final value creation. Try going to a Build-a-Bear store with a young person and not become part of the process of creating a new bear. Interesting as well is the number of bears built by grandparents for themselves or others.

We need to understand more about connected consumers. All evidence suggests that consumers will increasingly drive performance as the global digital economy matures.

Consumer Anatomy

It will come as no surprise to the business reader that demographics matter. The fundamental driver of the responsive supply chain business model is the challenge of delivering products and product services to consumers when and where they are demanded. In 2006, the U.S. population reached 300 million and is projected to gain another 100 million in 37 years, or sooner. In addition to growing faster, the population is projected to increasingly concentrate in metropolitan areas along coastlines. From a logistical perspective, this means that the United States will consist of geographically more dense and more concentrated populations in destination markets. On a global basis, U.S. projected population growth is not as vigorous as that of China, India, and Africa, with slower growth projected for Europe and Japan. In the cases of China and India, which both have current populations of more than one billion people, gross domestic products are growing two to three times faster than the GDP of the United States and Europe. Each country will continue to experience growing consumerism as it simultaneously navigates through its version of an Industrial Revolution driven by information technology, at a speed unimagined 10 years ago. What is demographically significant is understanding who these new consumers around the globe are, how they will respond to connectivity, and what goods and services they will purchase.

The core of today's consumer market, however, remains in the United States, Europe, and Japan and is dominated by the rapidly graying baby boomer generation. The boomer population bubble occurred as a result of World War II postponement in family creation. The boomers are now entering their sixties and are staying more active because of desire and need. What is most important to emerging supply chains is that the post–World War II bubble has spawned three significantly different subsequent generations when it comes to work, play, and consumption. The first group following the peak years of the post–World War II baby boom, typically labeled Generation X, became the initial wave of technology-oriented consumers. Gen Xers entered the work world as computers and e-mails were becoming commonplace. In short, this was the first generation to be raised in the emerging or dawning years of the Information Age.

Generation X's younger siblings or children, Generation Y, became the first real generation fully raised in the Information Age. For their entire lives, Gen Yers have encountered the good and the bad of information technology. They have grown up with all the information sharing capabilities of using the Internet and instant messaging. For most readers, this is old news. What may not be old news, however, is the way the Gen X and a significant segment of the Gen Y population act as consumers. They enjoy being connected and engaged in the process.

Adding to this emerging consumer bubble is the rapidly growing twenty-first-century youth, the Now Generation, born in the past two decades, who has a substantially different approach to technology and how it relates to consumption. These latest-to-arrive consumers display little or no interest in the wonder of technology; they just accept it and expect it to perform. In short, they think digital rather than analog, they process simultaneous rather than sequential, they typically multitask, and they are totally comfortable with participation in electronic networks and communities. These attributes have combined to create an even greater expectation to be technically connected during the value creation processes. This rapidly growing segment of the population is equipped in every way to be active participants in the supply chain process. As evidenced by the magnitude of Web-based versus in-store retailing during the 2007 holiday season, there is growing evidence that they may, in fact, demand participation.

One driving force, and perhaps the most important, behind the responsive supply chain business model is that it fits the expectations of connected consumers. The responsive supply chain business model is built on cross-functional and cross-organizational integrated management. It is fueled by the collaborative synergy of participating businesses. It is networked based and driven by shared information. In short, it fits the profile of many boomers, maturing Gen Xers, emerging Gen Yers, and the new Now wave of twenty-first-century consumers. Several key aspects of the responsive supply chain business model are developed in greater detail in the chapters that follow. Unless the responsive supply chain business model serves all consumers in a meaningful and sustainable way, it will not emerge to dominate business practice in the Information Age.

Extreme Competition for Consumer Loyalty

The free market system has grown and continues to thrive on consumer choice. The performance and proliferation of this system has dominated twentieth-century political and social agendas. It will be indispensable to the twenty-first century. The significant difference is that the new economy has an information and consumer focus, not an industrial focus. The competitive stage for the decades ahead will be best characterized as "extreme competition for consumer loyalty." The end state will be far more dramatic than the manufacturing and retail revolutions of the twentieth century.

As commercial enterprises align in responsive supply chains, sustainable consumer engagement will become increasingly essential for survival. In today's world of dominant brands and massive retail chains, it has become far too easy to assume that consumers will accept standing in line, out-of-stocks, and other inconveniences associated with mass merchandising. This is all changing as we proceed into the world of digital commerce.

Assume that the connected consumer will use all channels of sale to his or her advantage to maximize time, preference, and analysis. These consumers are already limiting face-to-face shopping to selected merchandise, such as upscale purchases or selected experiences. They are crossing over channels at their convenience. Victoria's Secret Direct markets are developed by distributing more than 360 million catalogs per year as well as direct connectivity through the Internet. The company offers both telephonic call centers and Web-based ordering by use of an order pad that facilitates browsing through electronic catalog page images in a way and time that fit a customer's choice. Since Victoria's Secret's Web site was established, more than half of its customers, without promotion or incentive, have migrated their ordering to the Internet. Increasingly, connected consumers use the Web site to purchase merchandise after they have viewed the physical catalog in their homes or elsewhere. In short, the connected consumer picks their most comfortable time to browse, shop, and order.

Other consumers believe that the ultimate solution is using the Web to graze and shop. Most all branded items purchased on a day-to-day basis are and will increasingly be available via Web-based technology. One has only to look at the success of QVC, selling both on television and using the Internet, to see how consumers are redefining experiences they like. Consumers will be able to routinize such shopping by use of computerized standing orders. Economical last-mile solutions that combine high-speed consumer pickup or convenient home delivery are supporting and radically changing the shopping experience.

Items purchased at irregular intervals, such as appliances, autos, and furniture, may be among the easiest to purchase online. Search engines for electronics, computers, and cameras are already matching product specifications—across brands—to customer expectations while providing comparative pricing and feature analysis. Other durables are sure to follow. Selected durables will increasingly be assembled or customized to order and delivered direct to consumer homes. We are already seeing the impact of direct marketing, with the continual growth of companies such as Penske and Excel delivering directly to consumer homes.

While shopping without a retail store experience may seem extreme to some existing retail merchants, consider the following facts: (1) all the essential technology is here today; (2) consumers (X, Y, and Now generations) know how to use technology, are not afraid to use it, and, in fact, enjoy using it; (3) most all firms that manufacture consumer durables currently offer Internet-based shopping; and (4) most firms that manufacture consumer durables have nationwide last-mile delivery and installation services currently established. In short, the capability is in place, and consumer acceptance is growing annually.

Even this early in the emerging Information Age, it is clear that consumers are beginning to transform traditional shopping behavior. In fact, they seem to be ahead of industry in embracing new technology. The emerging generation of shoppers does not get great satisfaction out of the traditional shopping experience for everyday household needs and standardized consumer durables. Whereas their great-grandmother enjoyed the daily walk to A&P, their grandmother experienced the evolution of self-service shopping, and their mother experienced the challenges of full-time employment while being forced to shop at retail stores during crowded peak hours. Tomorrow's consumers will be even less patient. Emerging consumers are psychologically and technologically equipped to move to the next shopping model: technology-based consumer connectivity. Internet-based ordering of groceries at local supermarkets for pickup in the parking lot at a scheduled time is being introduced to satisfy the Generation X, Y, and Now consumers who value their limited free time and children-related activities more than a surcharge for local order fulfillment. Mass consumer engagement will not happen overnight, but with only a few exceptions, today's progressive retailers and manufacturers are deep into crafting ways to access and exploit consumer connectivity. The Information Age raises new and challenging segmentation opportunities.

Segmentation and Fragmentation

Twentieth-century marketing was based on sound principles of accessing mass markets. The marketing concept that emerged after World War II clearly focused on meeting consumer needs and requirements. Such needs and requirements were viewed as being more fundamental or basic than products. The marketing concept acknowledged that different consumers have different needs, which, to be fully understood, must be viewed from their unique perspectives. Once such needs are understood, products and services can be developed to match and satisfy these unique requirements. To be successful, marketers of products and services learned to identify and access groups of consumers who had similar preferences. These groups, called "market segments," became the targets of sustainable marketing efforts. Segmentation became the key to successful marketing.

For a market segment to be sustainable, three attributes are required. First, the segment needs to have sufficient size to justify costs associated with product development and marketing. Second, a segment needs to be measurable to allow evaluation of its profit growth potential. Finally, the segment needs to be accessible. Accessibility to marketers means the ability to communicate with consumers and achieve distribution closure. The emergence of technology-driven accessibility raised new opportunities as well as challenges.

Segments that traditionally reflected demographic or geographical attributes are increasingly becoming accessible electronic clusters using blogs, chat rooms, and various forms of information exchange. Social-networking sites such as MySpace, Facebook, Tagged.com, Hi5, and Friendster offer convenient ways for consumers to search for new information and offer their opinions to all who care to listen.

Within a few short years, browsing and searching have expanded to include sharing of personal information and opinions. Widgets, which provide tiny messages to the blogs of connected consumers, or even to their personal computers, give automatic product and service alerts, thereby extending the reach of Web-based marketing. What ultimately will constitute an electronic segment may not be anchored in terms of any traditional market measures. Such information-based segments might best be described as geographically dispersed but electronically clustered consumers who most likely will never share physical proximity. In fact, customers previously considered out of reach because of high cost to service are becoming accessible and profitable.[2]

Technology-defined segments, or what might better be called electronic communities, will increasingly grow as a result of information connectivity. Two-way dialogue is exploding in terms of feedback and active electronic community involvement. In Chapter Eight, we will discuss how traditional two-way dialogue is morphing into many-to-many unbridled networks. Companies traditionally aspired to get as many consumer telephone numbers as possible to facilitate connectivity. Sending e-mail messages has replaced telephone calling because Web technology can touch more people and touch them faster. Consumers are staying more connected to their e-mails throughout their daily lives by cell/data phones and work computers. In terms of connectivity, consumers respond more often to e-mails than to telemarketing calls. At this stage, our understanding of the full ramification of a many-to-many network is in its infancy. However, electronic or information-based segments will be interactive and will embody the capability to network.

The position and power of consumers are rapidly changing. Their involvement in the marketing process is expanding to become that of negotiators and supply chain participants. Traditional market segmentation will increasingly be pushed toward one-to-one transactional connectivity framed within the rich context of a many-to-many shared-knowledge network. Is it possible that the consumers of tomorrow will negotiate customized contracts to satisfy their consumption requirements?

Finally, the connected consumer will pose significant challenges to the process and structure of operational consolidation. Consolidation has traditionally been used to achieve economy of scale in manufacturing and logistics. Improved consolidation was a significant driver

---

[2]   Chris Anderson, *The Long Tail* (New York: Hyperion Press, 2006).

of twentieth-century supply chain structure and strategy. What the Information Age is ushering in is extreme fragmentation! When a truck delivers and the driver installs a new washer and dryer, the size of the financial transaction justitifes customized delivery. In contrast, where is the scale associated with direct delivery of consumer products such as food, drugs, and beverages?

Part of the answer is found in a careful look at the direct-delivery models that exist today in pizza, newspaper, and parcel delivery. These models are dynamic. Most direct-delivery models have been designed to achieve new value-added capabilities. These capabilities lower the cost threshold for providing consumer convenience. Almost as fast as Blockbuster expanded the convenience of video delivery via mail service to include the convenience of local video store exchange, the direct digital world responded by introducing electronic delivery of a selected video library or theme packages to a connected consumer's television. The result was a direct marketing and distribution model capable of offering consumers near-effortless video selection and maximum convenience. Part of the answer is also found in the removal of uncertainty from the shopping equation made possible by consumer connectivity. Finally, part of the answer will increasingly be found in yet-to-be formulated collaborative networks of last-mile delivery. It is clear that the world is changing—the critical question is whether traditional business organizations can change their value propositions sufficiently fast to become significant participants in the global digital economy.

Segmentation in the Information Age will be operationalized much as it has been in the past. Segments will be characterized by operationally distinct consumption destinations sufficiently large to facilitate physical connectivity but sufficiently small to avoid averaging. The significant difference in the future will be the dynamic of constant change in behavior and membership. Expectations will be clear as a result of increase connectivity. Consumers will be better informed and capable of accessing better information. This knowledge will change the fundamental paradigms underlying an effective marketing strategy. It will increasingly be necessary for firms to understand the social networks that serve as the value foundations of connected consumers. Consumers will play an expanded role in shaping marketing innovation and strategy.

Consumer insight will drive product and product service design. The challenge will be the balancing of diseconomies of scale resulting from extreme fragmentation with the benefits of reduced uncertainty. To any executive schooled in the traditional dynamics of supply chain economics, reduced uncertainty translates to lower levels of speculative inventory. Clearly, the appropriate business model for meeting and exceeding consumer expectations will increasingly change as we proceed into the twenty-first century. Our position is that the best framework available thus far to meet and exploit this market potential is a responsive supply chain business model.

Customer Service and Beyond

It is clear that traditional concepts of customer service will need to change to meet the expectations of the connected consumer. Any reduction in uncertainty of consumer intentions will be accompanied by an increase in expectation concerning fail-safe performance. After all, the same information networks that support connectivity are capable of providing exact order-to-delivery status and precise operational performance tracking.

The traditional customer service model focused on three levels of measurement, namely, inventory availability, operational performance, and reliability. These will all remain important measures for score-carding or tracking how well a preferred supplier meets the expectations of a connected consumer. Keep in mind that the consumer of the future will likely be connected to a retailer and/or wholesaler and/or manufacturer to meet repetitive buying needs. It's also important to remember that only the final consumer counts in a networked economy.

Availability is all about inventory being present in the time frame promised when the transaction is initiated. Availability measures relate to stock-out frequency; fill rate, which is the quantity percentage of desired to available products; and frequency of complete or perfect orders, which is the percentage of repetitive orders or shopping lists totally filled.

Operational performance is a set of metrics typically used to measure supply chain activity. In situations where suppliers are servicing customers, it is important to measure several operational attributes related to the order-to-delivery process. Two important measures are speed and consistency of order to delivery. Suppliers are also measured with respect to their flexibility to accommodate special requests for increase or decrease in quantities supplied. Also, how well a supplier recovers when operations do not meet agreed-to or anticipated behavior is typically measured.

The final aspect of customer service performance is reliability. When measuring reliability, the focus shifts to performance of the relationship over time, concerning such factors as the degree of risk mitigation, security, information, and general responsiveness to change. Reliability is all about sustainable performance and continuous improvement.

Traditional operational measures have focused on transactions between channel members as contrasted with consumer transactions. However, as noted above, issues of operational performance will increasingly be on the agenda of connected consumers. These issues will involve distribution of new orders and will increasingly be concerned with return and disposal of products. The pristine hypoallergenic perfume sold direct to connected consumers becomes regulated hazardous waste containing alcohol, glass, plastic, and cardboard, all of which need to be disposed of responsibly. It is important to keep in mind that direct distribution also means direct reverse logistics.

It is clear that consumer expectations are framed independent of the realities of complex supply chain management. In the past few holiday seasons, consumers have expected to receive timely delivery regardless of when they placed orders. For example, online retailing has continued to grow significantly, with consumer ordering being postponed until closer and closer to the actual holiday. As a result, operational volumes have increased exponentially, with an expectation of all orders being delivered in time to be unwrapped by happy gift recipients.

In combination, availability, operational performance, and reliability have served to mold customer and, to a lesser degree, consumer expectations during the Industrial Age. While most progressive firms have been committed to continuous customer service improvement, overall leadership drive to achieve specified service levels has been low. Firms across the supply chain have been committed to maintaining inventories to assure meeting some typically undefined level of sales activity. However, traditional performance has been far from fail-safe. The pendulum of the twenty-first century is casting a shadow on these Industrial Age perceptions and practices. Increasingly, firms will be expected to commit to perfect order or guarantee consumer availability performance to lean operations and reduce risk. The extensive operation ramifications of this are discussed in Chapter Five, "Operational Excellence." Suffice to say the operational performance bar is rising and will become even more challenging as the ratio of direct-to-consumer distribution increases.

Figure 4-1 provides a summary of meeting and exceeding customer expectations. Whereas customer service focuses on a supplier's operational performance, measures of satisfaction and success represent the customer's perspective. In light of what was said earlier about consumer connectivity, it becomes clear that the operational challenges of the future will rapidly change in favor of satisfaction and success strategies.

Figure 4–1   Meeting and Exceeding Customer Expectations

· **CUSTOMER SERVICE**
  – Performance meeting a firm's internal operating standards.

· **CUSTOMER SATISFACTION**
  – Performance meeting or exceeding customer expectations.

· **CUSTOMER SUCCESS**
  – Performance that facilitates customer long-term success.

Along a traditional channel of distribution, there are purchase points at which inventory changes ownership. When merchandise assortments are developed and moved physically closer to consumers, value is added. The continual debate in the apparel industry is about whether "tops sell bottoms" or the other way around. The fact that together they create synergy and added value and, in combination, drive multiple item sales is not debatable. This distribution process serves to give products time and place value. However, as noted earlier, all traditional channel activity is in anticipation of consumption. The twenty-first-century challenge is how to create consumer value as channel alignment becomes increasingly direct. It appears clear that marketing and distribution initiatives targeted to a network segment of connected consumers will require significant modification in today's best practices in order to build agile, relevant, and sustainable business-to-consumer relationships.

Measuring Engagement

Measuring successful consumer and customer engagement requires a comprehensive value performance model. The EERS model offers one such perspective. The first "E" stands for effectiveness, the second "E" efficiency, the "R" relevancy, and the "S" sustainability. Each attribute is discussed.

The attribute of effectiveness means that a customer commitment is fulfilled. In short, the expectation is satisfied as a result of doing the right things to generate and maintain loyalty. If the correct product or service is delivered at the time specified for a commensurate price, to the correct location, damage free, then the order-to-delivery process is judged effective. While the work effort required on the part of the supplier to achieve effectiveness may have been much greater and more costly than originally anticipated, the delivery mission is judged effective because the value creation process met the receiving party's, customer's, or consumer's expectation.

Efficiency is all about total cost to serve. Thus, efficiency never stands alone. Efficiency reinforces effectiveness as a result of doing the right or desired things well. A firm must, first of all, be effective in order for efficiency to make a difference. If two firms can provide identical products and supporting services, then the difference between the two would be comparative efficiency. Thus, any engagement can be both efficient and effective. But the process of servicing a customer can never be efficient unless it is also effective. If a firm develops a low-cost or highly efficient delivery model, such efficiency must be accompanied by timely, complete order delivery and presentation at the desired destination. As one senior business executive put the relationship, "Efficiency rules if a process doesn't touch the customer." If the process touches the customer, effectiveness is the first consideration, and efficiency becomes a secondary consideration. Naturally, part of the leadership challenge is to achieve both simultaneously. This seems to be a customer service message that many twentieth-century firms failed to fully comprehend. In the emerging world of direct connectivity, such inadequate performance will increasingly be shared among customer communities via home pages, widgets, or blogs. In today's connected world, your service performance will become legendary at lighting speed whether it delights or disappoints the customer.

Relevancy is best captured by the phrase "Have it your way." Relevancy creates precise value by doing the right things well but, even more important, in the way desired by a specific customer or consumer. All customers are different. So, relevancy means connectivity designed to facilitate customized operations. To a grocery retailer, relevancy may be warehouse delivery at a specific time to facilitate cross-dock redistribution. To consumers, given the growing practice of direct marketing, relevancy is all about combining product availability and value and facilitating successful consumption. Thus, relevancy takes on many different configurations when viewed from a connected consumer perspective. An example of how connected consumers can respond was illustrated by the speed of using the Internet to create a congressional drug crisis when senior citizens ordered their prescription drugs from Canada at lower cost. Medicare D became a reality in record time. If senior citizens can change that quickly, Generations X, Y, and Now will be able to affectively shift their preference and purchasing impact in hours and days versus weeks and months.

Sustainability is all about maintaining combinations of effectiveness, efficiency, and relevancy over time. A commercial world characterized by high-volume repetitive purchases will not be able to depend on expedited delivery of individual orders to meet customer and consumer expectations. Successful distribution, in a connected world, could be viewed as analogous to a trapeze artist performing without a safety net. In a directly connected business model, speculative or just-in-case inventories will not exist. A premium will be placed on a supplier's capability to rapidly meet customers' or consumers' expectations by delivering a product or a product assortment at a competitive price to the right place (effectiveness) at lowest delivered cost (efficiency) according to customized specification (relevancy) every time engaged (sustainability). Connected consumers have and will continue to have more comparable information about price/value, cost of production, where friendly sources are, delivery cost options, and past performance. Figure 4-2 provides a graphical illustration of the EERS value performance model.

In the first decades of the Information Age, business is beginning to transform away from the best practices of the Industrial Age. The speed of such transformations is likely to accelerate. Traditional channels of distribution are being revamped in an effort to become increasingly responsive. Consumers are becoming increasingly involved because service propositions create value. The key to successful consumer involvement is a fundamental and unyielding belief that exact performance will create loyalty. Consumer loyalty is best viewed as a process, not an event.

For decades, successful business has focused on perfecting order-to-delivery cycle performance. One great insight of the twentieth century was to view the order cycle as a manageable process. Many

Figure 4–2   The EERS Value Performance Model

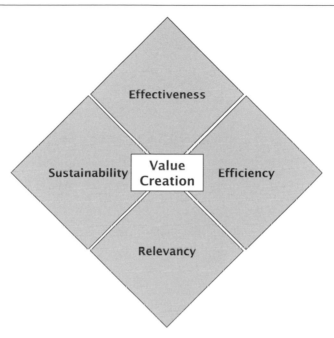

successful firms adopted the order-to-delivery cycle as the fundamental way to gauge operational success. This well-established paradigm appears to be changing.

The twenty-first-century business leader increasingly will understand that traditional perceptions concerning order and order management really don't matter. Understanding that the best way to resolve order problems is to eliminate orders, twenty-first-century managers will increasingly seek connective arrangements with customers and supply chain collaborators. A connective arrangement is when a supplier and a buyer of a product or service have fused operations around shared demand-sensing signals.

To illustrate, assume that firm A supplies firm B with a specific set of parts and components used in the assembly of a specific consumer product. Direct visibility of firm A into firm B's inventory status and consumer ordering process could eliminate the need for firm

B to maintain an inventory of parts, components, or finished goods. Rapid delivery of exactly the parts and components needed by firm B to assemble a product to customer order or consumer demand could eliminate expensive duplicated inventories while also increasing the flexibility of firm B to customize products to exacting customer/consumer specifications. To some readers, such connectivity may appear "theoretical"—the illustration is, in fact, based on Honda's responsive supply chain business model that has been functioning for more than a decade. Similarly, the efficient consumer response (ECR) and efficient health care consumer response (EHCR) models in existence for more than a decade have done the same thing for food retailers and selected hospitals throughout the United States and globally.

The EERS value model offers a balanced approach to viewing the collaborative interface between business firms engaged in a supply chain as well as connectivity with consumers. Managing EERS value across the emerging structure of twenty-first-century distribution requires creative thinking. New models are needed to understand how to manage connectivity across the supply chain. It is also essential to explore new ways to exploit direct connectivity in mass consumer marketing. In Chapter Five, we will discuss how the EERS framework can be used to understand operational excellence.

Some creative thought leaders are concerned with the need to avoid developing emotionally detached consumers. They feel that today's highly automated electronic processes, such as online banking, are creating customers who do not "feel" the benefits of connectivity. Others debate the benefits of convenience, accuracy, and security as driving unprecedented levels of value. It would seem that the answer to the debate rests in the evidence of how fast consumers have adopted online banking, travel reservations, and shopping. Additionally, digitizing music meant that people no longer needed to buy the physical CD but rather they could electronically buy only the songs they wanted. The result was a total transformation of the music industry. Physical products were eliminated, along with many of the stores that used to sell music. Again, the great driver of radical change was disruptive technology, which enabled buyers to bypass CDs completely.

After decades of false starts, companies that provide in-home delivery of groceries, such as Peapod and selected others, are finally gaining a sustainable footprint in the tedious process called grocery shopping. Years of studying position on physical shelves to "sell" a product will have to be rethought. Marketers will need to think about new ways to differentiate, to encourage impulse buying, or to "promote" new products to connected consumers. Traditional marketing best practices are not sufficient to connect to twenty-first-century digitized consumers. In reality, the maturity of consumer direct marketing and distribution, while in their infancy, depends on perfection of the underlying doctrines of the responsive supply chain business model.

The second imperative of ratcheting supply chain mobilization is adopting a new and demanding viewpoint concerning operational excellence—the focus of Chapter Five. In this chapter, a great deal of time has been devoted to the fundamental difference between a customer and a consumer in the value creation process. It should be clear that twenty-first-century technology is rapidly including the consumer as part of the mix of commercial activity. The point has been repeatedly made that nothing of sustainable value happens until products and services are purchased and consumed. From this point forward, the term "customer" will be used to conveniently describe all purchase points throughout the supply chain. However, the reader is asked to always keep in mind the fundamental importance of connected consumers in driving the overall distributive process.

Chapter Five

Operational Excellence

"A close study of corporate failure suggests that, acts of God aside, most companies flounder for one simple reason: managerial error." [1]

—Ram Charan and Jerry Useen

G iven an in-depth understanding of customer connectivity, we see that transformation proceeds when a firm's leadership makes a serious commitment to sustainable operational excellence. Operational excellence is the second transformation imperative. A commitment to operational excellence requires that all levels of an organization face the reality of what constitutes today's operating performance. In terms of servicing new as well as existing customers, very few firms even come close to enjoying operational excellence.

Facing Today's Operating Brutality

It's 4:30 on Sunday afternoon. A typical family is about to start getting "logistically" prepared for the week ahead. One serious aspect of this preparation is family grocery shopping. A family of five will spend an average of $141 per week on a wide variety of grocery-store-purchased merchandise.[2] Time is, of course, a critical resource for both the wife and the husband, who constitute today's typical

---

[1]   Ram Charan and Jerry Useen, "Why Companies Fail," *Fortune*, May 27, 2002, p. 52.

[2]   Food Marketing Institute, *U.S. Grocery Shopper Trends*, 2006, p. 68.

working couple. Sunday afternoon is most often the day to "stock up." Being well aware of consumer needs, many supermarket chains have extended hours and even break new promotional advertising effective Sunday morning. Other less consumer-sensitive chains select other days of the week to introduce promotions. It's odd that when asked why such is the case, executives in these traditional firms justify their business model and inventory replenishment practices by using the rationale that "it better fits our procurement and warehouse operational work schedule." In either case, the retailers' distribution operations seem to lack sensitivity to the importance of the Sunday shopping trip to consumers. What is at stake in the consumers' minds amounts to trading valuable leisure time in order to perform what amounts to a work task, namely, grocery shopping. What is about to occur some 52 Sundays a year is what we call the great "out-of-stock paradox." Six to 12 percent of retail goods are out of stock at any given time and as much as 20 percent during peak shopping hours. Why is it that, in an era characterized by superior operational potential, customer shopping activity matches perfectly with the weekly period of the greatest product out-of-stock on retail shelves? Of course, the traditional managerial explanation is shopping intensity and inability to perform weekend merchandise replenishment.

Behind this weekly stock breakdown is a serious mismatch of supply chain logistical replenishment operations and retail store merchandising. Conventional methods and measures of warehouse and store operating efficiency simply don't deploy resources to best satisfy periods of peak in-store demand. In most situations, the product out of stock on a store shelf is in adequate supply at a nearby warehouse. In fact, in many situations, the out-of-stock product can be found in the store's back room or in a semi trailer positioned at a store's receiving dock. Only in some limited number of situations is the product in fact out of stock throughout the retailer's overall system.

In terms of servicing consumers at other than grocery stores, the track record is even more dismal. It is unfortunately more the case than one might expect that selling floor out-of-stock products can be found buried in the back of the store. In seasonal products, such failures to replenish selling areas often lead to markdowns as the season or holiday passes prime selling time. The digital transformation journey requires a realistic assessment of existing operational competency. It is critical for a firm's senior leadership to establish a sustainable commitment to the EERS value proposition introduced at the conclusion of the preceding chapter.

The "out-of-stock paradox" is simply the result of not having the right product (desired by the shoppers) at the right place (store shelf) when the consumers want it (which is every time they shop). The magnitude of this paradox can be staggering. Some consumers report that as many as 25 to 30 items they planned to purchase were not available when they shopped. These items span from promotional products to those consumed every day. While consumers may resolve many purchasing problems by switching brands or sizes, they rarely depart retail grocery stores completely satisfied with their shopping experience. Take the time to ask them and you will understand better why, in the overall scheme of things, food purchased ready to eat now approaches nearly 60 percent of a family's total food expenditures.

The operating reality of business is that many leaders fail to view and measure their operations from a consumer's perspective. The yardsticks used, such as year-over-year same-store sales and sales as compared with forecast, are operational measures, not measures of satisfaction. The expectations of consumers are specific. The reality is that averages don't measure specifics!

While averages are a way to achieve a general view of operational competency, they fail to focus on specific breakdowns. A breakdown is a situation when the firm fails to satisfy a specific customer's expectations. The "expectation" might be an explicit promise to deliver a product at a specific time. Such explicit promises are normal events in most business-to-business transactions. From consumers' perspectives, the expectation is based on the implied promise that if they come to the retail store, the products they desire will be available. Regardless of whether the promise is explicit or implied, when a firm fails to meet customer expectations, damage is done, good will is deteriorated, and loyalty erodes to some degree. Failure to view operations in terms of the impact on specific consumer expectations is among the greatest failures in modern business leadership. Jim Collins, author of *Good to Great*, refers to accurate self-assessment as the "litmus test or the pivot point" when senior leadership faces the brutal facts head-on with corrective action rather than attempting to explain such failures away.[3]

The consequences of repeated service disappointment may not be immediate. In the case of consumers, a silent protest may occur as, one by one, formally loyal shoppers seek new and more reliable alternate products and different shopping venues and experiences. Such protest, with the growing support of Web-based experience sharing via online communities, blogs, and widgets, is likely to grow in intensity and magnitude and become less silent as consumer connectivity increases.

In business-to-business situations, when performance fails, future orders may be canceled and the customer may rebid the business with a new supplier. Rebidding the business typically launches a series of high-cost concessions by the former supplier, who is fighting to

---

[3]   James Collins, *Good to Great* (New York: Harper Collins Publishers Inc., 2001).

retain the business. At the end of this cycle, all too often, the only tangible result is a consumer price increase.

The operating reality is that business competing in the twenty-first-century Information Age needs precise operational measurement and a new level of commitment to achieve and maintain operational excellence. Simply stated, all aspects of day-to-day operations must be deaveraged. Each and every aspect of operations needs to be measured and managed. Whereas such precise measurement was not possible a few years ago, today's information technology provides the foundation for ratcheting operational excellence. As we will elaborated shortly, operational excellence is an overall enterprise commitment to performing each and every aspect of work related to each and every facet of a customer's order with full accountability for achieving and sustaining satisfactory results. It is enterprise commitment to perfect performance throughout the full journey from order arrival to consumer satisfaction. It does not stop at the factory or the shipping door of a distribution warehouse or the back door of a retail store. It goes directly to where and when the consumers see the product, possibly touch it, and, as appropriate, even smell it. Assuming purchase and consumption, then and only then is the distribution process complete. While the notion of perfect execution is not uncommon to surgical practices and space shuttle launches, a similar commitment to operational excellence is incomprehensible to most business executives. However, expectations are rapidly changing. Some executives are "facing the brutal operating reality." Even more important, some are true believers and are doing something about changing traditional operational performance.

Facing operating reality requires acceptance of the fact that few senior executives have even a remote idea of their firms' operating performance when viewed by a specific customer or on a unique product basis. Resource decisions are made every day without consideration for customer sustainability. Today, using supply chain visibility technology, it is possible to track all units of a product as they move from the factory and distribution centers to retail store back rooms. Most in positions of senior leadership would be shocked to find out that firms across a variety of traditional industries completely serve fewer than 50 percent of all orders. Thus, reality gets lost in averages and statistics related to channel complexity or in a supply chain journey half-traveled. We will talk a great deal about the discipline of perfect order and product retail availability throughout the forthcoming pages.

Anyone who has been in the battle understands the reality of today's operating world. This brief introduction serves to illustrate why traditional expectations concerning what constitutes leading-edge performance must rapidly change. New firms that truly get the message are emerging and are raising the performance bar. What served as best practices yesterday can become a barrier to achieving superior performance today. The journey that the best of the best are embarking upon we have decided to call "operational excellence."

The Journey to Operational Excellence

Initiatives to ratchet performance start with setting aside or discharging several long-standing beliefs concerning what level constitutes operational excellence. What is required is an altered operational image of what constitutes success. In the context of operational excellence, success must be measured as a fully satisfied customer one order or purchase at a time, order after order, time after time. Operational excellence builds loyalty by continuous commitment to taking care of all order details the right way, each and every time. This focused commitment requires establishing and maintaining a consistent operational course from purchase until consumption. Many firms fall victim to what might be called the "strategy du jour." New strategic initiatives or promotions, one after another, compete in their attempt to attract new business with existing and new consumers. However, strategy highlighted by promotional hype often loses sight of the basics of operational excellence. Operational excellence is about sustainable commitment to performance at or beyond customer expectation. It requires that several long-standing operational perspectives be permanently discarded.

A common belief is that commitment to superior performance will cost a great deal more than operating at lower or less ambitious levels. In other words, most managers believe some reasonable limit exists beyond which it's neither profitable nor does it make good business sense to provide additional customer-valued service. Take, for example, the traditional belief concerning item fill rate. The traditional belief is that supporting a goal of high fill rates will require very large supportive inventories. Large inventories, in turn, translate into high risk and high operational costs. Such logic may lead to success if the goal is minimal inventory investment. But what if the goal is to simultaneously achieve maximum consumer satisfaction and minimum total cost to serve?

Students, at least those who have not yet been baptized in traditional ideas of performance, find it incomprehensible that business leadership would encourage behavior designed to limit customer product availability. In fact, most business executives would deny such behavior. However, these same executives develop and enforce operation goals and performance measures based on two-sigma levels of achievement. Two-sigma-driven inventory availability seeks to service 95 percent of all requests. When applied to availability, this means that between 2.5 and 5 percent of all customer requests will, "by design," not be operationally satisfied. The performance result is greatly magnified if the total order consists of multiple items. For example, if the order consists of 10 separate products each having 95 percent availability, the chances of achieving a perfect order would be approximately 60 percent. It's difficult to achieve total customer satisfaction if targeted performance levels build in guaranteed failure!

Beyond performance, operational circumstances tending to damaged customer relations are amplified by the cost of recovery. What is the real cost of failure to serve? At the minimum, a firm that fails to fill an order faces a lost sale. The real consequence might be a lost customer. The cost associated with service failure, resulting in lost customers, is far greater than the lost transaction revenue. Failure to properly service order availability as promised often ends up involving recovery cost that far exceeds the profit potential of the original transaction. In short, failure to serve may turn an otherwise profitable sale into a loss! Resolution of a service discrepancy often requires special administration, expedited replacement product delivery, and unique customer service administration and accommodations. In many business-to-business situations, failure to serve can have a major impact on a customer's planned operations and can result in supplier cost penalties. The total cost of failure can erode a customer's profitability and loyalty. Lack of available products and assortments can, over time, have a major impact on retail selling prices and markdowns resulting in reduced margins.

Learning from Failure

Perhaps the greatest irony in today's performance measurement systems is that they typically do not identify, highlight, or document failure situations or the reasons why such failures occur. Failures to serve generate a negative impact and cost to resolve. Even performance measurement systems that capture and isolate the impact of service failures seldom report impact in terms of specific customers. Rather, what managers see are average performance statistics across a group of products or a class of customers. While such averages may reflect the aggregated trend, they do nothing to help management keep its finger on the pulse of a firm's most important customers, nor do they help identify connective solutions.

What is needed is measurement of failure. Such failure measurement needs to be augmented by root cause analysis that is focused on identifying why the failure occurred. What was the precise cause of the failure? What corrective action was required to prevent repeat occurrences? Has the corrective action been taken? What did it cost? Measurement of failure is all about targeted performance measurement that highlights order-to-order service compliance or purchase-to-purchase service compliance for specific consumers, not averages. What is needed are specific numbers and actions related to specific customers and specific orders, resulting in a no-holds-barred look at the specific facts, no matter how ugly. The rationale is rather simple. To resolve deficiencies, it is necessary to cut to the facts and correct specifics. Information technology available today is capable of monitoring and reporting exacting operational performance to the most precise detail across the entire supply chain. From a technological viewpoint, business is ready to generate "brutal" operating honesty. The question is just how ready is senior leadership to view and act on the information?

Beyond Benchmarking

During the past several decades, it has become fashionable for managers to identify firms considered "best in class" to benchmark how comparatively they perform common work. The practice of benchmarking has benefited many firms by helping identify new processes or practices that are transferable between companies. Sometimes benchmarking can be successfully used to proliferate best practice across operating divisions within a single firm. More often, it is used to gain a close look at identifying and duplicating how an industry leader operates. In other cases, it simply serves to justify existing operational practices.

The fallacy of benchmarking is that it creates a mind-set built on the belief that someone else has discovered the best way that your firm should perform a specific act of work. What it fails to achieve is an answer to the more basic question of what value this specific work contributes to your customers and your operational excellence. In short, the fallacy of benchmarking is that it may result in adoption and institutionalization of a best practice related to performing a task or process that, when viewed from a customer's perspective, adds minimal or no value.

A case in point is the extensive time that firms traditionally devoted to benchmarking and establishing best warehouse receiving and storage practices. Such obsession in making the warehouse operate better caused several firms to fail to identify and grasp the potential benefits of direct-to-customer inventory cross-docking. These firms were so committed to operating the warehouse better that they failed to see new opportunities available to totally eliminate the need for maintaining traditional warehouse operations being enabled by emerging information technology. Many warehouses today and the products they hold were built on the premises of the twentieth century and have outlived their Industrial Age purpose. The twenty-first-century model built on information technology should result in simplification and not added complexity and layers. In the future, a large part of supply chain inventory will be continually moving toward customers, with its whereabouts always known and its planned usage part of achieving a responsive consumer-based system. As Peter Drucker was fond of saying, "There is nothing so inefficient as making something more efficient that should not be done at all."

The argument against benchmarking is not one of throwing the baby out with the bathwater. A great deal can be learned about the experience curve related to performing essential tasks. However, operational excellence requires management to think outside the box and relate the motivation driving every process to a business end goal. Why do we do this? What value does it provide customers? Does it improve our overall performance? These are typical questions not answered by benchmarking.

Beyond Best Practice

The challenge to achieving operational excellence is to establish the correct mind-set throughout the leadership team within an enterprise. From senior leadership to those responsible for frontline execution, an enterprise needs to be driven by compelling commitment to continuously improved performance. The challenge is to emphasize continued execution of the best-known performance while introducing new practices designed to improve operational performance and leverage customer solidarity. These new practices must result in a sustainable value proposition. At least three traditional and often-quoted managerial paradigms are becoming increasingly questionable from the perspective of a twenty-first-century leader.

"If it ain't broke, don't fix it." Perhaps in the days of Charles Wilson, an icon at General Motors and later Secretary of Defense, this famous statement was appropriate. However, the twenty-first-century manager is continuously involved in identifying and replacing

traditional practices that continue to work well with new practices
that work substantially better. That's what leadership is all about: fixing
things that are working well and are not "broke" according to today's
standards so that they far exceed traditional performance expectations. Reinventing the brick-and-mortar enterprise is all about fixing
things that are not broken but that are losing their relevancy. In a very
real way, creative adoption of digital capability is the burning platform
of the twenty-first-century organization.

"If you can't measure it, you can't manage it." The late Edward
Demming, one of the undisputed quality gurus, was famous for calling this corporate legend pure nonsense. Demming persuasively
argued that the most important things a business needs to do in
order to achieve success can't be measured. In fact, Demming felt
that many essential things, such as total cost and customer satisfaction and simple cross-divisional cost-to-cost trade-offs, could not
be adequately measured. Nevertheless, Demming felt that continued
improvement depends upon these key efforts being managed. From
the outset of the twenty-first century, managers are accepting the
challenge of forging new frontiers in cross-functional integration
despite difficult or near-impossible measurement clarity.

"The customer's always right." In the spirit of creating an attitude
of meeting expectations and gaining loyalty, it is fashionable to position the customer as the "king." However, meeting and establishing customer expectations are two quite different things. Customers,
especially connected consumers, are not always right. Certainly, in a
forward-looking way, customers do not always know the next thing
they will like or need. We all lived without portable and simpler accessories for some time until innovation introduced new needs. The discussion at the beginning of the book involved digital cell phones, data
phones, and movie and still-picture cameras generating a deck full of

information and communication capability linking users instantly to almost any place in the world. Fewer today remember that "portable" movie cameras started out the size of an attaché case. Original "portable" telephones were the size of a shoebox. And now today's consumers are sure they need all of the above in one device smaller than the size of a wallet? A major responsibility of a supplier is to help customers better understand and take advantage of new opportunities. The reality is that innovation in industries such as information technology, automotive, aerospace, and even mass retailing can often be traced to insight and knowledge obtained from suppliers. Such fusion of core competencies across the supply chain is what fuels the ratchet effect. The simple fact of the matter is that twenty-first-century leadership does not have a best practice road map.

The New Value Proposition

In Chapter Four, business strategies of the twenty-first century were positioned to achieve effectiveness, efficiency, relevancy, and sustainability (the EERS value performance model). It is now timely to elaborate the essential features of the EERS value model in greater depth.

Since the Industrial Revolution, firms have sought to increase efficiency. In the sense used here, efficiency is about doing things well. It's a ratio of input to output that seeks to make the best use of limited resources. Effectiveness is all about doing the right things. An outgrowth of the focus on marketing that dominated post–World War II, effectiveness established new terms in the business vocabulary such as "customer service," "satisfaction," and "delight." Most of these concepts had more sizzle than content.

The twenty-first-century value proposition is building on the spirit of efficiency and effectiveness by adding the meaningful dimension of relevancy. Relevancy introduces and sustains the powerful notion of customer success. Customer success is about assuring that organizations that invent, make, and distribute products and related services connect with those people who consume products and services. In short, those who build business success and profitable growth by operating upstream in the supply chain can be successful only if, at the end of the process, the combined effort makes consumers successful. While having the appearance of being elusive, relevancy is a surprisingly simple concept. In an operational sense, relevancy is what gives focus to the synergism of efficiency and effectiveness.

Take, for example, the capability of Whirlpool to make delivery and installation of appliances in customer homes, ranging from the congestion of Manhattan to remote vacation homes located in northern Michigan. The ability of Whirlpool's Quality Express to promise and execute home delivery within a very small delivery time window has changed the face of selling appliances. The traditional practice of purchasing appliances at retail stores with disjoined delivery has been augmented with a customer-relevant delivery and installation service that is even capable of removing and disposing old appliances. A major feature of such relevancy is instructing consumers on how to best operate and maintain the appliance.

Another example is the very successful creation of the Geek Squad at Best Buy, which accommodated the needs of consumers shopping in its stores. The consumers wanted more than product availability at the best price. They wanted help with their purchases of electronic computers and video/audio home systems, as well as help installing and "consuming" them. They wanted to eliminate the complexity of the equipment and have a reliable supplier of services, starting at the time of purchase and continuing for some time thereafter. Relevancy solidifies the total supply chain into a value creation orchestration. In fact, supply chain competency becomes a significant differentiator or creator of brand equity in the overall value proposition. As seen above, relevancy can also create entirely new and profitable businesses.

The final aspect of superior performance is sustainability. While most operations can be ratcheted to achieve a high level of performance to resolve a specific service request, sustainability is about continuous performance over time at or above industry average. A sustainable supply chain is one that performs uniformly the same way or in a better way day in and day out. It is the essence of marketable value. UPS, FedEx, DHL, and others sell delivery value to consumers who expect guaranteed next-morning delivery. Effectiveness, efficiency, and relevancy are meaningful competencies only if they are sustainable. Thus, a major plank falls in place. Operational excellence builds by combining EERS capabilities to support a new value proposition. This new value proposition involves several commitments.

Commitment to Operational Perfection

The first commitment is to operational perfection. The emerging operational attitude is that each and every aspect of all prescribed behavior should have equal priority commitment. While acknowledging Pareto's law, this commitment to excellence seeks to eliminate the 80/20 phenomenon from supply chain operations.

To refresh, Pareto, a famous Italian philosopher, observed that, in most situations, very few events tend to dominate the overall characteristic of a universe; hence, the creation of the 80/20 law, which states that 20 percent of the items in a universe of events account for 80 percent of the activity. Pareto's observation has been repeatedly proven in performance distributions related to such varied aspects of business as 20 percent of customers representing 80 percent of sales or 20 percent of the products representing 80 percent of the sales activity. The Pareto logic stands behind widely adopted classification rules such as the ABC inventory model.

The challenge of "commitment to perfection" is not to question the validity of Pareto's law; rather, it is to eliminate its applicability to supply chain performance when it comes to achieving operational excellence. In other words, commitment to operational perfection seeks to eliminate the events that result in 80/20 distributions. It's about simplification and continual striving toward real-time synchronization to avoid exposure to failure. Processes can be designed to eliminate steps. For example, in inventory management, the commitment to perfection is manifested in stock keeping unit (SKU) rationalization. SKU proliferation can be avoided by utilizing rigid discipline concerning adding new products. Perhaps new products should be authorized only when low-volume and low-profit SKUs are eliminated.

However, commitment to perfection is not limited to visible events such as inventory or customers. The quest for perfection also involves far less visible opportunities found in processes such as managing customer order to delivery or retail order to purchase. Here, both the frequency of the event (some firms process thousands of orders or purchases daily) and the systematic nature of the process cry for rationalization. It is essential in complex and less visible processes to establish a priority framework to identify those events capable of affecting the fundamental value propositions of an enterprise. Once these events, those capable of ratcheting sustainable success, are identified, they must be targeted for perfection. In essence, the goal becomes to manage Pareto's ideology out of the value proposition.

Commitment to Continuous Improvement

Perfection will not be achieved overnight. The second commitment is to continuous improvement. The complexity of interlocking processes along a supply chain commands a realistic perspective of how difficult perfection is to achieve. The challenge is to establish attainable goals and engage to achieve continuous improvement. This requires a new mind-set regarding performance measurement. Success will be in small increments at irregular intervals. The key is to assure that success is the result of continuous improvement and that it is sustainable.

The twenty-first-century leader needs to reevaluate the traditional and entrenched performance metrics used in the enterprise. Firms engaged in a digital transformation are empowering new organizations committed to implementing new and holistic processes. The metric framework of the global digital economy enterprise, discussed in Chapter Eleven, must span both cross-functional integration and cross-organizational collaboration to measure all key activities relevant to the ultimate consumer. Such a comprehensive performance evaluation framework also needs to focus on continuous improvement.

Finally, traditional notions concerning what constitutes leading performance need to be repositioned. It's reasonable, in the age of the responsive supply chain business model, that traditional measures of what constitutes an industry will be totally redefined. For example, what industry is GE all about, or, to put it differently, does it matter, and who cares? One needs only to talk to GE's competitors, Whirlpool in appliances, Rolls-Royce in jet engines, and Honeywell in medical equipment, to realize that GE, as well as its managerial commitment, transcends the global economy. Such models of the modern enterprise require new visions concerning creating and sustaining leadership independent of the specifics of individual industries.

The new value proposition is about customer relevancy and connectivity in terms of perfection and continuous improvement. These attributes culminate into a firm's capability to achieve high levels of perfect order/purchase performance while continuously identifying, acting on, and measuring the root cause of failure. This ability to evaluate and sustain performance rests at the heart of becoming operationally excellent.

Commitment to Perfect Order Performance

The final commitment is to perfect order execution. The dogmatic persistence of taking connective action and staying the course by providing key customers and consumers an increasing frequency of perfect orders or purchases is the ratcheting force of operational excellence.

The perfect order is positioned as the vortex of operational excellence. The end game or goal of operational excellence is to become the preferred participant in many supply chain collaborations. In final analysis, it is a small number of firms that become best in class and earn the opportunity to catapult to industry leadership.

What, then, is a perfect order? Simply stated, it is the precise performance of every element of work related to every facet of an order, from inception to delivery. This includes all aspects of administration, from order entry to delivery or sale in compliance with specifications, incentives, and agreements. A perfect order means achievement of all preorder promises or purchase expectations precisely to specification or, in the case of retail, consumer aspiration.

The perfect order is a key concept in operational excellence. The elements of what constitutes a perfect order are easy to identify. View the order-to-delivery process as containing all events or elements of work extending from order creation to delivery. Achievement of a perfect order requires that each and every element of work be completed as originally planned. Because order or sales fulfillment typically involves activities of two or more independent businesses, by definition, perfect order execution is cross-enterprise. For example, a single order or sales fulfillment could involve the combined efforts of the customer, a public warehouse, a transportation carrier, and a company that conducts the sale, plus one or more companies performing financing or related services. As a result, the achievement of perfect order execution must be a masterful application of cross-organizational collaboration. Despite this complexity, one organization, typically the enterprise selling to the consumer, is the firm viewed as being responsible for achieving and maintaining operational excellence. While no data exist to substantiate the fact, it is common belief that perfect order achievement across most industries is substantially below 50 percent. In other words, less than one-half of all orders processed in today's business environment are actually delivered to exacting specification.

Perfect order execution is a difficult task. The administrative assessment of what goes wrong is even more difficult. What is required is root cause identification of each and every order-fulfillment-related deficiency. Whereas it takes only one defect to render an order imperfect, an individual fulfillment may be flawed by multiple defects. Root cause analysis means that the origin of each defect needs to be isolated. In other words, an across-the-board determination of what caused the deficiency needs to be identified, the root cause of failure isolated, and corrective action taken to prevent a repetitive problem.

Given the information technology available to most business operations a decade ago, the idea of perfect order execution was viewed as a theoretical "mission impossible." Today, technology is available to allow precise measurement and make such commitments to excellence increasingly a necessity.

Five Pillars of Operational Excellence

The twenty-first-century enterprise can be viewed as simultaneously achieving five pillars essential for operational excellence. A firm that achieves performance sustainability regarding these five pillars is viewed as having achieved the goals of ratcheting and stands on the threshold of catapulting to higher and more profitable growth.

Figure 5-1 illustrates the five pillars of operational excellence. It is important to understand the relationship between each area of focus.

Figure 5-1   Five Pillars of Operational Excellence

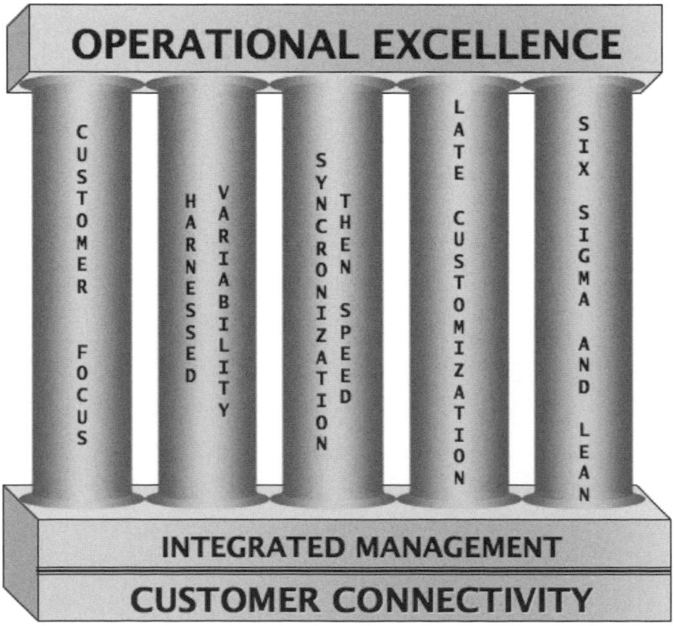

Similar to a building, the durability of the structure depends upon the strength of its supporting columns. The top of the structure is operational excellence. The five pillars reflect the strength to achieve such excellence.

Customer Focus

As we developed in Chapter Four, all initiatives, all behaviors, all resources—basically, all of anything that drives success—must be focused on the imperative of consumer (customer) connectivity. Consumption ultimately drives all strategy. Customers hold veto power over all marketing initiatives. It must be crystal clear that the customer is the individual or family unit that actually uses the end product or service being sold. The customer is the entity introducing new and continued revenue as goods and services are purchased and consumed. Once consumed, such goods and services cannot be economically reconstituted in their original form. Thus, a customer could be an individual eating a product or purchasing and using a house, an automobile, or an airplane ticket. The point is simple: all focus must be on consumption.

This is where the EERS value proposition influences behavior. All else happening in the supply chain depends on and is driven by this focus on customer connectivity. For this simple reason, information is driving traditionally anticipatory business systems to become more responsive. At the heart of this transformation is the growing connectivity of customers being driven by the inclusiveness of Web-based transacting. It is the customer who ultimately exercises the power to purchase with very defined expectations at Dell, Amazon, or Victoria's Secret. Thus, across an entire supply chain, the customer enables the need for elaborate alignment of independent business organizations. All sales to and between businesses organizations participating in any channel arrangement in final analysis depend on consumption. Understanding this shift in emphasis from channel of distribution structure to customer connectivity is a major differentiator of the Information Age.

Harnessed Variability

In terms of achieving operational excellence, the enemy of performance is variance. Any form of supply chain variability requires that additional resources be deployed in order to achieve predictability. Operational excellence is all about being predictable within your supply chain domain while retaining sufficient agility and capability to flexibly respond to customer demand. The logistics of supply chain operations transcends and connects multiple enterprise operations. Lead times and resource levels within the complete supply chain must be exacting and, most of all, predictable to assure operational performance. When performance is not predictable, resources such as manufacturing or assembly capacity, additional product inventories, or system lead times must be allocated to protect against operational breakdown. These resources are deployed to smooth out and overcome variance. But, each of these options introduces a new level of resources and risk.

The traditional practice is to participate in forecasting in an effort to predict the variance likely to be encountered during a specified operating period. The alternative, becoming increasingly feasible in the Information Age, is real-time performance monitoring and maximum responsiveness to eliminate variance. The greater the customer connectivity, the lower the incident of variance across the supply chain. This is why, in fashion-based industries, significant ongoing research efforts are completed to understand what drives consumer behavior. It is the fundamental reason why companies seek connectivity with customers.

Synchronized—then Speed

Fast is exciting and may be fashionable, but it also may not be relevant. Anyone who has ever served in the military is well aware of the practice of "hurry up and wait." The primary aspect of timing in a twenty-first-century enterprise is to achieve synchronization. The key to maximize operational performance is to rapidly achieve and then maintain momentum. This capability to maintain momentum serves to eliminate dwell. Dwell is best defined as the incident of valuable resources, such as people, inventory, or transportation capacity, sitting idle in anticipation of future use. No experienced business manager needs to be reminded of the host of bad things that can happen to an operation dominated by excessive dwell. The costs associated with stop, dwell, and start represent maximum situations of energy consumption. Thus, most operational managers inherently understand that, to the maximum extent possible, goods in motion should be maintained in motion during the value adding process. For example, the ideal distributive arrangement is one that accomplishes all product sorting and customization during the time the order is being transported to the final destination. Merging final assembly components of a product while they are being transported or during final delivery can eliminate costly warehousing and reduce finished product or service obsolescence. Such merging has become a hallmark of leading electronic, furniture, and fashion companies. Speed is important because time is money and market innovation has a short shelf life and depreciating sales price point. Companies such as Dell, HP, Motorola, Steelcase, Coach, and many others have this belief built into their standard operation practices. However, synchronization remains the key to response efficiency.

Late Customization

The Industrial Age best solved problems by developing complex and complicated machine solutions. In the Information Age, the focus is to reduce such complexity by replacement with simpler and more dependable digital solutions that have a high degree of interchangeability. This quest to be flexible rests at the heart of a broad range of value-added services (VASs). Any VAS that increases the combined impact of a firm's EERS value proposition serves to move a basic service or product away from being a commodity toward becoming a specialty or a solution. A standard product or service modified to become a specialty or a solution increases value in the eyes of the customer. Examples of this are most of the computers, printers, and telephones we buy today. Most are feature configured and assembled near the ultimate consumer market. This late customization uses the latest available components and information to configure the product in each local market.

Late customization, sometimes called postponement, comes in many different forms in the digital enterprise. When strategic information is freely exchanged among firms engaged in a supply chain, the possibility of delaying or postponing differentiation in the assembly and movement of final products becomes increasingly feasible. Assembly of other products is being postponed until customer specifications are finalized. These real-time responsiveness concepts are more fully discussed in Chapter Seven. Once again, technology-driven collaborative processes translate into responsiveness.

Six Sigma and Lean

The final pillar of operational excellence is best captured by the rigors of six sigma and lean commitment. Six-sigma perfection is most often associated with quality initiatives, and its popularity has generated a revolution in measurement tolerance. In fact, many managers have become specialists (black and green belts) in proliferating extreme perfection in execution throughout manufacture, assembly, and product delivery. Under the six-sigma framework, the incident of acceptable failure is 3.4 defects per million. Keep in mind, as discussed earlier, the two-sigma standard typical of traditional supply chain operations results in between 2.5 and 5 defects per 100 events!

In terms of operational excellence, the adoption of six-sigma mentalities simply means "get it and keep it right." This requires getting outside the four walls of an enterprise and applying the same rigor across supply chain operations. While this may be an extreme stretch goal for most traditional supply chains, the momentum toward such perfection is the focus and reality of perfect order execution. These lofty goals seem far more realistic, given the operational capabilities inherent in response-based continuous improvement. The foundation of integrated management is the topic of Chapter Six, the last of the ratcheting chapters.

Chapter Six
Integrative Management

> *"What is so astonishing in 2000 is that most companies still find it almost more than they can bear to adapt their structures and practices to those universally accepted realities."*[1]
>
> —Geoffey Colvin

Subjects close to the heart of most executives are leadership and organizational structure. Leadership is all about stimulating and motivating the creative talents of knowledge workers. Organization deals with ways to structure work assignments to enable customer value creation. While the challenge of leadership will not be directly discussed until later in the book, the question of how to organizationally structure knowledge workers to achieve maximum synergy is every bit a leadership challenge. The reality is that the organizational structures of most brick-and-mortar enterprises are operationally in shambles. The managerial challenge is to facilitate, enable, and implement integrative processes. This we call "integrative management."

A major managerial accomplishment of the twentieth century was the design and deployment of organizations to implement Frederick Taylor's concepts of "scientific management."[2] The "scientific" organization structure was designed to harness the benefits of specialization

---

[1]   Geoffey Colvin, "Managing in the Info Era," *Fortune*, March 6, 2003.

[2]   Frederick W. Taylor, *Scientific Management* (New York: W. W. Norton, 1967).

and facilitate maximum economy of scale in pursuit of unprecedented productivity. The result was the birth of vertical specialization, siloed functionality, and management using a hierarchical command-and-control organization structure. Each functional organization was responsible for performing a meaningful unit of work. Performance metrics were developed to measure accomplishment. Best practices were identified to assure leading-edge or best-in-class performance. The result was that many complex organizations were vertically structured in command-and-control layers to facilitate performance of essential tasks and objectives, thereby enabling them to harness the fruits of the Industrial Revolution.

Similar to most transition enabling frameworks, over time, the doctrines of "scientific management" began to outlive their usefulness. By the late twentieth century, the rapid development of knowledge workers and the widespread availability of information technology combined to increasingly challenge the continued relevancy of these vertical, or hierarchical, organization structures. Despite countless articles and books declaring the command-and-control organization model obsolete, vertical organization hierarchies continue to survive in the twenty-first century. Why?

The most persuasive answers are that business leaders could not justify an alternative structure, did not know how to implement a new model without jeopardizing current operations, or simply did not believe that a different organizational arrangement was necessary. The deficiency of the most successful twentieth-century enterprises was failure to continue to excel operationally. The operating reality is that when servicing customers, very few well-established firms even come close to enjoying operational excellence as discussed in Chapter Five. The challenge is to commit and empower initiatives to gain and maintain operational excellence. Although the benefits may come slowly, over time, sincere commitment to operational excellence will gain momentum. To leverage the power of operational excellence, we introduced the ratchet effect, the sustained power of continuous improvement and sustainability. Despite everything discussed earlier, the power structure of most traditional companies has remained in vertical organization units structured around products, geographical areas, functions, and, in some situations, customers.

Most senior managers understand that organizational structures dominated by functional silos just don't cut it performance wise when the challenge is to manage end-to-end customer-focused processes. The increasing obsolescence of traditional organization structures is not news. They also are aware that cross-functional integrated management is essential to leveraging synergistic performance. On the basis of countless discussions across a wide spectrum of industries, it is also clear to us that senior leadership is fully aware of the challenges associated with enabling widespread process integration. The barrier is one of migration: how does one transition an organization traditionally structured around functional specialization to one focused on customer value creation processes while at the same time maintaining and improving business results?

The complete answer to organizational alignment needs to be understood and designed with the uniqueness of specific companies and industries in mind. We will, however, share general thoughts on how it might be conceived and how one might begin to implement the change, given current organizational models.

Organizational adaptation and migration are, and will during the foreseeable future remain, the most complex challenges facing today's business leaders. The alignment and deployment of knowledge workers in an information-rich environment is one of the main factors rendering digitizing a long-term journey. What will be found in this chapter are guidelines concerning how to engage the opportunity. The leadership challenge starts with understanding the eight key horizontal processes. The initial step in developing an organization structure to drive integrative management is gaining an in-depth understanding of the horizontal processes that are essential to successful value creation and stainable business operations.

Horizontal Processes

To facilitate integrative management, it is useful to envision business organization in terms of fundamental horizontal processes. The processes are specified as horizontal because two or more traditional functional organizations typically have shared responsibility for process achievement. Eight key horizontal processes represent candidates for extraction or liberation from the vertical, or functional, hierarchy of the typical enterprise.[3] The reality is that integrated execution of all eight of the core processes depends on successful collaboration with customers and suppliers, discussed later in this book. Thus, replacing the traditional functional business model with the responsive supply chain business model ultimately must expand performance of the eight basic processes within and beyond the operations of the four walls of the individual enterprise. Figure 6-1 presents a brief definition of each process.

Demand Planning

A fundamental cross-organizational process is demand planning. Demand planning is about what to sell, make, and buy and when. Because most business organizations must undertake value creation

---

[3]   This section is adapted from Donald J. Bowersox, David J. Doss, and M. Bixby Cooper, *Supply Chain Logistics Management* (Boston: McGraw-Hill/Irwin Companies, Inc., 2007).

Figure 6-1   Eight Core Supply-Chain-Integrated Processes

Demand Planning
Demand assessment to achieve maximum customer responsiveness.

Customer Relationship
Development and administration of customer relationships to facilitate strategic information sharing, joint planning, and integrated operations.

Order Fulfillment
Execution of superior and sustainable order-to-delivery performance and related services.

Product Launch
Participation in product and product service development, promotion and lean launch.

Manufacturing
Production strategy support and facilitation of postponement throughout the supply chain.

Supplier Relationship
Development and administration of supplier relationships to facilitate strategic information sharing, joint planning, and integrated operations.

Product Support
Life cycle repair and support of products. Includes warranty, replacement, maintenance, and repair.

Reverse Movement
Return and disposition of inventories in a cost-effective and secure manner.

in anticipation of future demand for their services or products, it remains important to make an assessment of activities likely to materialize. In most firms, forecasting and demand planning are critical processes. They should be based on enterprise-wide connected plans that ensure that each department's objectives are aligned to ultimately produce the desired amount of end products and product services at the agreed-to times. Firms have process issues when all interconnected departments' activities are not based on the same overall sales and inventory plan and do not consider individual department capacity, agility, and flexibility. Firms have traditionally not been very accurate when it comes to forecasting what their customers are going to purchase.

As a general rule, the more precise or specific the forecast, the greater the difficulty in developing an accurate projection. While it may not be too difficult to forecast the overall quantity of automobiles a manufacturer, or even a dealer, will sell in a model year, it is extremely difficult to forecast specific models, colors, and accessory packages. It is even more difficult to forecast specific model sales by geographical market or specific time frames. This difficulty in developing successful forecasts has long been an operations management dilemma for most firms.

On the one hand, forecasts with associated product support plans are essential to successful operations, including buying, making, storing, and moving products and performing product support services necessary to satisfy demand. On the other hand, managers within most functional areas do not trust the overall or aggregate forecasts with which they are presented.

A great deal of their lack of trust in forecasting is directly related to the fact that their incentive compensation is driven by actual performance, in contrast to plan and budget. But what are plan and budget, and how do they align with original sales and supportive plans of the company? As a result, the typical firm finds managers creating many different forecasts and related plans. These individual forecasts and plans tend to drive business performance as departmental leaders seek to best position their organizations for functional success. In one business organization visited by one of the authors, a total of eight different forecasts for the same business operational period were being used to drive operations and to communicate to interested parties. Most firms don't have one forecast and one set of related departmental plans because unit managers don't have confidence in forecasting integrity.

Naturally, senior leadership is constantly seeking new and better ways to develop cross-functional forecasts and plans. A planning process designed to achieve successful cross-functional planning is sales and operations planning (S&OP). Advanced S&OP processes use cross-functional inputs at the senior leadership level to arrive at quantification of anticipatory needs. Some firms have incorporated customer input into the planning process by using collaborative planning and forecasting replenishment (CPFR), which is promoted and coordinated by the voluntary industry standards organization (VICS). The goal is to reach a planned response for all supporting activities of the company, including selling, distributing, manufacturing, and procuring necessary materials or products. The end objective is a statement of anticipatory actions to be adhered to by all functions involved. In short, an S&OP process utilizes cross-function collaboration to create one joint operational plan for all operating units of an organization.

Such a holistic perspective is designed to facilitate functional collaboration across and between operating areas. For successful S&OP implementation, it is typically necessary to adopt one incentive compensation plan for all functional managers based on overall enterprise achievement.

While efforts to arrive at a statement of shared expectations are admirable, the fact remains that anticipatory, or forecast-based, plans are seldom correct. However, most business leaders agree that a standardized S&OP process is preferable to each function generating a unique view of future requirements. At the end of the demand planning process, one shared vision should drive cross-functional performance. In many ways, the most important of the eight processes, getting demand planning right, is the most difficult process to perfect. Such difficulty is a result of deficiency in both technique and procedure. The difficulty in generating successful S&OP results within an enterprise and across an enterprise's supply chain is the primary force driving greater emphasis on developing demand sensing and response capabilities both with consumers and from shared planning with trading partners, suppliers, and even suppliers' suppliers. Minimizing the impact of the anticipatory challenge rests at the core of developing a responsive supply chain business model.

Customer Relationship

In a typical vertical organization, numerous management units have responsibility for bits and pieces of the customer relationship process. Others are often involved in the customer experience but are not organizationally or performance wise held responsible. It's not unusual for as many as six different functional organizations to maintain regular dialogue with some part of a customer's organization. For example, R&D, marketing, sales, order fulfillment, logistics, engineering, accounting, and legal all have legitimate reasons to contact or be contacted by customers. Most all of these groups need to establish and maintain ongoing customer relationships to establish initial expectations, reinforce ongoing and changing needs, entice purchases, administer orders, monitor consumption, and ensure overall satisfaction.

Leadership is increasingly realizing that customers positively respond to a single point of contact (SPOC). Supported by a comprehensive customer information database, one person or organization, often referred to as the "one face to the customer," serves as the contact point for an integrated cross-functional team dedicated to providing customers complete and coordinated information. Such clarity and focused responsibility for managing the relationship process are integral to achieving operational integration.

With technology facilitating SPOC, cross-functional account teams have become a reasonable solution for managing customer relationships. In some organizations, account teams have moved from a project-based focus to being permanently assigned the responsibility of managing the total life cycle of a customer relationship.

The growing connectivity of customers with suppliers having complex organizations raises additional challenges. Connectivity using Web-based ordering and payment is a relatively straightforward proposition. However, dealing with all aspects of customer service related to post-transaction administration is a more complex issue.

Relationship management with customers is one of the most challenging problems and opportunities of twenty-first-century enterprise. Many firms have created "voice of the customer" relationship management systems to support full interface with customers. Such relationship management systems provide customer profiles, performance achievements and past shortfalls, availability issues, and, where necessary, regulatory compliance information.

Many firms have off-shored customer response functionality. This practice has created growing consumer resistance to talking with a person in another country when seeking to resolve a local problem. These connective systems were created for improved efficiency but often failed to consider effectiveness, relevancy, and sustainability (EERS). The implementation of outsourced centers must take into consideration how such centers fit into overall customer relationship management. Customer dissatisfaction with such arrangements creates competitive opportunities.

Order Fulfillment

For organizations implementing integrative processes, harnessing the cross-functional order-to-delivery process constitutes an essential starting point. The process of order fulfillment includes all activities from customer purchase commitment to product delivery and administrative closure. The order fulfillment process is the natural framework for implementing a perfect order initiative to drive operational excellence. The classic *Harvard Business Review* article "Staple Yourself to an Order" illustrates the many different ways a consumer or customer order can bounce between functional organizational units and even get lost while being processed within a typical enterprise.[4]

No other process is as critical as order fulfillment because it directly relates to a firm's revenue stream. However, leaders should keep in mind that traditional order fulfillment processes were established at a time when digital information technology was hardly a thought in anyone's mind. Thus, order processing is one process that is highly fragmented and even broken in many brick-and-mortar companies. The idea that future increases in business-to-business as well as customer-to-business connectivity could eliminate the need to have traditional orders is no longer a far-fetched idea. As one executive put it, "The best way to manage order processing is to eliminate the customer order." The potential for such innovation is discussed in Chapter Eight. In the twenty-first century, what should the new paradigm for carrying out order fulfillment processes across companies be, and what will the multicompany organizations look like? What is the new language for transacting business in the digital world? These are all issues that must be addressed in planning and executing a comprehensive digital transformation.

Product Launch

The processes of new product design and introduction are clearly linked to creating customer value. The typical design and approval of a new product offering require input from engineering, packag-

---

[4]   Benson P. Shapiro, V. Kasturi Rangan, and John J. Sviokla, "Staple Yourself to an Order," *Harvard Business Review*, July–August 1992 (Reprint July 2004).

ing, marketing, logistics, manufacturing, finance, legal, and others. Deciding how and where to deploy R&D resources, what products to launch, and how to undertake initial market distribution requires the best collective judgment across the supply chain.

In many companies, new integrated processes have been created to expand the search for innovative opportunities while accelerating go-to-market time frames, with kill or invest milestones, to maximize resource utilization and idea generation. The high rate of new product failure and the high cost of failure recovery and damage control require comprehensive cross-functional coordination and oversight. Unless the new product development and launch processes are liberated from traditional functional control and positioned as integrated processes, results will continue to be disappointing. Innovation requires the capability to continually cast a wide net to capture new and improved ideas. It also needs a filtering and funneling process that drives decisive go/no-go review throughout the process to maximize creation of new products and ensure that supply chain resources are focused on the most promising ideas. Today, in the consumer and fashion industries, in order to maintain the pace of innovation, more than half of all new products are expected to originate from trading partners' suggestions.

At the same time, someone needs to decide which products to kill and remove from the supply chain. For example, the unbridled growth of stock keeping units, often called SKU proliferation, is one of industry's greatest areas of operational failure. It is not unusual to see very few SKUs accounting for a vast majority of a firm's sales. Likewise, many SKUs experience near zero annual movement. As discussed earlier, one challenge of twenty-first-century leadership is to manage Pareto's law out of all processes, including new product development and launch. No other processes are more victimized by vertical, or silo, management than new product development and launch. Most firms require a comprehensive review of how new product development is organized and integrated across the enterprise and how the associated horizontal processes are satisfying their raison d'être for the enterprise.

Manufacturing

Across most industries and in many firms, the most horizontally integrated process is manufacturing and its related support activities. While more typically viewed as a process, manufacturing still may or may not be complimentary to an enterprise's overall integrated management. Because of the significant amount of attention to the efficiency of the manufacturing process during the Industrial Age, most firms place great value on gaining and maintaining economy of scale. Most firms that dominated early-twentieth-century commerce were engaged in transforming raw materials into finished products. Since World War II, industry has increasingly trended toward supplementing basic manufacturing with a range of value-added services.

The critical manufacturing issues of the twenty-first century relate to maintaining scale economy while simultaneously increasing flexibility. Many companies in the consumer industry have had to rethink their run length and line changeover practices to better accommodate customer demand while simultaneously staying within economic scale and the profit "sweet spot." In addition to economy of scale, the growing advantages of outsourcing and off-shoring are serving to revolutionize traditional concepts concerning what constitutes best manufacturing practice.

A major factor for a firm seeking to become more connected to customers is learning how to increase agility and flexibility in an effort to rapidly accommodate specialized customer requests. In a world where inventory is viewed as a necessary evil to be avoided at all costs, those firms mastering flexible manufacturing are better positioned to support responsive, or pull, strategies. To be flexible means a firm has perfected ways to accommodate customer request for product modification and customization at late stages of the order-to-delivery process. Increasingly, firms are outsourcing performance of selected services in order to accommodate customer requests for unique product customization.

An example of outsourced just-in-time manufacturing includes the automated weekly replenishment of oxford shirts at JC Penny stores by offshore manufacturers. These manufacturers receive store sales and inventory information electronically and manage inventory levels, manufacturing plans, and delivery of shirts to all stores. Similarly, offshore factories in the apparel industry are now able, for the same unit cost, to manufacture multiple sizes and colors of intimate apparel on a single production line. This capability allows manufacturing and assembly of mixed-size cases of apparel sufficiently large to enable economical shipments direct to retail stores from overseas factories.

Thus, manufacturing principles representing the bedrock of the Industrial Era are being radically rethought. Manufacturing competency will increasingly be measured by how rapidly a firm is capable of accommodating a unique product configured to meet a specific customer's specification. For some products, customization will increasingly be performed throughout the supply chain at varied locations not limited to factories. New best practices will emerge to guide this configuration and customization process.

Supplier Relationship

Just as customer relationship management seeks to focus on demand facing units of an organization, supplier relationship seeks clarity and relational management of the procurement process. Today, progressive firms no longer approach procurement as simply an opportunity to increase profits by forcing price reductions and operational concessions from suppliers. They understand that the fundamental goal of strategic procurement is to sustain manufacturing and related business operations at the lowest total cost. This minimum total cost must be achieved while adding more manufacturing or product innovation, speed, flexibility, and agility to the product creation process. These goals are typically best achieved by collaborating with key suppliers in an effort to identify and implement win-win arrangements.

Such strategic sourcing and lowest total cost procurement are achieved and sustained only by a comprehensive and coordinated program to manage total spend. In addition, the scope of strategic procurement is being expanded to focus on all company expenditures. There is growing awareness that expenditures for materials and related services typically account for less than half of the total cost incurred to support sales. For example, the same techniques used today to monitor and manage material procurement are starting to be applied to retail store costs such as store packaging, store displays, advertising, and promotion material. Tiffany and Co. and Victoria's Secret are two brands where this visual leverage within the store experience and related packaging has proven appealing to consumers. Additionally, enterprise costs of legal, consulting, technology, and accounting services are increasingly being viewed as manageable purchases. Many companies are starting to partner with suppliers to realize synergies in product R&D innovation, manufacturing, supply chain, and non-product services.

Most firms are both buyers and suppliers when viewed from an overall supply chain perspective. The only participants in any supply chain having a unique position are consumers. A consumer makes purchases for personal consumption. All other participants in a supply chain are buying in anticipation of a future sale of either the same product or a manufactured product that incorporates the purchased material or component. Most organizations gain significant advantage during their part of the value creation process as a result of synergistic collaboration with key suppliers.

Product Support

Most products are sold with explicit promises concerning performance. Such guarantees typically warrant performance over a specified time. During the warranty period, firms usually offer repair services and information to assist customers in learning how to best use the products. In other situations, products require specific supplies in order to continue to perform over extended time. These supplies may be products such as ink or paper, razor blades, or preventative maintenance. The process of product support can affect several different parts of an organization. For example, careful management of the warranty process may be a primary source of ideas for new product development or modification of existing products.

In a similar sense, postsales product support may have a direct influence on future purchases. Customers who feel they have received outstanding support are far more likely to purchase new models or replacement products from the same supplier. Brand loyalty is significantly influenced by product support.

Many firms outsource product support to third-party service providers. Firms specializing in package delivery often develop the competencies necessary to perform product service and support for their customers as an outsourced service. In such situations, customers may think they are returning a product for repair to the firm where they purchased it, via FedEx, UPS, or another firm that specializes in package delivery. The product may actually be shipped to a repair facility operated by the transportation company and then returned directly to the customer following repair. The use of such third-party repair specialists is common in the computer, medical, and electronic industries.

In many industries, the performance of aftermarket repair represents a large and profitable business. Some auto dealerships report greater profits from providing comprehensive repair and general service to customers than they do selling new and used automobiles. What happens to products and customer opinions following the initial product sale is of prime interest to a large number of managers within an organization, ranging from marketing and sales, to new product development, to manufacturing and purchasing. Product support is an activity of critical cross-functional importance to most firms.

Reverse Movement

For a variety of reasons, products may be subjected to reverse movement from consumers back to the original manufacturer. In other situations, manufacturers return materials and component parts to their suppliers. One such reverse movement was noted in the earlier discussion of product support.

Reverse logistics in the United States is estimated to be in excess of a $60-billion annual industry. The fact of the matter is that all firms are required by law to stand behind and guaranty products sold to consumers. When products have not been sold by the stated "best sold by" date, the common practice is for the manufacturer to reimburse retailers for the product and associated reverse logistical expense. Several 3PLs specialize in providing reverse logistics services. Such services may include product disposition to salvage or, when appropriate, resell via clearance outlets, auctions, charities, and Web-based marketing. For example, some of the "best if sold by" dates on food products are based on time frames designed to protect a brand's standard for taste and freshness, and after the date has passed, the products are not harmful if consumed. For some of these products, the grocery industry expedites transfer to food banks for use by charities. For other types of products, some firms will disassemble products to recover parts and components that can be reused or marketed.

Reverse logistics competency is essential to accomplish successful product recalls. Whenever a product is deemed unsafe for use in manufacturing or for consumption, the associated supply chain members face the need to rapidly move the product involved out of harm's way. Such recalls, even from retailer shelves, can be performed in a matter of hours in highly structured supply chains. A case in point is ConAgra's recent recall of frozen pot pies and Peter Pan peanut butter as a result of potential salmonella contamination.

Naturally, all forms of reverse movement are of concern to a wide range of managerial groups within an enterprise. Information leading to a recall or withdrawal impacts many departments and government agencies. The recall directive as well as all corrective actions must be managed from a total enterprise perspective.

In summary, all eight core processes are integral to how organizations create value. Each process identifies a vital operational effort that must be managed across the functional boundaries of enterprise departments and across the supply chain. To varying degrees, all eight of these processes involve suppliers, trading partners, and consumers. Therefore, in final analysis, the eight processes enable the responsive supply chain business model. All eight processes deal with important aspects of integrated management. Each represents a legitimate horizontal platform for generating the momentum necessary to exploit the benefits of operational ratcheting. Learning and organizing for the successful execution of these eight processes are at the heart of integrative management.

Integrative Management Framework

It is clear that new organization models are necessary to maximize the integrated performance of a digital enterprise. When strategic objectives focus on final consumers, the logic of traditional vertical enterprise structure designed around functional efficiency soon loses relevancy. Achieving the integrated performance requires a new and innovative organizational design. This new organization structure must coordinate the successful execution of the eight core horizontal processes in collaboration with supply chain partners.

This new structure must be designed to direct and maintain velocity of five key enterprise value creation flows. The five key flows are information, product, service, finance, and knowledge. These flows need to be coordinated within an enterprise and positioned for maximum interoperability with suppliers, trading partners, and, most important, customers.

The five key flows serve to integrate all participating firms in a responsive supply chain. Information flow provides the intelligence to direct and maintain operations. Product flow is all about positioning inventory availability at the right place at the right time, with minimum risk exposure. Service is the coordination of all value enhancing activities that increase the attractiveness of a firm's product offering. Finance is the management of assets throughout the process and the focus on price/value and maintaining liquidity. Knowledge involves the in-depth understanding of markets, products, and processes that firms must share both within the four walls of an enterprise and with supply chain collaborators. The fear of sharing all forms of knowledge represents one of the largest barriers to implementing integrated management.

The integrated enterprise, Figure 6-2, is viewed as having five centers of knowledge and expertise. The synergy of integrating these centers is what creates and drives a company's core competency. The centers encapsulating all activities and processes of an enterprise are (1) human resource management, (2) customer relationship management, (3) operational management, (4) financial stewardship, and (5) process measurement and motivation. These centers replace the traditional line-and-command organization structure with overlapping knowledge centers that provide essential support for core processes. All five of these key centers of excellence and expertise are discussed in the varied chapters of this book.

An experienced reader will recognize these five centers as key ingredients of a traditional organization model. The difference is found in the orientation and focus of emphasis. Instead of being

Figure 6-2   Integrated Digital Organizational Framework

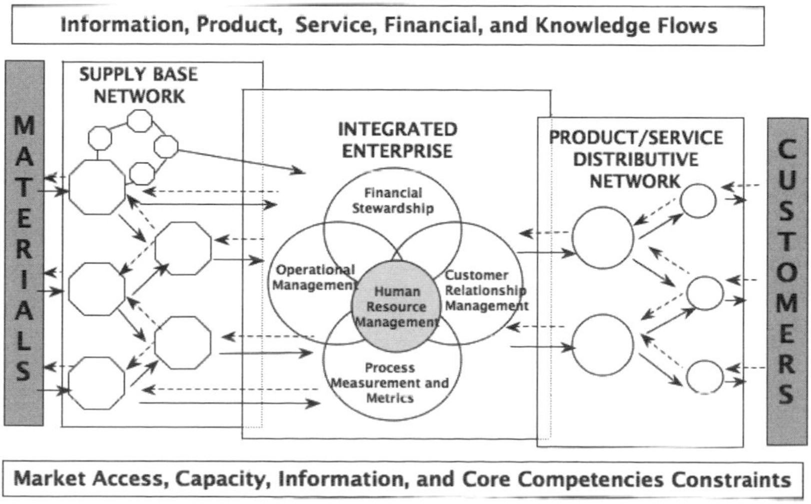

positioned as line or staff functions, as is typical in a traditional organization, each center represents a process-focused organization that is an integral part of day-to-day operations. For example, human resource management and financial stewardship are directly involved in day-to-day operational execution. The reason is simple: each of these key processes has a direct impact on successful supply chain execution, and each is directly involved with customers and suppliers.

It is interesting to note the lack of presence of a traditional data processing organization in Figure 6-2. As discussed throughout the earlier chapters, information technology must be positioned as a fundamental part and shared resource among all organizational units of a digital enterprise. Cross-functional technology user groups are viewed as collaborating with a combination of external or internal technology service providers. As noted earlier, the trend is clearly toward the outsourcing of the operation of technology platforms. Internal challenges are related to successful integration of cross-process applications.

The traditional functional organizational structure's preoccupation with products, territories, or industries needs to be replaced with direct lines of communication and activity transcending the supply chain. Key processes unique to achieving the value proposition of each enterprise should receive leadership from the experience and expert centers. The precise combination of the eight fundamental processes and organizational relationships that any given enterprise will configure and sustain depends upon the nature of its specific customer engagements and the degree to which the integrated enterprise is collaboratively and operationally extended into supply, distribution, or customer supply chain operating relationships. The blueprint is simple but daunting. The digital firm is focused to provide a maximum impact in areas capable of leading to competitive superiority, which we refer to as core competencies. A firm may also internalize selected processes not representing areas of core competency but considered essential to operational success. These essential competencies are referred to as core necessities. Everything else, while needed, could be considered candidates for outsourcing or cross-enterprise collaboration with external members of a firm's supply chain.

Finally, the scope of any extended enterprise faces constraints. These constraints serve as boundaries concerning the operational scope of the enterprise. These boundaries can be modified by a variety of strategies, ranging from research and development to merger and acquisition. Siemans Corporation and IBM are prime examples of global enterprises that have repeatedly redefined their constraining boundaries during the past decade. While constraints can take many different forms, the most obvious ones are knowledge related to market access, capacity, information, and core competencies.

The essence of the digital enterprise is developing an organization structure that allows it to ratchet operational expertise throughout the supply chain. This ratcheting capability is based on consumer connectivity, operational excellence, and integrative process management, all focused on gaining and maintaining customer centricity. These concepts of structure and horizontal processes are not comfortable to many leaders who gained senior status working in a command-and-control environment. The concluding section reviews in greater depth the challenges of mobilizing integrated process management.

Mobilizing Integrated Process Management

The fact of the matter is that, for decades, rigid functional organizations worked. In fact, they worked sufficiently well to achieve the highest level of economic development known in recorded history. The fundamental force driving command-and-control organizations was specialization. The enabling concept was grouping knowledge related to performing a specific job or element of work into an organizational unit, most often called a department. Departments are the organizational structures empowered to maximize efficiency. These organizational units are driven by initiatives designed to achieve maximum economy of scale. Departments became the knowledge centers of the Industrial Age.

While most of the above logic makes sense, the missing attribute is a mechanism to drive connectivity. The linking of departments into a value creation process has always been more or less assumed a natural outcome. Departments that performed related work have typically been located in close proximity to each other, in the belief that "closeness" would facilitate end-to-end performance. For example, several related departments were combined to create a factory or a warehouse. Typically, such departmental clusters became the budgetary control points and planning units for command-and-control organizations.

It is what is not being said about these structures that has become the Achilles' heal of functionalism, namely, (1) each department was encouraged to excel and was rewarded for excelling as a result of having full authority and responsibility for performing its unique work; (2) despite the fact that related departments worked to achieve best-in-class performance, no mechanism, except planning and control, existed to assure the creation of a superior holistic effort; and (3) the functional separation principle assumed that trade-offs having the potential of creating either synergism or degradation would be nonexistent or would be automatically integrated. The historical fact of the matter is that implementation of scientific management advancements of the Industrial Age were sufficiently integrated to result in unprecedented efficiency. However, most good things reach their limits.

Progressively, during the last several decades of the twentieth century, the shortcomings of traditional organization structure emerged. Whereas many experts advocated adoption of new managerial practices to maximize the impact of business process engineering and emerging information connectivity, old organizational structures were held firmly in place. In retrospect, this structural rigidity seems to have been driven by a failure to create comprehensive organizational change strategies. Facing and mobilizing rigid organizations to enable process management requires commitment to at least three leadership initiatives: (1) core process liberation, (2) change management, and (3) metric-reward alignment.

Core Process Liberation

One highly visible aspect of traditional, or vertical, organizations is that they confirm their importance and sustainability by maintaining ownership over resources deployed to a specific product, customer, geographical area, or function. These resource kingdoms, better described as powerful functional domains, need to be challenged and replaced by focusing control on core processes. As noted earlier, a core process is identified as a sequence of work that creates value. Ideally, firms will establish unique value propositions or differentials by performing core processes in a manner that creates customer loyalty. It is these core processes, not traditional functions, that represent the important and sustainable competencies of an enterprise.

One initiative for focusing and mobilizing the traditional organizational gridlock is to break out or liberate the eight core processes discussed earlier and their related competencies from their traditional functional organizational structure. For example, cross-functional responsibility to logistically service key or enterprise customers may be liberated from specific business units and reassigned to a shared-services distribution organization. Johnson & Johnson has retained an autonomous structure of individual manufacturing companies while at the same time creating a shared-enterprise organization responsible for supply chain competency. Thus, the perceived benefits of vertical management were retained while enjoying the synergy of integrated supply chain order-to-delivery performance. As a result of such core processes, liberation, and shared services, large customers, such as Target and Walgreens, benefited from integrated cross-enterprise J&J logistics.

At Zara, a very successful vertically integrated fashion retailer in Europe, the company has organized itself around customers by product group. For example, one of its formal business teams, women's clothes, is in one office in one large section of a building. Sitting side by side along a row of long tables are all of the functional representatives responsible for design, merchandising, sales planning and operations, production, logistics, and finance. They interact by the hour on what is selling, where, for how much, what they should be making more or less of, and what new designs will be the next products to sell, in real time, face to face, with the latest information on sales, inventory, and production. Additionally, at the end of the long tables in the office, there is a CADCAM where product prototypes approved by the team can be electronically transmitted to manufacturing in order to make samples for review. Behind the CADCAM, work tables exist for cutting sample fabric, which is then handed to a team of adjacent sewers. Within hours, ideas shaped by current feedback from stores and new design creations are turned into samples for review, revision, or approval for future sales. When approved, electronic product specifications are transferred directly to factories, where the product is made and delivered to stores within weeks. For some companies, integrated management is not a remote concept but an emerging reality.

Change Management

Rather than hoping that cross-functional trade-offs will positively aggregate, management can take steps to organizationally facilitate integration. The rapid emergence of supply chain organizations throughout industry illustrates an increasingly popular structural approach designed to achieve cross-functional process integration. Such organization models group responsibility for customer relationship, manufacturing, procurement, and logistics into a single organization having end-to-end performance responsibility for customer order-to-product delivery. Enabling such process-focused organization creates the ability to service a customer on an integrated basis while improving the capability to identify and manage total cost to serve. The integrative management of overall order to delivery assures that no specific function is emphasized at the expense of the overall process.

Identifying process owners and contributors can achieve a similar integrative benefit. Unlike establishing formal organizational responsibility, the process is identified and highlighted as an activity cutting across the operating domains of several different traditional departments. Integrated operational processes need to be coordinated by a specific process owner. Elevating the process to high visibility has the potential short-term benefit of achieving operational integration without commitment to permanent organizational modification. In the longer run, more permanent organizational arrangements may be desirable.

Metric-Reward Alignment

Regardless of the specific initiative to enable process management, little substance will occur unless the traditional metric and reward structure is modified and aligned. As a general rule, employees complete the work they are measured on and are compensated to perform. For any form of integrated behavior to become institutionalized, it is essential to establish a set of relevant metrics capable of measuring successful process implementation. Likewise, pay and other incentives must be directly related to achieving the desired results to assure that the process-related work is sustainable. It is also important to start to align metrics on customer and operational excellence for the overall enterprise. Additionally, in a world characterized by distributed leadership, team purpose and goals need to be the primary focus of reward systems. Rewards need to drive modified behavior in the short term to help support the team's focus on longer-term goals.

Such metric-reward alignment typically is more difficult to establish than identifying the process to be liberated from the command-and-control organizational hierarchy. Metrics and rewards are well grounded in the accounting and auditing practices of an enterprise. Even prior to the extra oversight required by Sarbanes-Oxley legislation and subsequent expanded rulings, it was difficult to modify measurement and pay practices. One fundamental facet of accounting standardization is maintaining period-to-period consistency. Such attributes do not encourage either process isolation or special metric-reward alignment. Once again, the forces of rigidity inherent in the traditional functional organizational structure typically make facing and mobilizing change extremely difficult.

In conclusion, one might rightfully ask, "Why not simply move to a twenty-first-century organization structure and thereby avoid the many inherent barriers faced when introducing integrative management?" The reason, thus far, has been an inability to articulate a comprehensive transformation process and to describe a sustainable end-state organization structure. While it is clear that increased attention to integrated key process management is desirable, no single overall organizational model has been universally accepted. This widespread adoption of enterprise resource planning (ERP) software in the late 1990s involved far-reaching organizational implications that initially appeared to offer a first step toward achieving cross-functional integration. However, a combination of software problems and organizational rigidity caused less than satisfactory results. Some feel that the evolution of organization structure from vertical to horizontal is such a difficult transformation that it constitutes a "mission impossible." This has created the belief among some students of structural change that revamping the vertical hierarchy organization into a horizontal configuration will ultimately require total destruction of the twentieth-century organization model. We believe that the answer rests in developing a better understanding of how to integrate management using horizontal processes to enable and catapult the twenty-first-century enterprise.

Part Three
Catapulting

Supply Chain Engagement

Catapulting is an effort to ultimately leverage the combined benefits of the final three imperatives: real-time responsiveness, information network synergism, and cross-enterprise collaboration. The result is a responsive supply chain business model appropriately viewed as a virtual union of real-time companies sharing resources to achieve unprecedented consumer satisfaction. The potential and desired results of supply chain engagement are introduced as the "network effect." In essence, firms participating in a collaborative supply chain are visualized as nodes in a virtual network of responsive enterprises synergistically integrating knowledge, intellectual capital, financial resources, and core competencies. Each "chain" of collaborating firms has the opportunity to jointly redefine industry boundaries and potentially establish new industry leadership.

The end state is collaborative-driven performance, wherein all participating firms are aligned in a manner allowing each to maximize agreed-to and well-defined roles while also pursuing their individual goals. Working in planned unison, a collaborative supply chain has the potential to fuel an unprecedented level of success across industries and to redefine global competition.

Part Three contains three chapters. Chapter Seven discusses how the model for creating value changes as firms become increasingly responsive. Real-time responsiveness (from push to pull), the fourth imperative, represents the essential transformation for successful catapulting. In Chapter Eight, the explosive fifth imperative of leveraging networks is discussed. The power of many firms communicating simultaneously with many others is positioned as an emerging but untested communication model having an unprecedented potential impact. Finally, by Chapter Nine, the stage has been set to fully discuss the all-important sixth imperative, collaboration, which integrates and drives the responsive supply chain business model.

Chapter Seven
Real-Time Responsiveness

*"With the great number of new products being intro-
duced, shorter product life cycles and more special
event promotions, it is extremely difficult to 'predict'
today's consumers."*[1]

—Jean V. Murphy

Digital transformation provides the opportunity to drive a major paradigm shift in the basic nature and timing of how business operations are conducted. The nineteenth-century operational model that served economic development well from the Industrial Revolution forward is best characterized as anticipatory. As noted earlier, this anticipatory, or push, information model was baked into the original ERP logic and software. The holy grail of an anticipatory business structure was, and always will be, the forecast. To this end, anticipatory-based business organizations continue to expend countless resources in the unfailing hope that, some day, they will get the forecast right. They assume that if the forecast is accurate, good things will automatically follow. All firms in a traditional channel of distribution have always performed their unique tasks driven by the shared expectation that the union of their anticipatory work will ultimately create value. In reality, seldom does the statistical forecast present a correct assessment of what customers want or will purchase. What often occurs is the launching of a bullwhip dynamic as managers'

---

[1] Jean V. Murphy, "Global Logistics and Supply Chain Strategies," August 2006, p. 44.

anticipatory corrective actions chase and collide with inventory levels across the supply chain. The fact of the matter is that as a result of lack of forecast accuracy, supply chain managers really don't know whether the right products and associated quantities are being stocked at the right locations in anticipation of sales. This has significant implications for inventory level, turns, and eventual obsolescence.

The major paradigm shift emerging as the Information Age unfolds is the growing potential to develop and implement increasingly faster and more responsive business operations. In short, the time is arriving wherein it will be technologically possible to conduct a majority of business operations in a manner allowing firms to identify exactly what a specific consumer desires, or is at least willing to accept, and then be able to deliver the product and related services sufficiently fast to satisfy customer expectations.

A dramatic example of how innovative thinking can drive real-time responsiveness was demonstrated by a charity home building contest sponsored by the San Diego Home Builder's Association some years back. The contest pitted two teams against each other to determine how fast they could each complete a custom-built home to code from scratch. One purpose of the contest was to demonstrate the power of cross-functional collaboration, parallel planning, and conformance to real-time quality management. The contest began with pouring concrete footings and floors and finished with a fully landscaped and furnished home having a legal certificate of occupancy. Whenever this story is shared with audiences, their best guess of a possible time frame for this contest is many days to even weeks. In the contest, the Home Builder's Association teams set their target to complete a custom-built home in four hours. The winning team completed a home in two hours and 59 minutes!

The contest opened many business leaders' minds to how real-time responsiveness can change existing paradigms concerning how time adds value to a very conventional process and product. The contest stimulated the marketing and custom construction of moderately priced homes in fractions of the time characteristic of conventional building. As Paul Harvey so often said, "and now the rest of the story": the proof of concept was demonstrated by the commercial success of Kaufman and Broad Home Construction in Detroit, Los Angles, Phoenix, and Chicago.

A selected group of firms that are developing successful supply chain business models think that the era of response-based business performance has arrived. In contrast, many conventional consumer durable manufacturers continue to produce and assemble products to forecast, thereby enduring the risk and expense of 100 or more days of value-added inventory stocked forward in their anticipatory supply chains. The impressive growth in Internet-based retailing supports the realization that things are changing. All of this is happening despite the fact that only a limited number of consumers are currently engaged as active supply chain participants.

The significant change in the way executives operationalize timing represents a transformation away from dependence on a forecast-driven business structure. In a forecast based business model, all value—and its associated risk—is in anticipation of demand. In contrast, response-based business models perform risky actions only when targeted to satisfy specific customer requirements. Response-based business structures rely upon rapid and accurate identification of a customer's precise purchase preference, followed by lightening-like accommodation and fulfillment. Response-based supply chain business models exploit the full capabilities of all collaborating firms, jointly orchestrating customized customer solutions.

A key competency essential to enabling maximum responsiveness is the ability to accommodate specific customer requests as late as possible in the value creation process. Firms capable of withholding final and risky product design, manufacturing, and anticipatory distribution are best positioned to make a maximum impact on purchase decisions. Firms such as Kellogg's, Whirlpool, and Colgate have transformed the way manufacturing lines are run to accommodate changeover from days to hours. Today, line changeover in many consumer goods packaging plants look more like the lighting-fast Indianapolis 500 gas refills and tire changes—they are completed in seconds. A high degree of responsiveness enables a firm to offer customers a wide assortment of unique products without loss of scale or incurring the risk or expense associated with anticipatory manufacturing and distribution. The capability to introduce such maximum responsiveness is increasingly being enabled by here-today information technology.

Figure 7-1 provides an illustration of a typical anticipatory supply chain. The channel diagram illustrates several independent businesses linked together to accommodate servicing customers. In anticipation of future purchase, inventory is positioned at varied locations along the supply chain. Each participating business forecasts—or perhaps a better name is guesses—inventory assortments to stock in anticipation of a future sale. Because all of the businesses are independent entities, the traditional practice has been not to share information concerning sales or inventory levels. The result is a sup-

Figure 7-1   Anticipatory (Push) Supply Chain

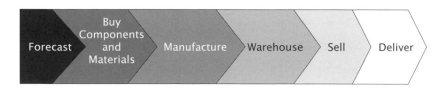

- **Forecast Driven**
- **Push Mentality – Allocation Paced**

ply chain characterized by wide variations in inventory levels and extensive promotional activities. Some argue that this inefficiency is good for consumers, who become the beneficiaries of markdowns and promotional sales, such as bargain-basement sales, designed to clear excess or slow-moving inventory. We belong to the school that believes that lower prices result from efficiency, as opposed to mistakes and inefficiency.

The argument favoring a response-based distribution arrangement is based on the value of achieving efficiency, effectiveness, relevancy, and sustainability (EERS). The supporting logic is as follows. If information were shared between participating firms in a channel, then a great deal of the anticipation would be replaced with facts. In a collaborative environment, it would not be necessary to forecast what others are planning to do or what they are planning to buy. In fact, if firms linked together in supply chain arrangements openly shared information, they would be ideally positioned to develop joint operating plans. Now, link in consumers and all doubt would be removed from the equation. However, consumers have not traditionally been active participants in channels. This leaves the firms seeking more responsiveness to consumer demand two alternatives.

First, programs can be mobilized to encourage direct consumer involvement. This is the logic behind special incentives, purchase points, and loyalty programs. They serve to link consumers directly into distribution arrangements, thereby reducing the need to stock retail inventory in anticipation of purchase. In some situations, these direct-purchase programs allow several days or even weeks for consumer product delivery. In some extreme situations, the delivery window is sufficiently long to allow a product to be manufactured and then to be delivered within the time promised. Wouldn't it be great for worldwide resource conservation and efficiency if this type of response-based distribution could be worked out for food?

The second form of response-based distribution is based on development and perfection of response capabilities that allow a product to be rapidly customized to exact consumer specifications. The logic is simple—the processes are not so simple. Figure 7-2 illustrates a response-based supply chain arrangement. In Figure 7-2, the product is sold and then assembled to exact customer specifications and delivered within an accepted time. This direct-distribution model has been popularized by firms in the computer industry, such as Dell and Hewlett-Packard.

Figure 7-2   **Responsive (Pull) Supply Chain**

- **Collaborative**
- **Pull Mentality – Requirements Paced**

The fact of the matter is that response-based distribution requires consumers to wait for product availability. While any distribution arrangement involving delivery will require consumer wait time, the time gap is shrinking. The ability to electronically link consumers into the distribution structure is growing as more Internet-based arrangements are developed and implemented. The capability to more rapidly and efficiently navigate the last mile of distribution is closing the time gap between purchase and availability to consume.

Thus far in the twenty-first century, the state of supply chain transformation from anticipatory to response based has been slow but steady. As noted earlier, the pendulum is swinging in favor of greater responsiveness. Increased responsiveness is bringing down the cost of both variety and availability to consumers as a result of pushing the location of product differentiation down the distribution channel closer to consumers. Better understanding of the potential of response-based distribution starts with understanding the importance of raising the performance bar.

Raising the Performance Bar

Six-sigma, cost-to-serve, and top-line growth initiatives are all directly related to responsiveness. Perhaps these initiatives are best positioned as essential prerequisites to developing the responsiveness necessary to catapult a firm toward higher levels of industry leadership. It is important to keep in mind that these capabilities are more directional than absolute. In other words, to achieve industry leadership, it is essential to be measurably better than competitors in achieving each of the following essential attributes.

From Two to Six Sigma Revisited

Earlier, we discussed the two-sigma mentality that has dominated traditional managerial thinking with respect to supply chain performance. The discussions related to the five pillars of operational excellence and understanding the importance of the EERS value performance model are essential prerequisites to raising the performance bar. Without a commitment to perfect order execution, all initiatives to increase responsiveness will ultimately fall short. The reasoning is simple. When consumers participate in supply chain arrangements, they become partners. Consumers participating in the supply chain process commit to specific purchases earlier than required in other distribution arrangements. This surrendering of some of their purchasing independence helps reduce overall channel uncertainty. The consumer reward for early commitment can't be broken promises of product availability or delivery. Unless manufacturing and distribution firms are fully committed to the responsibilities inherent in launching more perfect operations, the initiative will fail. Commitment to move a firm's performance increasingly closer to a sustainable six-sigma level is essential in achieving increased responsiveness.

Reducing Total Cost-to-Serve

Understanding the total cost-to-serve and embracing a commitment to continuous reduction are important to responsiveness. In Chapter Six, the importance of understanding and implementing cross-functional or horizontal processes was highlighted. Eight horizontal processes were discussed. These eight processes combine to represent an integrative management framework. Unless this cross-functional framework represents the core of a firm's operating structure, the true total cost-to-serve a customer in a responsive manner will not be apparent. In fact, reliance on traditional functional cost accounting will most likely result in any effort to increase responsiveness being ultimately aborted. Identifying the total cost-to-serve requires inclusiveness of all costs associated with preparation and execution of the end-to-end process of bringing a product or service to market.

Many traditional costs related to distribution performance are difficult to identify because classification by traditional accounting standards places them into unrelated accounts. This methodology satisfies uniform accounting notation but does nothing to add value or help managers understand the true cost of a transaction. Additionally, in many distributive arrangements, select costs are absorbed by other channel members who receive corresponding allowances and discounts. These allowances and discounts may be accounted for by netting down gross sales. The simple fact of the matter is that far too many firms don't have the slightest idea of their true total cost-to-serve a customer. When firms are faced with partial accounting for their traditional cost-to-serve, comparisons to comprehensive end-to-end cost-to-serve will most often seem high and will most likely not represent an attractive alternative. This redistribution of cost to improve alignment is critical to identifying and reducing the true total cost to serve specific customers. It is also clear that for a firm to become increasingly more operationally responsive, the total cost to serve can't be substantially increased unless revenue is positively affected.

Growing Top-Line Revenue

Will customers pay more for more responsive and unique or customized service? This is a complex question faced by many executives who ponder the risks and benefits of increasing responsiveness. The answer ranges from "maybe for a short time" to "probably not." In limited situations, the customized product and added service benefits are of sufficient value to a customer to command higher prices. Fashion-based products and services typically fall into this category. In the case of fashion, the consumer is willing to pay for newness only for a short period of time, mostly because of copies and enhanced products rapidly driving down perceived value. This is best illustrated in fashion apparel or electronics. Few would argue that the cost of purchasing prepared food is economical when compared to buying groceries. The differential comes in service and convenience. In the case of products, some premium price may be justified in the eyes of consumers if the product meets their exact expectations.

However, the greatest potential for growing top-line revenue is found in a firm's ability to, more often than competitors, be able to provide customers precisely what they desire to purchase and when they desire to purchase it. In short, top-line revenue growth is directly correlated to service excellence. While it is doubtful that customers will pay substantially more to purchase a given product, they will pay for convenience, and they are more likely to purchase from a supplier having a track record of responsiveness. Thus, more-responsive distribution arrangements are better positioned to meet specific customer desires, and as a result, they enjoy greater unit sales. Increased top-line revenue will result because these well-positioned firms enjoy more sales.

It's All about Timing

How, then, does a firm utilize emerging information technology to become more responsive? It all starts with the realization that many products are identical in construction until they become unique as a result of adding features or functionality. Features and functionality can be in the form of product or packaging differences. Before developing a structure to discuss product modification, let's briefly look at an example.

Assume, as a pharmaceutical manufacturer, that you are faced with the distribution of branded products to the European market. Despite many similarities among members of the Common Market Alliance and the adoption of a standardized monetary system based on the euro, nations are different in terms of language, tradition, and, to some significant degree, regulation. As a manufacturer, you have at least two options concerning how to best distribute products to these linked but independent European markets.

First, you can use the traditional anticipatory supply chain model. Under the traditional model, you would forecast each nation's demand for specific pharmaceutical products, which would then be manufactured and packaged. These products would be shipped to your European distribution center in anticipation of future sale. Once the inventory was stocked, the operators of the facility would wait for orders to materialize from your sales force or agent. What, in fact, you would be doing is following the best practice of an anticipatory supply chain.

Second, you could establish a packaging capability at the distribution center. Products in this supply chain design would be shipped to the distribution center in bulk. Once orders were received from specific customers in individual countries, products would be precisely packaged to each order's specification. Thus, all bulk inventory of a specific product would be available to meet the requirements of any order from any country without the restriction of previous forecasting and anticipatory packaging. Whereas a forecast would still be required, it would be a forecast of overall or aggregate market requirement, as compared with an individual or specific one for each specific product for each country. Anyone familiar with forecasting understands the value of being able to aggregate demand data.

Let's dream a step further. Assume that the product in question is typically sold in tablet, capsule, caplet, pill, and lozenge forms. In other words, the identical product is sold in each country in up to five different configurations and in differently sized packages. If it were possible to shape the desired formulation of the compound into the requested product configuration, such as a tablet or pill, at the distribution center, then even more aggregation would be enjoyed. While the packaging and formulation of the product at the distribution center would surely be more expensive on a unit basis than if completed back at the factory, what might be gained in terms of the total cost-to-serve a customer? Perhaps more important, how likely would the comparative total cost be fully captured in the typical accounting system?

Some challenges related to comparative total costing are reserved for later discussion. The important point is the realization that twenty-first-century information technology is making new and more response-based supply chain arrangement a reasonable alternative. Distribution timing has three important dimensions. Two of the dimensions, postponement and customization, are here today. The third, acceleration, remains on the conceptual drawing board.

Postponement

The concept of postponement was initially popularized by the marketing pioneer Wroe Alderson. In 1957, Alderson wrote a forward-looking book entitled *Marketing Behavior and Executive Action*.[2] The book introduced both form and time postponement. The idea was conceptually very basic: never do anything today that you can put off until tomorrow because you may obtain more information concerning precise customer expectations. However, given the prevailing attitude concerning what constituted best practice of the day, operationalizing postponement was very controversial. The idea was to postpone the shape or form of a product until a customer order was in hand and then manufacture to the precise specification of the customer. Postponement would, in the eyes of Alderson, substantially reduce risk associated with anticipation. Preaching into the prevailing wind of mass manufacturing and against the established doctrines of industrial best practice, Alderson had the tenacity to tee up the idea that doing what the customer wanted might be more significant and profitable than enjoying economy of scale.

---

[2]   Wroe Alderson, *Marketing Behavior and Executive Action* (Homewood, IL: Richard Irwin, Inc., 1957).

Alderson also foresaw opportunities to postpone timing related to movement of products. In short, if firms didn't move products in anticipation of need but rather in response to need, then getting the right products to the right markets could be dramatically improved.

While few initially saw the wisdom of Aldersonian logic, some significant changes in traditional practices did materialize. For example, many firms began to realize the practice of forward shipment of inventories into market-located warehouses served to fragment inventory. While such consolidated shipments resulted in lower transportation charges, they also served to spread inventory thin across the total market in anticipation of a future sale but not in response to an actual sale. Many firms began to take advantage of smaller direct-to-customer shipments in response to actual orders or demand rather than shipment-to-warehouse inventory in anticipation of future orders. For example, today, offshore apparel manufacturing firms are capable of manufacturing assorted-sized products on single production lines, creating store-ready case packs that can be economically distributed directly to retail store locations. Such direct distribution is economically justified when minimizing overall inventory investments, reducing markdowns, and achieving increased product availability. Is it any wonder that package distribution firms such as UPS and FedEx flourished during the last decades of the twentieth century?

The benefits of postponement have also revolutionized some traditional manufacturing practices. A prime example is retail paint manufacturing and distribution. Just a few short decades ago, it was common practice to manufacture and package all colors and sizes of paint exclusively at the manufacturing plant. The operative paradigm in the paint industry was that factory mixing was essential to maintain color integrity and product quality. The unintended consequence was a typical retail paint store experiencing as many as 50 percent of planned stock units (SKUs) out of stock at any given time. In short, it was a forecasting nightmare. Then, one firm decided to postpone mixing paint until the customer came into the store and placed an order. In addition to their fears of product quality deterioration, many who opposed the new concept were concerned about the willingness of consumers to wait in the store while paint was being mixed to order. How wrong could experts be?

The reality is that consumers were so pleased to get the color and size of paint they wanted that waiting for the paint to be mixed was far less inconvenient than making trips to other paint stores to seek the desired color. In fact, few involved anticipated that the unintended by-product of this revolutionary practice would form the foundation of the multi-billion-dollar consumer home improvement industry. Consumers, while waiting for their paint to be custom mixed, were inclined to shop for do-it-yourself products.

A half a century has elapsed since Alderson wrote about the potential of postponement. In Alderson's day, the technology for fully operationalized postponement concepts was nonexistent; today's limitation is leadership vision.

Customization

Closely related to postponement is the concept of customization. Whereas postponement is related to changes in a product's form or time of movement, customization is reserved for very specific modification of a product to satisfy specific desires of the new owner. The famous Burger King advertising slogan "Have It Your Way," designed to differentiate from McDonald's original "One Way Fits All," best captures the spirit of customization. In many ways, traditional marketing and distribution practices embodied customization. Some readers will recall the days of home delivery of milk. It was not unusual for the route delivery person to alter the exact product mix delivered by the day of the week in an effort to customize delivery to accommodate consumption patterns. The gasoline service station of the 1950s featured a service representative who customized your gasoline purchase, checked oil and tires, washed windows, and maybe even provided you with a soft drink. The fact that gasoline was well under a dollar per gallon was taken for granted.

Mass merchandising of the late twentieth century eliminated most customization from retail transactions. However, a significant growth took place in introducing customization services into wholesale, retail, and third-party distribution service providers. At each of these levels in the distribution channel, firms began to change product configurations and assortments to meet specific desires of specific customers. The value-added industry gradually became a major part of the supply chain. A later section of this chapter will expand upon value-added services because they are a primary force driving contemporary supply chain structure and strategy. At this point, let's think of customization as creating product variety by wrapping unique value-added services around a mass-manufactured product. Customization uses value-added services to create a user-specific product, thereby increasing base product flexibility and responsiveness.

Acceleration

Alderson also briefly talked about acceleration. If a series of actions could serve to postpone, Alderson argued, it also seemed logical that a corollary set of principles would serve to accelerate the distributive process. While Alderson was content to offer high-level speculation concerning the potential of acceleration, others carried the idea forward. In contemporary supply chain practice, the concept of vendor-managed inventory (VMI) offers an example of acceleration. When a supplier manages inventory status at a customer's business, the supplier is, in essence, anticipating future requirements by carefully tracking current use of the product. VMI provides a form of early warning concerning when product inventory will need to be replenished. It also provides early warning concerning when usage of the product is increasing or declining in comparison to the usage of other products in the category. The efficient consumer response (ECR) initiative used by Wal-Mart and its top 200 suppliers transformed the practices of many companies to include VMI capable to accommodate the ebb and flow of consumer takeaway. Armed with inventory trend information, businesses could incorporate corrective action in the form of either postponement or acceleration in planning future replenishment. It appears that the uncharted waters of acceleration offer the potential to improve both understanding and anticipation of customer requirements. To some unknown degree, the power to fully operationalize acceleration may rest in understanding the full ramifications of the "network effect" discussed in the next chapter.

Value-Added Services

The provision of value-added services (VASs) has become a major twenty-first-century service industry. In the broadest perspective, a VAS is anything that adds value to a product or product service from the perspective of the customer. A VAS converts a generic product from a commodity to a specialty. After the VAS is performed, the original product increases in value from the customer's perspective. The trend toward performing increased VASs during the distribution process began to rapidly grow during the last quarter of the twentieth century. The VAS industry is projected to continue to experience double-digit growth.

What exactly, then, is a VAS? An analogy can be made to the work of a tailor. When a tailor makes last-minute alterations and

adjustments to fit a suit for a specific customer, it becomes precisely what that customer desires. When a service provider modifies a
product to fit the exact specifications of either a retailer or a consumer, then a VAS has been performed. Once a VAS is performed, the
product is customized to the specifications of one specific customer
or customer group. In the eyes of that customer, value has been added. The potential range of VASs is unlimited. Many manufacturers
are developing products using modular designs. The basic modular product is designed to facilitate quick conversion by addition of
accessories or interchange of functional modules.

From our viewpoint, a VAS is any activity that increases the
attractiveness of the product from the perspective of the purchaser.
The broad range of VAS activities can be grouped into five categories: (1) assembly, (2) installation, (3) operations, (4) information,
and (5) product modification.

Assembly is, as the name implies, a VAS that completes the final
configuration of a product. When a tier-one supplier selects a color-
coordinated wheel, mounts and inflates a tire, balances the tire on the
rim, and installs the braking apparatus for automotive assembly, that
supplier is performing value-added assembly. Such integrated activity has replaced many traditional jobs associated with automotive
assembly. Countless forms of value-added assembly services exist at
the manufacturing and distribution levels of complex supply chains.
Such services range from assembly of retail store-specific promotional displays to the configuration of customization kits to facilitate
rapid product modification. Most concepts of lean manufacturing
depend on a network of value-added assembly service providers to
achieve desired results.

Installation is a form of VAS customizing products to the specifications of a specific user. Home delivery and installation of appliances is a prime example. Forms of value-added installation are also

common in the communication and computer industries. The functionality of a product can be substantially changed as a result of customization and installation.

Several unique forms of VAS are operational in nature. While transport of a shipment may be a basic service required to complete ownership exchange, many VASs may also be performed during the transportation process. For example, products may be sorted as they are transported. Such sorting may be performed as products flow across a carrier's dock or across a distribution warehouse cross dock. A major operational challenge within a supply chain is synchronization of products as they are being transported between shipment origins and destination. When companies use in-transit VASs, products can be merged, sorted, sequenced, and segregated as they are being transported from multiple origins to a final destination. A common example today is the delivery of computers and electronics that arrive at your home in multiple cartons. In all likelihood, this consolidated delivery started as shipments of individual components, such as a computer chassis, keyboard, monitor, and printer, originating from different locations. The result is that individual products shipped from multiple origins arrive as a just-in-time assortment at destination. In a broader sense, operational VASs may involve the performance of essential operating and technology applications. Transportation management, warehousing operations, inventory management, order processing, credit card administration, and customer service administration all are operational areas of potential VAS outsourcing.

A special category of VAS, while closely related to operations, is the performance of information support. ISO certification, testing, and monitoring all represent VASs. This category of information-based services is increasing as a direct result of the added security and risk involved in the operation of global supply chains.

A final form of VAS is directly related to product modification in support of marketing and sales. These modifications may be in such diverse areas as packaging, functionality, and pricing. While product modifications are similar to some of the other VAS categories, they are unique in the sense that they are completed as a planned part of the manufacturing and distribution process. Another way to look at the modification category of VAS is to view it as a decentralized extension to manufacturing. If value-added modifications are performed at a location close to the point of purchase, they can be precisely aligned with customer requirements. Examples of value-added packaging are shrink-wrapping and labeling to meet customer expectations.

The famous "bright can" of tomatoes or a "plain box" of USDA-grade frozen green beans are examples of products often private labeled at distribution warehouses to accommodate market demand. Product functionality modification deals with adding specific components or parts to a product to satisfy an individual customer's specifications. For example, one retailer may wish to include batteries with a product while another may not. Finally, it is becoming common practice for employees at distribution warehouses to add prices, mark specific products with special tags, and even record serial numbers for purpose of store-specific recalls. These and countless other forms of customer-specific product modification are examples of VASs most efficiently performed in the distribution network to accommodate local specifications.

Naturally, any attempt to classify VASs will have overlaps. In fact, any effort to classify different services into neat categories tends to defeat the basic objective of what value-added customization is all about. The driving force behind value-added accommodation is developing a way to meet the growing desire for unique, differentiated, and customized products in the marketplace while retaining the advantages of mass manufacturing. The perfection of value-added strategies translates postponement, customization, and even acceleration into improved order fill rates and availability of a broad range of customized product and product service assortments. The bottom line in the case of VAS is the direct impact on top-line revenue.

Branding and Beyond

For decades, few observers made a major connection between a firm's product branding and supply chain performance. The brand was viewed as the result of astute marketing. Some observers are beginning to link a firm's branding success with supply chain performance. A good way to better understand this connectivity is to take a fresh look at how firms are increasingly being evaluated in the marketplace.

Yesterday's and Tomorrow's Differentiators

It is becoming increasingly clear that how a firm differentiates itself from competitors in the eyes of its key customers is rapidly changing. An interesting way to gauge the impact of this change is a brief review of yesterday's and tomorrow's differentiators.

Leaders in the twentieth century were deeply concerned with achieving improved operating performance. As noted earlier, few were concerned with perfect orders or availability, and most were satisfied if they could maintain continuous performance at a two-sigma level of achievement. Yesterday's supply chain differentiators were performance measures achieved by firms that were considered twentieth-century operational leaders. These firms offered what was then considered superior or leading-edge service. They enjoyed operating efficiency, they were sensitive to inventory deployment, and they were risk avoidant. In other words, they were viewed, by the standard of the day, to be best in class.

Traditional performance attributes are now being viewed as prerequisites. In other words, operational excellence is increasingly viewed as the price of admission in the twenty-first-century competitive environment. Tomorrow's differentiators include all of yesterday's performance attributes plus responsiveness, agility, speed, flexibility, postponement, customization, and, increasingly, acceleration. Today's firm, operating in the threshold years of the twenty-first century, is learning how to compete in a more exacting world. Those who raise the performance bar will set the future standard of competition. Such leading-edge or superior performance represents the earned brand of operational excellence.

Earlier, we discussed the five pillars of twenty-first-century operational excellence, identified as simultaneously achieving customer focus, harnessed variability, synchronization then speed, late customization, and six-sigma lean. Sustainable performance of the five operational pillars develops into a unique "brand of operational excellence." In short, firms that achieve brand awareness based on operational excellence are viewed as representing superior product quality and reliability and are consistently meeting or exceeding customer expectations. These high-performing firms are viewed across industries as the best of the best in supply chain performance. They have earned the competitive position of brand leader.

Targeting, Branding, and Brand Extension

Branding superiority is an important attribute in day-to-day operations. It positions a firm with respect to customer expectations. In short, the brand represents a promise that a firm's supply chain will perform to a level that adds value for the customer. This value can be as simple as delivering the right products to the right place at the right time, every time. In a distribution sense, users of a specific brand of products take for granted that the products they desire will always be available. The expectation is "always"—not some of the time or most of the time. If VASs are involved in the transaction, the customers have confidence that they will be performed as specified. In short, the brand equity related to supply chain excellence serves to frame a believable and sustainable transactional relationship.

In terms of brand targeting, it is important to remember that supply chain services are performed, not manufactured. As noted earlier, VASs are specific to the customer or customer group. As such, VASs must be customized or targeted to each unique buying specification. These specifications will change over time and will require a dynamic adjustment of the VAS platform to the operational specifics confronted.

Timely, accurate delivery, precise inventory control, and the capability to rapidly respond to unexpected challenges are all difficult to observe or measure until after the essential service has or has not been performed. It is this focus on achieving solutions that builds brand equity. It is the focus on solutions that identifies one service provider as being distinctively superior in comparison to competitors. In the mix of selecting supply chain partners, a brand's reputation for operational excellence is of fundamental importance. In the case of marketing service capabilities, firms that are leading-edge service providers typically target customers who place a premium on superior performance. Branding supply chain capability is becoming a major attribute in twenty-first-century operational excellence.

Finally, in terms of brand extension, supply chain excellence can help achieve rapid acceptance of a product or service. Becton Dickinson and Company (BD) offers customer services and products that compliment the medical and diagnostic products they sell. The supply chain service products are marketed and sold along with physical health care products, to facilitate their go-to-market strategy.

The idea of brand extension is important to the introduction of new products and services, new market segments, and product utilization and repurchase by the customer. The growing belief is that product or operational superiority earned in one situation is transferable between segments and even between industries. P&G has an established competency to manufacture and distribute household cleaning products. Building on these proven competencies, P&G showed an example of brand extension in its decision to introduce a line of industrial cleaning products. Because of long-standing success in the household market, P&G's proven product and supply chain capabilities were instantly viewed as being credible by buyers in the industrial market sector.

When the brand involves the performance of a service, it may have even greater extension capability than when products are involved. Selected supply chain service providers have developed strong reputations for providing and maintaining excellence service. Some years ago, a survey was conducted to measure which 3PL firms had the strongest reputations for excellence among users of this category of services. Respondents were asked to identify and rank those 3PL firms that, in their opinion, provided the best range of supply chain services. To the researchers' surprise, two outstanding transportation companies, American President Line and Schneider National Trucking, were identified by a significant number of respondents as deserving to be ranked among the top-10 3PLs. Neither of these transportation firms at that time participated in the 3PL business. Both were exclusively high-achievement transportation service providers. Shortly after, both transportation firms successfully entered the 3PL industry and are leading integrated service providers today.

It is clear that brand extension was a positive factor in the case of these two firms.

Concluding Statement

Responsiveness results from a combination of commitment, positioning, and competency. The attributes necessary to catapult to leadership in the twenty-first century are remarkably different from those that existed during the twentieth century. The transition from an anticipatory-based economy to one dominated by responsiveness has begun. Some firms are moving quickly along the transformation journey; others haven't started. This is not a short trip, and not all firms are making or will make equal progress on the journey. A major transformation challenge is to begin to unravel the mysteries of competing in an information-intensive networked environment. In Chapter Eight, our attention turns to the magic and uncharted mystery of networks.

Chapter Eight
Leveraging Networks

"The new economy is founded on the forces of technologies and the increasing importance of intangible assets such as relationships and knowledge. This is powering revolutionary new value propositions that delight customers while delivering exceptional economics and sustainable differentiation for the innovator."[1]

—Ralph Drayer

The word "network" has many meanings in contemporary language. Most of us think of television and radio networks when we hear the word. In this chapter, we will explore several meanings of the word "network" that are related to supply chains. Our intent is to better understand how twenty-first-century Web-based communication networks are changing and will increasingly continue to change the landscape of best business practices. While the network impact story is still playing out, it is becoming increasingly clear that the traditional business best practice model is being irrevocably modified. What remains to be seen is just how far sweeping the impact of the "network effect" will be on the structure and conduct of society. The impact technology networks may have on business could well represent one of the most visible dimensions of change.

---

[1] Ralph Drayer, Founder and Chairman, Supply Chain Insights LLC, and former Chief Logistics Officer, The Procter & Gamble Company.

Communication Models

Each of us is an active member of many different communication communities. We grow up learning the written and spoken language of the nations we inhabit. From that point forward in life, we are engaged in many different communication models. A brief review of the structure of communication models will help establish the unique and far-reaching impact networks and their communities are likely to have on future supply chain structure and strategy.

Traditional: One-to-One

The one-to-one communication model is the basic format for inter-personal communication. Everyone who functions without medical deficiency or other limitation learns to communicate in the one-to-one mode early in life. While effective for interpersonal communication, this traditional model is limited in commercial application to order entry and transaction administration. It is important to keep in mind the fact that most business organizations use this fundamental model for internal employee communication and when communicating with customers. Consequently, most systems used in business were developed to support traditional one-to-one communication.

Broadcast: One-to-Many

The broadcast communication model has been popularized by radio and television. As such, we all became familiar with listening and, for the past six decades since television was commercialized, watching and listening from an early age. Our first experience with school burns the broadcast model into our behavioral and learning patterns forever. In elementary school, the teacher uses this model to influence behavior and maintain control. By higher education, we have become experts in listening to the so-called lecture. One must add that we all transcend this early stage of life with the ability to listen with a discriminatory ear to the fact and fiction of the broadcast.

Throughout our adult years, we continue to receive a substantial amount of information via the broadcast model. Most all social, religious, and professional institutions make widespread use of this model. Thus, some of us became proficient in being both a speaker and a member of an audience. At times, we go out of the way to encourage discussion groups in order to share viewpoints in an effort to better understand the widespread ramifications of the subject at hand. This becomes our first introduction to the many-to-many structured communication model, which is discussed below. At this point, it is worthwhile to note that discussion groups are typically relatively small in size and consist of individuals who share somewhat common interest in the topic.

Hierarchical: Many-to-One

Many-to-one communication is used in our society less than the previous two models. The town meeting is an example of this communication model. An elected official meets to hear the opinions of constituents. Another example of many-to-one structured communications is when individuals provide responses to a survey. At times, business organizations structure customer feedback communication to obtain and better understand customer impressions or reactions to new product introductions or other business behavior. In a transactional sense, the auction where potential buyers enter either blind or open bids represents deployment of a many-to-one communication format.

Network: Many-to-Many

Network communication is the least understood of the four models. The idea of many communicating simultaneously with many others creates a feeling of chaos and a lack of a systematic or logical flow of ideas and information exchange. This is a model we need to understand a great deal more because it is rapidly becoming a common form of exchange among individuals and business organizations. It was not until information technology embraced the Internet that most became aware of the ability to rapidly communicate in a shared-information environment. Thus, despite the fact that the vast majority of today's population grew up in a vigorous communication environment, we all are newcomers to the network structure. We have all experienced a situation when all the people in a room or on a transportation vehicle are talking at once. In these crowded environments, little, if any, meaningful communication occurs. However, as discussed in Chapter Four, present and emerging technology of the Information Age is beginning to render meaningful simultaneous communication a reality.

Perhaps the most elusive dimension of the Information Age is what we call "network synergism," for lack of a better name. Simply stated, information disseminated in a shared environment is capable of creating a form of unbounded synergy when presented in real time to all participants and when it is available for all to engage in simultaneously from many different vantage points. In a business-to-business context, consider, for a moment, the potential operational advantage of all participants in a supply chain simultaneously knowing exactly what consumers have bought or are purchasing. Envision a dashboard that records precise customer purchase behavior by location as individual purchases are consummated. In some situations, participating customers, and even connected consumers, might be willing to share their future purchase intentions. Of what value would instantaneous aggregation of such data be to business managers, who, for decades, have tried to forecast such future activity without much success?

Now, go one step further: what if all businesses involved in an integrated supply chain had both an individual and a collective view of what wholesalers and retailers were most likely to buy in the future as a result of network connectivity concerning purchase plans and inventories? Because we are dreaming, how about one more step? Assume that final consumers, you and me, for example, were willing to share our purchase plans, at least for nonimpulse items or regularly consumed merchandise, in advance of actual purchase. While it is only remotely possible that such early-detection systems will become reality in the near future in consumer purchase environments, such information is being shared today between collaborating upstream supply chain members.

The significant and fundamental mind stretching point is that today's limitations to such information sharing arrangements are organizational, legal, and/or cultural, not technical. Most households in developed nations already have access to high-speed networks and computing capacity of sufficient power to participate in a shared network. In fact, many consumers currently participate in such networks using communication models dragged forward from the Industrial Age.

It is clear that the traditional communication models are changing. Figure 8-1 provides an illustration of the communication flows in each of the four basic models. From the simple-to-understand one-to-one model to the complex and confusing many-to-many model, messages of meaning can be communicated. Before undertaking a more in-depth discussion of the changing nature of communication, it will be useful to develop a better understanding of a technology-driven synergism called the "network effect."

Figure 8-1   Visualizing Communication Models

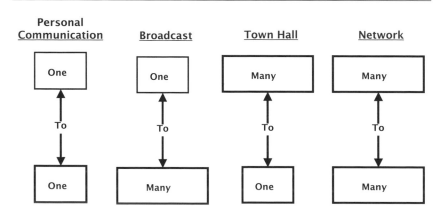

What Is the Network Effect?

The network effect is summed up as the synergism resulting from multiple participants simultaneously sharing operational experiences by using identical data formats and common data structures. It is, operating under a standardized work flow sequence with shared event visibility, collaborating firms and perhaps even individual consumers linked as members of a network to conduct joint real-time operations to achieve maximum efficiency, effectiveness, relevancy, and sustainability (EERS).

The network effect is a technologically stimulated synergism whereby connectivity becomes more valuable as more users join the network. As the user base expands, overall network participants benefit by access to more activity and an increasingly comprehensive real-time view of information. As the participating user base or community of users expands, the network becomes a linked or shared operating structure. In the case of business, the shared operating structure creates a standard, or protocol, for conducting business operations. To a significant degree, understanding the network effect is important to transforming an enterprise to a responsive supply chain business model. It is a key paradigm for shifting supply chain operating tempo from anticipatory to responsive.

Operating within a many-to-many framework, network communities assume new and different status. Individual communications are not events as they are typically positioned or structured in the other three models. Messages may be transmitted and received at random rather than in a structured or sequential manner. As such, the network functions as a continuous process. Participants are viewed as sending and receiving messages simultaneously to a broad community of connected participants. As such, the network is continuous, with no clearly identified start or end time. A many-to-many network is best viewed as a means to an end, instead of an end in itself.

In a commercial sense, a network can be shaped to achieve specific outputs or objectives at a point in time. However, such outputs should be viewed as point-in-time outputs and not terminal points. The network, viewed as a continuous process, will continue to develop and generate synergistic outputs across time. These fundamental attributes make a network a communication model much different from the other three traditional models. It is clear that we lack a great deal of understanding concerning how to deploy the collective power of a network.

Many individuals have experienced and participate in chat rooms. Base camps are common, wherein individuals and groups post messages and create information files, to-do lists, and project management paths. It is common for professionals (even in the supply chain space) to develop portals for information exchange and technical dialogue. The use of personal blogs represents a method of exchanging information in a networked environment.

A few examples of effective network deployment are the AMBER Alert Portal Consortium that stands ready to share information concerning abductions. Schlumberger's Human Resource Network contains postings and shares information among 32,000 employees in 80 countries. In a more proprietary application, IBM has developed a global human resource network that catalogs global talent. It is clear that there are many types of networks emerging in the twenty-first century. The question is which of the more common networks are relevant for the design and operation of the emerging responsive supply chain business model?

Network Communities

A "network community" is a structured group of participants that engage in regular information exchange. The concept of being a network community serves to bind communication participation. It follows that a specific network can be open or closed, with respect to who is able to join and when they are able to participate. This is an important distinction between open social and entrepreneurial network communities and closed business operational and transactional network communities.

Social and Entrepreneurial Networks

To help frame the business application, a few comments are appropriate concerning social and entrepreneurial networks. These two fundamental networks have been an integral part of society for the past several decades.

The social network consists of a number of individuals (nodes) and a set of relationships (ties) between individuals. This simple idea of viewing social interaction in the form of a network has developed into a respected academic and research field referred to as social network theory. From a research perspective, the field of social network theory builds on the fundamental belief that the actions of individual participants are less important than their relationships or ties with others in the network.

Many interesting generalizations concerning social structure and behavior have evolved from the social network perspective. As far back as the 1920s, it was hypothesized that everyone in the world is linked with everyone else by "six degrees of separation."[2] More recent experiments confirm that about five to seven degrees of separation connect two individuals when searching via the Internet.

Of course, the arrival of Internet technology has greatly increased the interaction of individuals and has expanded the workable size of the effective network. One of the most striking impacts of the Industrial Age was the expansion of individual social participation, in comparison to that of the Agricultural Age. The social network hub of the Agricultural Age was the farm community. In the Industrial Age, as travel became more commonplace, the network engaged a broader geographical linkage of related individuals. Now, in the early stages of the Information Age, we are becoming a global community.

While the degrees of separation may not change, it is clear that the ease of connectivity is vastly different. This ease of connectivity and the expansion in diversity of members have significant implications for the marketing strategy of a twenty-first-century enterprise.

The entrepreneurial network is a special subset of a social network consisting of the formal linkage of highly skilled individuals. Entrepreneurial network membership consists of professionals and individuals focused on launching new and innovative forms of commercial activity. The network serves as the structure for innovation, talent, and capital to drive new organizational development. It is also a primary source for new product and service development.

---

[2]   Clifford F. Lynch, "Leveraging the Power of Networks for Optimal Supply Chain Efficiencies" *IO*, May 2005, pp. 11–14.

The entrepreneurial network has special meaning to the business environment because of its direct focus on change leadership. In an operational sense, the entrepreneurial network displays the same attributes as a social network. Likewise, its scope and depth have been magnified by the advent of technology-based information exchange. Similar to the social network, the entrepreneurial network is a primary resource for the twenty-first-century enterprise.

Operational and Proprietary Networks

Whereas social and entrepreneurial networks have an indirect linkage to twenty-first-century business, operational and proprietary networks represent the architectural foundation of the responsive supply chain business model. To start, it is important to understand two fundamental concepts related to information technology that serve to illustrate how the Internet is affecting the development of networks: (1) open source (OS) and (2) software as a service (SaaS). With respect to the following discussion, the simplifying assumption is that Web-based technology provides the delivery platform for both OS and SaaS.

OS represents a perspective on software development that treats computer code as "open source" and available to anyone who desires to modify or improve the code. As such, OS stands in direct conflict with proprietary source and execution code common in twentieth-century technology. Proprietary code was either developed by a user or purchased from software vendors. Prior to the availability of the Internet, it was common practice for firms to either write their own code (legacy systems) or purchase code in the form of performance systems (i.e., ERP). OS code is available free on the Internet.

The first major or widespread availability of OS software was the Linux operating system. A variety of other major software source codes have become part of the OS movement. As one would expect, the notion of OS raises serious issues related to traditional concepts regarding intellectual property rights. Thomas L. Friedman presented an interesting review of OS as he discussed the fourth of his now-famous "flatteners." He defines and describes "open sourcing as self-organizing collaborative communities."[3] While the debate continues on the long-range impact OS will have on all forms of intellectual property, the fact remains that the world of functional software will never be the same, as firms position their computer resources to support the growing emergence of the responsive supply chain business model.

SaaS represents a new distribution model for software vendors to deliver their proprietary software to clients. "Under the SaaS model, software vendors host their respective applications on remote servers, and customers access the program through virtually any Internet connection and web browser."[4] The important operational point is that application users do not have to install, run, or maintain the software. From a software vendor perspective, Salesforce.com was among the first to gain popularity in selling a hosted Web-based application. While hosting has been around for a number of years in the form of the traditional service bureau, the idea of hosting Internet-based transaction systems is new to the twenty-first century. While early adopters accepted SaaS solutions for stand-alone or horizontal applications, some hesitance remains concerning conversion of mainstream business computing to this delivery model. However, development of advanced Internet-based network opportunities, the capabilities of Internet2, and increasing network security may soon change this perspective. The result is likely to be a rapid growth in operational networks.

---

3   Thomas L. Friedman, op. cit., pp. 81–103.

4   "Software as a Service," *CIBC World Markets,* January 13, 2006, p. 2.

Operational Networks

The operational network is one in which the community of users joins together to share experiences and resources. While not essential, most operational networks gaining attention are being offered on a SaaS basis. The operational network is an open system in the sense that participation is not limited to firms engaged in a specific or proprietary supply chain. Participants in an operational network have a common need and seek the synergy of resolving that need by working with a shared community. A prime example of an operational network is an on-demand transportation management system (TMS).

A firm engaged in using an on-demand TMS links its transportation requirements and carriers together via the Web-based host application service. In this sense, the system functions similar to a traditional TMS. The initial result is information to assist in the management of a firm's transportation operations. LeanLogistics is an example of a firm providing TMS on a SaaS basis. As more firms join the shared application, the network expands in terms of the number of shippers, carriers, and shipments involved. As a by-product of day-to-day operations across a number of shippers and carriers, a transactional database begins to emerge that has both historical and real-time value.

In a historical sense, shipping patterns and carrier capacity become visible across the network of participating (hosted) companies. Data mining holds the potential to significantly raise the level of shared efficiency by increasing carrier availability and reducing deadhead (empty) miles.

The real-time benefits of being in the operational network are synergistic for all participants. All participants have access to key operating information and are expected to act in a manner they perceive to be in their best interest. The capability of the network to serve as a holistic link between the many participants increases the potential efficiency for all members. In addition, the database or shared information and knowledge reservoir opens the door to raising the overall level of each firm's individual operations. In the case of LeanLogistics, the inclusion of key retailers and their largest suppliers in the same TMS network opens the strategic opportunity for unprecedented shipment consolidation and supply chain collaboration.

At this early stage of development, the number of operational networks is limited primarily to the management of service transactions. As noted earlier, the primary applications are in sales force and transportation management. Other developing applications are in human resource management, purchasing, real estate, and travel systems. While the on-demand features are appealing, the ace in the hole of on-demand shared operating systems is the inherent advantage gained from the synergistic network effect. Most experts predict a rapid increase in the range and scale of SaaS operational networks.

Proprietary Networks

The proprietary network consists of a number of firms that are voluntarily linked to operate in an information perspective as a single enterprise. This type of a network builds upon awareness that all of the firms involved are interdependent. These firms are voluntarily linked in an effort to jointly create a substantial impact in terms of market presence. The operating model is a concept of a value union that enables fast and flexible joined performance. The network represents a series of customer- and supplier-linked operations and shared information flow. This model has been around for a number of years and typically operates under the leadership of a dominant enterprise. Most major retailers host a proprietary network to facilitate operations with major suppliers. Wal-Mart is among the leaders in providing two-way communication with suppliers. In other situations, a manufacturer such as Kohler may have sufficient brand power to align suppliers and some distributors into a managed network. These networks are closed in the sense that access is only gained by doing business with the hosting enterprise. A typical retailer, wholesaler, or manufacturer engaged in national distribution will most likely participate in several of these proprietary networks. Each network uses an Internet-based proprietary extranet, with access restricted by a firewall. Thus, each network arrangement is a closed system with participation limited to specified members.

The important point is that proprietary networks are common today and can be expected to become an increasingly dominant force in business for the foreseeable future. However, on the not-so-distant horizon is the emergence of voluntary networks. These emerging networks consist of a union of specialized firms joined together in a transactional network. Such voluntary networks have the joint capability that when linked together, they can technologically gain the scale and scope necessary to be competitive in markets traditionally dominated by major retailers or manufacturers. In a marketing sense, these new collaborative ventures will be the archetypes of the twentieth-century cooperatives reincarnated in a form and structure leveraging twenty-first-century information technology networks. They are coming—the question is "When?"

Doing Business in a Many-to-Many Network

Doing business in a many-to-many network means that most firms will be linked in either an operational or a proprietary arrangement. Either type of engagement implies a set of expectations and rules. These expectations and rules may evolve from either the administrator of the operational arrangement or the dominant firm in a proprietary arrangement. In each situation, four unique operating characteristics serve to differentiate day-to-day networked operations from the more traditional business arrangements.

Everyone Owns the Customer

Perhaps the most unique aspect of a networked business arrangement is that everyone performing as a member of the network owns a share of the customer. The network exists for one fundamental reason, and that reason is to service the consumer, who is the source of revenue. As noted earlier, unless the distribution process enables consumption, no sustainable value is achieved. While the traditional view of a business channel is that the dominant enterprise has command of customer loyalty, the perspective shifts to a shared customer ownership in a many-to-many network environment.

Ubiquitous Information

A unique feature of many-to-many networks is open architecture with respect for information sharing. The fact that the arrangement is a network means that all participants have access to all information all of the time. Data reservoirs exist wherein everyone has access to common information, and all participants are expected to act or execute according to predescribed roles. This feature of open information access is what a network is all about. Likewise, it is extensive information sharing that drives the emergence of the network effect.

Shared Processes

The transition from functional to process operations is one of the primary transformations required to digitize. In Chapter Six, the eight fundamental processes required for integrated supply chain operations were detailed. These eight processes remain the essential operating objectives in both operational and proprietary networks.

The essential difference, when compared with an individual firm, is the ability to share responsibility for performing the work involved in essential processes across a networked supply chain. Of course, this is where outsourcing and insourcing become key alternatives in joint operational design. Given the network structure, the framework is established for effective sharing in the performance of key processes in a manner that results in less duplicate effort and redundancy. In a network arrangement, the sense of joint mission and available information is positioned to facilitate shared processes.

Shared Risk and Reward

In today's voluntary arrangements, it is common practice to share risk. All members of a supply chain arrangement understand their specific performance responsibility and embrace the risk associated with that performance. Less likely to be understood and shared is the reward for extraordinary achievement. More often than not, one or a few businesses involved in the arrangement are positioned to be rewarded while all in the process confront risk. This inequality of sharing reward has been one of the major impediments to implementing voluntary business collaborations. Businesses associated with both the operational and the proprietary network models provide a framework to resolve this dilemma. Simply put, the shared nature of processes related to the mission and the availability of ubiquitous information combine to focus both responsibility and reward. This existence of shared risk and reward is clearly one of the main differentiators in a networked operating arrangement.

Doing Business Without Orders

To illustrate some potential advantages of an operational or a proprietary network, let's assume that participants have linked their enterprises and have decided to conduct business without the traditional practice of repeatedly creating inventory replenishment orders. In the new network arrangement, traditional orders are replaced by a collaborative agreement specifying in detail the desired results and the operational responsibilities of each participating firm. A shared desire for consumer satisfaction drives the sustainable retailer/manufacturer relationship. Other supply chain participants, such as transportation carriers and 3PL distribution companies, understand the collaborative structure and have voluntarily committed to become sustainable business associates. In the arrangement, shared revenue and clearly specified performance expectations rule day-to-day operations.

While much development would be required to make an orderless supply chain relationship a reality, two facts seem indisputable. First, the technology necessary to make the orderless relationship a reality is available today. Second, the systems, processes, imagination, and regulation common in the twentieth-century supply chain are inadequate to make this relatively simple business model work. Let's first look at today's commonly implemented best order-to-delivery practices. Then, we will explore a leading-edge networked alternative.

A Look at Today's Best Practice

To make the proposed orderless network achieve its operating goal, many of today's fundamentals, or what are considered best practices, would have to radically change. With a few exceptions, emerging twenty-first-century technology has been harnessed by implementation within a twentieth-century best practice framework. Let's look at today's typical grocery-manufacturer-to-retailer order-to-delivery process.

A traditional grocery manufacturer and a leading retailer can be observed repeatedly creating near-identical inventory replenishment orders week after week. These orders, commonly referred to as sales transactions, become the pacemaker of the marketing and inventory replenishment process. These inventory replenishment orders are diligently tracked and become the operating nucleus of the business relationship.

Orders result in inventory deliveries, and, ultimately, invoices are generated to facilitate inventory ownership transfer from the manufacturer to the retailer. In most situations, products physically flow from a manufacturer's distribution center to the retailer's distribution warehouses. This overall process, from start to finish, typically requires from three to five or more days, depending on geography and degree of technical sophistication. To move the products involved from the manufacturer's warehouse to the retailer's warehouse, for-hire trucking companies typically are responsible for timely and damage-free delivery. Because ownership transfer is taking place, the invoices related to revenue, discounts, allowances, and payment terms become items of extreme importance. The orders serve as the focus for accountability and control.

When engaged in ownership transfer, Sarbanes-Oxley regulations require precise adherence to standardize rules concerning (1) when an order in fact becomes an order and (2) when, from a legal perspective, a shipment becomes a shipment. While these regulatory constraints have more affect at the end of an operating period or at the end of a fiscal year, consistency and strict adherence to a standardized process is a year-round mandate. Despite this tight regulatory structure and the loose operating arrangement between manufacturer, retailer, and carriers, more progressive firms are trying to achieve perfect order execution. We talked about perfect orders earlier—suffice it to say that achieving a high percentage of perfect orders is a near-impossible mission, given the operating structure described above. In fact, the industry average is generally recognized to be less than 50 percent perfect orders.

Because uncertainty exists, both the manufacturer and retailer engage in forecasting what they consider will be the most likely future sales level. Shipments are planned to satisfy this level of expectation and are completed in anticipation of planned sales becoming reality. In a leap of faith, the forecast and even individual firms' plans are often shared between all participants in the channel arrangement. Collaborative planning, forecasting, and replenishment (CPFR) efforts are common to help reduce distortion between manufacturer and retailer planning perspectives. Despite this effort on the part of all parties to reduce uncertainty and share expectations, a great deal typically goes wrong.

The first level of disconnect is what was planned in comparison to what actually happens. Chapter Five opened with a discussion of Sunday afternoon in a typical supermarket. The reality is that traditional distribution systems, while incorporating the best practice of yesterday supported by today's technology, just don't get the job done. In addition to retail out-of-stocks, the typical distribution center operation also experiences out-of-stocks. Despite shared plans, a great deal of inventory just does not arrive in time to fully operationalize the plan. In addition, individual shipments may experience over, short, or damage (OS&D) because work was not performed to specification during the distribution process or damage occurred during handling or transportation. Put simply, people make errors in judgment and in work. Likewise, handling and transportation can create product damage.

The information system that supports the order-to-delivery process also has problems. Here, the problems are driven not nearly as much by failure to capture accurate information as they are by reconciliation of all the detail involved. For accurate accountability and control, all aspects of an order must be reconciled. The physical count

must be accurate to the specific case level and proper price and promotional allowances applied. If case count at point of receipt fails to
match that at point of shipment, the difference needs to be reconciled and the transaction value adjusted. Discussion of all the things
that can possibly go wrong while performing order to delivery could
continue; suffice it to say that accounting requires that every detail
related to every case involved in each and every transaction be reconciled to the satisfaction of all concerned parties, which, in this simple
distribution arrangement, involves the manufacturer, the carrier, and
the retailer's distribution warehouse. Such detailed reconciliation is
necessitated by the fact that three independent business organizations are involved in the transaction. Each has a different ownership
base, and each must protect its independent financial integrity.

While firms that engage in traditional distribution channel
arrangements aspire to an overall goal of achieving perfect order
performance, achieving such operational status is extremely difficult.
A great deal can go wrong in the order-to-delivery process, and it
typically does. In addition to the delivery cycle from manufacturer
to retail warehouse, the products involved still need to be processed
through the retailer's warehouse or be cross-docked for delivery to
a retail store. Thus, an additional order-to-delivery cycle is introduced to achieve retail store inventory replenishment. Finally, at the
retail store, products must be placed on the retail shelf for consumer
access. Of course, all of these steps in the distribution process create
opportunities for error and require transactional reconciliation while
adding no consumer value. When viewed in detail, it is truly remarkable that this traditional replenishment process has resulted in the
highest standard of living ever known to the human race.

The operating results, while marginally improved by adoption
of new information technology and streamlined (best practice)
processes, fail to capture the full potential of what might be if the

overall process was reinvented. While today's information networks can provide real-time event monitoring and status across a global supply chain, firms continue to perpetuate sequential and redundant work processes. It is not unusual to hear supply chain executives talk about an extremely high number of orders that require some type of non-value-added reconciliation at a cost that significantly reduces profitability for all concerned. However, while costly, such reconciliation does balance the books down to the last penny! Given today's technology, let's look ahead to what could be tomorrow's distributive best practice.

A Look Ahead: Using Technology to Change Today's Best Practice

Fully deploying today's available technology requires a careful reexamination of what are considered today's best practices. Assume a different order of relationships between firms engaged in the supply chain. Assume a network containing the same firms discussed earlier, namely, a grocery manufacturer, a retailer, and a transportation company. However, in this assumed scenario, let's position the working relationship between these firms as one characterized by "acknowledged dependency." The firms involved view themselves as jointly engaged in and committed to the success of a shared network having the mission of achieving the highest possible level of consumer retail shelf availability for the products involved.

In this network, the retailer involved is directly connected by information technology to all other participants in the distribution arrangement. The retailer is electronically sharing sales and inventory status. As sales materialize, all members in the shared operational network are provided exact quantity and sizes of products sold to consumers as well as current and planned inventory status. In this arrangement, the retailer and the manufacturer jointly determine the desired shelf inventory, given their shared view of future events. For example, if a particular season supports larger or smaller shelf inventory for a specific product and related size assortment, this is jointly determined by the retailer and the manufacturer, and all implications of the plan are shared with all connected parties, including the carrier. From this point forward, it becomes the responsibility of the manufacturer to be sure that the work necessary to achieve the plan is performed and to make any adjustments necessary based on retail sales.

In such a shared-performance-driven network, no product replenishment orders would be necessary. The merchandising plan and approved adjustments based on consumption would drive and pace desired performance. The overall focus and goal for network participants would be maximum consumer-product-on-shelf availability. The financial scoreboard, given achievement of the service goal, would be maintaining lowest possible end-to-end total cost-to-serve. In fact, all the pomp and circumstance of ordering, corrective action, reconciliation, and payment would not be necessary because there would not be orders to correct. The complexity of pricing and promotional arrangements would be replaced by agreement on a net price (no discounts, no allowances, and no adjustments) to be paid by electronic fund transfer at a specific agreed-to time. With respect to OS&D, an operating agreement based on trust, self-auditing, and shared responsibility has proven to work well between highly collaborative enterprises.

When people view the excessive detail and redundancy involved in traditional channels of distribution, they are forced to wonder just how firms were able to reach the levels of performance they did. Today, given available technology, ample opportunities exist to rethink the traditional way transactional systems have worked in the past. It's clear that a great deal more needs to be said about collaboration in the next chapter.

Chapter Nine
Collaboration: Creating Legendary Relationships

"Technology doesn't make collaboration. Processes don't guarantee it. Although both are important, it's ultimately the human interface and trust that it can engender that build a truly collaborative relationship."[1]

—Robert E. Sabath and John Fontanella

and

"Without collaboration, the supply chain will be nothing more than a collection of companies each following its own pathway."[2]

—Rick Blasgen

Twenty-first-century global business is increasingly becoming competition among extended enterprises seeking integrative benefits by leveraging collaborative relationships. The key word is "collaboration," not "ownership." In a true collaborative relationship, participants enjoy trust and are committed to sharing both risk and reward. Such indispensable relationships are increasingly being facilitated by the scope and functionality of available information technology.

---

[1] Robert E. Sabath and John Fontanella, *Supply Chain Management Review*, July/August 2002, p. 28.

[2] Rick Blasgen, CEO, Council of Supply Chain Management Professionals.

Collaboration and Enterprise Extension

Few words in the business vocabulary have experienced more rapid and expansive use than "collaboration." A quick search using Google confirms multimillions of sources, called hits, which grow by the hour. Why so much interest in collaborating after so many years of competing? The purpose of this chapter is to understand what collaboration is all about and why it is considered a fundamental cornerstone of catapulting a firm into a state of supply chain engagement. Before discussing collaboration, it is important to clarify differences between cooperation and coordination. Cooperation and coordination are, at times, mistakenly used interchangeably with collaboration.

Cooperation is characterized by informal relationships that exist without any jointly defined mission, structure, or planning effort. It describes the many historical buy-sell transaction-based relationships used throughout time with suppliers and customers. Information is shared as needed, and authority is retained by each party in the transaction, so there is virtually no shared risk. Resources as well as rewards are normally separate and private.

The process of coordination is characterized by more formal relationships and understanding of compatible but not aligned missions. Some planning and division of roles are normally required, and communication channels are established. Authority still rests with each individual organization, but there is some increased risk to all participants. Resources are generally available to all participants, and rewards are mutually acknowledged.

The dictionary offers two somewhat opposite definitions of collaboration. One is "to assist another," and the other is "to work with the enemy." Both have relevancy to twenty-first-century supply chains. A different dictionary defines collaboration as "the ability to work together in an intellectual and operational manner." This definition implies that collaboration is a managed process with clear implementation goals. Further, it implies that the act of collaborating requires leadership and strategy. In contemporary usage, collaboration explicitly implies a mutually beneficial and well-defined relationship entered into by separate organizations or individuals to achieve common goals. The relationship includes a jointly developed structure, shared responsibility, mutual authority, and accountability regarding resources and rewards. Collaboration, unlike cooperation or coordination, connotes a more durable and pervasive relationship characterized by expected behavior. Collaboration brings previously separated organizations into a new structure, with full commitment to a common mission. Such relationships require comprehensive planning and well-defined communication channels at all operating levels. Risk is increased because each member of the collaboration contributes resources and reputation. In collaborative arrangements, resources are pooled or jointly secured, and product and rewards are shared.

Digital transformation is, in part, about revamping a firm's supply chain strategy to capitalize on collaborative arrangements. Thus, interorganizational development is a significant part of a digital transformation. In addition to reinventing internal work processes, companies are challenged to extend their operational range and impact through a collaborative process that includes customers and all types of suppliers. In the twenty-first century, firms have the legal authorization and opportunity to leverage their competencies and capabilities with other firms with which they regularly conduct business operations. Because of rapidly expanding connective technologies, firms can develop and increasingly participate in, as well as lead, collaborative arrangements.

For decades, the model for buying and selling merchandise between firms has been referred to as a channel of distribution. In distribution channel arrangements, firms seek profits while participating as loose-ly linked voluntary buyers and sellers of merchandise and services. Such firms are loosely connected by their pursuit of joint opportunity and mutual desire for success. However, in traditional channels of distribution, no formal linkages existed to provide firms participat-ing in such loosely affiliated arrangements incentives to encourage sustainability. The operational bond in such traditional arrangements has been limited primarily to each buy-sell transaction.

Unless business managers or owners involved felt that their transactions achieved a favorable outcome, they most likely would not continue to participate in the buy-sell process. The word "bid-ding" best captures the typical atmosphere of the traditional buy-sell process. The bid or exchange price represents the compensation for which one is willing to perform a service or transfer ownership of a product or material. Use of a bidding process reflects an emphasis on negotiation, as opposed to collaboration. Perhaps most important, in typical bid situations, few incentives other than exchange price exist to streamline or improve the operational efficiency of the joint busi-ness arrangement.

Such traditional arrangements are best described as loosely orga-nized trading relationships. In a traditional channel of distribution, all of the participants are expected to look out for their own welfare. History has proven that such power-based arrangements typically represent an exercise in suboptimization. The reality is that the vast majority of transactions occurring in today's distributive channels are conducted using the traditional buy-sell market models. The very foundation of negotiation is based on the expectation that one party will gain at the expense of the other. The benefits and synergies of working together to achieve a higher level of efficiency, effective-ness, relevancy, and sustainability are lost in these traditional channel arrangements. Yes, once again, we come face to face with the EERS model.

Information technology and managerial willingness to explore the benefits of collaboration are changing the traditional channel of distribution model. The responsive supply chain business model is characterized by sustainable collaborative relationships between participating channel members. Even at the existing embryonic stage of development, one is able to observe new collaborative business models emerging. Firms such as Hewlett-Packard, Motorola, and Cisco are reinventing themselves as supply-chain-wide comprehensive service and knowledge providers. Their new operating model is built on collaborative planning and execution based on leveraging joined capabilities. IBM established a network of contract manufacturers, such as Celestica and Solectron, to specialize in performing the traditional tasks of manufacturing technology equipment. This collaborative process leading to highest-order specialization is appropriately called "enterprise extension."

Enterprise extension is defined as the process of two or more firms joining resources to complete a shared business process. The connective forces of enterprise extension are built on information sharing, joint strategic and operational planning, and specialized execution. Such collaboration represents the vortex of the responsive supply chain business model. More important, it also reflects the early manifestation and implementation of a many-to-many communication network.

Enterprise extension incorporates a variety of ways and means business leaders develop and nurture long-term operational arrangements with customers, material suppliers, and service suppliers. Voluntary enterprise extensions are long-term arrangements designed to fuse, leverage, and synergize the resources of two or more participating firms. Firms participating in such arrangements are positioned to focus or specialize on their areas of maximum expertise. The enterprises at the frontier of this movement are exploring the ways and means of synergistic value creation. To develop successful business relationships, leaders of involved enterprises must learn how to share rewards, as well as risks, resulting from participating in a collaborative supply chain.

The concept of enterprise extension finds its historical roots in, of all places, ownership-based vertical integration. Early Industrial Age business models were forced to emphasize ownership control to assure sustainable performance. The early doctrines of the Industrial Age, embodied in Taylorism and Fordism, were founded in the vision of control. As discussed earlier, Henry Ford, at the height of the Industrial Revolution, envisioned an automotive empire based in self-sufficiency. Ford's goal was to own and operate and, thereby, guarantee continuous performance of every facet of work required to build a "horseless carriage." By the early 1900s, Ford's enterprise extended from rubber plantations and iron ore mines to ships, railroads, and dealership showrooms. At the River Rouge plant, consisting of more than 2,000 acres and more than 100,000 employees, Ford boasted of being able to convert iron ore into an automobile in as few as 28 hours. While grand in concept, the vision of control via ownership failed in the long run to sustain the enterprise-wide expertise and performance Ford had envisioned. Over time, the icons of the Industrial Age began to realize that the key to efficiency was specialization. Most continue today to struggle with the initial reinvention of their enterprises—let alone the new challenges of digitizing.

As we enter the twenty-first century, examples of extended enterprises remain rare, but they are becoming more common and visible. New names such as Visiton and Cat Logistics are joining old but repositioned names such as Motorola, Volkswagen, Honda, Siemens,

Dell, Hewlett-Packard, P&G, Kimberly-Clark, and scores of others as the enterprise extension age begins to emerge. Long-standing business icons such as Kodak, Ford, and General Motors continue the long and tremulous transformation journey. Other former household names such as Westinghouse, Digital Equipment, U.S. Steel, Polaroid, and K-Mart are but a few once-prominent firms that failed to transform and have passed from the business scene.

For even the smallest firm, access to grid processing offers access to state-of-the-art information technology. Grid processing consists of using the computation powers of technology service providers. Such providers offer powerful networks of computing power available on demand. Thus, computer power can be a service purchased as needed, similar to electricity or natural gas. On-demand access to network processing capacity combined with the growing availability of software as a service (SaaS) means that the danger of computing brownout, network capacity, or risk and expense associated with the traditional time to install software are no longer constraints for either the largest or the smallest firm.

As twentieth-century command-and-control information systems are replaced with open and shared-access networks, the range of potential supply chain participants greatly expands. This range of potential participants includes all types of manufacturers, material and component suppliers, service firms, 3PL transportation and warehouse companies, wholesalers, retailers, and even consumers. Is it possible that competitors could also be included as collaborative participants? Only time will tell, but legal authorization enabling collaboration between companies that otherwise would be competitors was approved on a restricted basis with the passage of the 1984 National Cooperative Research Act. Amendments passed in 1993 and 2004 expanded and liberalized provisions related to the scope of permissible collaborative arrangements between competitors. It is interesting to note that these acts were passed into law during the twilight years of the Industrial Age.

Learning to direct collaborative business operations using a communication structure wherein both information and knowledge are fully distributed and equally assessable in real time to all participants constitutes an emerging and generally unexplored business model. Enabling and directing a collaborative supply chain initiative is no small task for a leader schooled in the traditional command-and-control information paradigm of "tell your own key employees only the strategic information they need to know to perform their jobs" management age.

The notion of the extended enterprise has been talked about in the business literature for several decades. However, the information technology necessary to enable such widespread collaboration has not. One of the greatest barriers to exploring adoption and implementation of the responsive supply chain business model has been an unwillingness to share knowledge as well as strategic and operational information between channel participants—hording, if you will. Most managers have difficulty even when it comes to sharing historical information with trading partners. Most conventional food retailers were shocked when Wal-Mart decided to make retail sales information at the individual store item level available to its key suppliers. Most of Wal-Mart's competitors followed the established industry practice of releasing such "proprietary" information only after it had been aggregated above the store level and, even then, only for a fee. It takes a great leap of faith in the power of collaboration to embrace and participate in the open environment characterized by sharing strategic information and forward-looking marketing and promotional plans. However, such unbridled information sharing is essential to make collaborative supply chains a reality. It is clear that we need to know a great deal more about the structure, strategy, and potential downside of collaborative business models. The operational manifesto for the collaborative responsive supply chain business model is still being written.

Understanding the Collaborative Framework

From the outset, it is important to recognize that there are many different collaboration models. In fact, as noted earlier, the transaction level in traditional buy-and-sell distribution channel structures is and will remain the operative structure for a significant portion of all commercial sales. A market mechanism and a structure of legal governance continue to facilitate the sell and buy process. Thus, vast real estate, stock, bond, retail to-consumer, and wholesale establishments continue to transfer ownership of goods and receipt of services using the legally structured market system. It is important to keep in mind that almost all sales to consumers occur in the traditional market system. However, as noted at several earlier points, this facet of consumer behavior is rapidly changing as a result of Web-based connectivity.

The collaborative structure for conducting business superimposes a relational framework guiding all transactions leading up to purchase for consumption. As discussed earlier, it is important to remember that consumption drives the free market system. When consumers decide to purchase or not to purchase a specific product, they exercise veto power over the continued success of all businesses participating in making a given product or service available for purchase. Thus, consumption, not buying and selling, is the sustaining force of the business process. The point was also made that, despite the growing magnitude of consumer Internet-facilitated purchases and growing evidence that consumers in select situations are willing to participate as channel members, the buy-and-sell process will remain market driven for the foreseeable future. The responsive supply chain business model, as we are beginning to understand it in today's market structure, is primarily business-to-business.

Within the business-to-business space, there are five collaborative models that can be observed in contemporary practice. All five of these models exhibit three main collaborative attributes. First, they all exhibit some degree of acknowledged dependency. Second, they all display a willingness to regularly share some level of strategic information. Finally, they all accept, share, and comply with some level of leadership or governance. As a result of these three attributes, firms engaged in a supply chain arrangement are cooperatively creating a union of resources that are capable of acting and behaving, to some degree, similar to a vertically integrated enterprise in the twentieth century. The fundamental difference in the union is based on voluntary collaboration, not ownership. The twenty-first-century model has shared leadership vision, a high degree of specialization, and an inherent capability to adapt and exploit market opportunity enabled by the orchestration of independent businesses.

The five collaborative business models are (1) contract, (2) outsource, (3) administered, (4) alliance, and (5) enterprise extension. These five models, as illustrated in Figure 9-1, differ with respect to acknowledged dependency, willingness to share information, the governance process, and leadership structure. These five collaborative models are independent of either the nation of a firm's domicile or the number of different nations involved in operational scope. In many ways, the best manner to think about a responsive supply chain business model in the world political sense is as a "stateless" collaboration.

Figure 9-1   Alternative Collaborative Structure

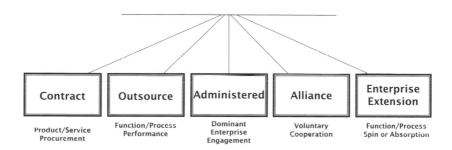

Contract	Outsource	Administered	Alliance	Enterprise Extension
Product/Service Procurement	Function/Process Performance	Dominant Enterprise Engagement	Voluntary Cooperation	Function/Process Spin or Absorption

Contracting

Contracting is when a firm selects to award a performance contract to another business firm. In command-and-control business models, contracting results from a managerial decision to focus and specialize a firm's internal processes on performing either proven core competencies or core necessities. A core competency is work a firm does as well or better than any other firm in its industry. Such core competencies are fundamental to a firm's basic value proposition. A core necessity is an activity or process that is important, maybe even essential, and that a firm's management decides it must perform in order to assure continued leadership in areas of core competency. All other activities judged as not being either core competencies or core necessities are candidates for contracting to an outside supplier. A common form of contracting is the use of for-hire transportation carriers, contract warehousing, and third-party logistics firms to perform essential distribution services.

The firm granting the contract desires to have specific work performed by another firm. As the name implies, the contract outlines in great detail the specifics of how and when the desired work will be completed. In most contracting situations, one firm, typically the firm granting the contract, enjoys a dominant power position. In some situations involving proprietary processes, scarce resources, or unique talents, the firm supplying, not the firm buying, may be the dominant enterprise. The typical contract is to perform a process or service over a specified period of time at an agreed-to price. Agreements are negotiated, with the contract specifying the time and price. While the actual contract may or may not be renewed, most situations at least have the expectation of a continued opportunity to enter bids. Contracting is common in heavy manufacturing and throughout the service industries.

In any contracting situation, the critical elements of acknowledged dependency and information sharing are limited. It is not uncommon for a given supplier to hold multiple contracts with firms that are direct competitors. Thus, both acknowledged dependency and willingness to share information are, to a significant degree, bridled on the part of participants. Typically, information sharing is limited to operational information essential for carrying out specified work. Finally, in terms of governance and leadership, the firm awarding the bid is in complete control. This, of course, is directly related to risk. The firm granting the contract is typically assuming all risk related to selling the end product. The firm winning the bid confronts limited risk related to performing specified services. Thus, all significant issues of leadership remain with the firm awarding the contract, and the process of governance is command and control, typical to the exercise of power within a single enterprise.

Outsourcing

Outsourcing represents a natural extension of contracting. The typical outsourcing arrangement represents a long-term commitment on the part of participating parties. Thus, significant points of difference between contracting and outsourcing are both the number and the duration of arrangements. Firms that outsource typically enter into arrangements that they anticipate will be sustainable over time. While contracts are normally guided by low-cost bidding, outsourcing is more often viewed as a partnership arrangement. Whereas contracting typically does not alter the internal operating capabilities of the granting firm, outsourcing typically does. The primary similarities between contracting and outsourcing are found in their operational direction, degree of shared risk, and the ability to reward is retained by the dominant firm, the one doing the contracting or outsourcing.

A primary difference between contracting and outsourcing is the anticipated time the relationship will continue. When a firm decides to outsource a function or a process, the typical expectation is that the work will remain outsourced from that time forward. While the supplier providing the outsource service may be changed, over time, the function or process is expected to remain outsourced. The firm outsourcing has typically decided that the operational area under consideration is not a core competency. The work involved, having been judged as not being a core competency by the granting firm, is awarded to a supplier with demonstrated ability to perform. The decision to outsource may be driven by one or all of the following factors: an inability to achieve scale economy, a lack of capacity, or the realization that the supplier can perform the specified work better than the granting firm.

In outsourced situations, acknowledged dependency is significantly higher than that involved in contract-to-contract bidding. Likewise, the degree and substance of information shared are significantly higher. In many industries, firms performing the outsourced work represent a primary source of research and development. Thus, new technology, product ideas, and innovations are expected to be generated and to flow from an established supplier network. This has been particularly true during the past few decades in the automotive industry. Interestingly, the ability of the Japanese automotive industry to more effectively incorporate such supply-based innovation, when compared to its U.S. counterpart, may directly relate to taking advantage of the solidarity of an outsourced, as opposed to a contracted, relationship.

Finally, the governance and leadership process is significantly different in an outsourced compared with a contracted relationship. The firm outsourcing is clearly the dominant establishment in an outsourced arrangement. But, just as the information shared becomes more proprietary, the managerial relationship becomes more of a two-way process. More feedback encourages a greater degree of collaboration. Thus, while the power structure remains command and control dominated by the firm granting the outsourcing opportunity, extensive feedback and collaborative management are typical. It is not unusual for regular meetings to be scheduled between frontline supervisors and functional specialists to facilitate day-to-day operations between the companies engaged in the outsourced arrangement.

It is important to clarify the growing practice of off-shoring that has grown in popularity during the past couple of decades. Off-shoring arrangements are popular in both contracting and outsourcing. Off-shoring simply means that the performance of contracts or outsourced work is awarded to a firm located in a different country. For example, when General Motors decides that parts or components of an engine are to be built to specifications by an outside firm it is contracting. When the responsibility for design, manufacturing, and quality for key components are delegated to a business associate or external supplier, on an ongoing basis, this is outsourcing. If the parent firm is U.S. based and the outsource partner is located in China or Mexico, both arrangements are examples of off-shoring. All of these easy-to-observe arrangements fall short of the collaborative supply chains being ushered in by twenty-first-century information technology.

Administered

An administered supply chain arrangement is one in which all participating companies have committed to work together in a highly coordinated way. Despite the fact that individual companies engaged in the relationship are independent, they look and act like they are members of the supply chain leader's organization. Firms that join an administered supply chain are committed to perform their specified duties as directed by the lead or dominant organization. Thus, a supplier of a product or service has the option not to participate in an administered supply chain. However, once the commitment is made to participate, there is no debate on what will be done or how it will be done. As one anonymous supplier to Wal-Mart stated, "Our future is to do or die, not to reason why." In short, he was saying that once his company decides to be a participant in the Wal-Mart supply chain and Wal-Mart agrees to include his company, it accepts the Wal-Mart game plan and rulebook. What that supplier has committed is willingness—acknowledged dependency—to follow the dominant enterprise and to perform the value-added functionality as agreed to and when specified by supply chain leadership.

To effectively function in an administered supply chain, it is clear that firms must share a great deal of operational and strategic information. Such information will be proprietary, and confidentiality is essential. Likewise, the prevailing expectation will be a two-way flow of important operational and strategic information between the participating companies. The leadership style in an administered business situation falls into the category of benevolent autocracy. The model is benevolent in the sense that all activities are directed to developing and maintaining a strong business operating capability. An administered supply chain is autocratic in the sense that all participating firms understand which enterprise is the home of the commander and chief! While many managers of participating product and service suppliers may be active participants on joint business strategy and operating committees, there is no doubt who chairs the committee and who has veto power.

Most strong retailers find success in developing and implementing administered supply chain models. Firms such as Kroger, Publix, Meijer, and Target maintained highly administered supply chain arrangements. Most of these firms conduct business with many of the same suppliers that distribute nationally branded consumer goods. Firms such as General Mills, Kellogg's, VF Corporation, P&G, Unilever, and Kimberly-Clark are operationally integrated with each of these top retailers. Many nationally branded manufacturers, of both consumer durables and package goods, have strong brands with consumer loyalty. The retail organization enjoys power derived from consumer store patronage. The manufacturers enjoy the power of consumer loyalty to their brands. Keeping in mind the fact that nothing of value happens until a product is consumed, it is not surprising that retailers typically dominate these administered channels. The manufacturers maintain a significant power counterbalance by virtue of their active participation in a number of different retail-administrated channels.

Alliance

An alliance occurs when two or more firms agree to undertake a joint initiative to manufacture and market a product. Alliances generally are structured around exclusive arrangements. Products are manufactured with the intent of being marketed exclusively under the auspiciousness of a single organization. Such marketing organizations may be cooperatives, industrial distributors, or retailers that own proprietary brands or private labels.

Other firms engaged in alliances may be manufacturing complex products. As firms move along the continuum toward exclusive arrangements, restrictions related to information sharing typically disappear. Alliance-based firms, while having separate ownership and independent operations, find value operating with the advantage of shared information and knowledge. In an alliance, firms commit to manage processes that span functional areas within their firms and link with trading partners and customers across organizational boundaries. Likewise, they clearly understand that profitable operations depend on successful operational execution on the part of all firms engaged in the alliance. A food distribution supplier, Martin-Brower, and a fast-food chain, McDonald's, will have individual success only if their alliance enjoys market success.

Aircraft companies such as Boeing have long followed the practice of collaborating with firms such as Rolls-Royce and General Electric in the design and assembly of jet engines These firms have a core competency in design and construction of jet power plants and many aspects of the associated fuel management systems. Given this expertise, it is highly unlikely that aircraft companies will venture into the engine business in the near future. In fact, on Boeing's newest plane, the 787 Dreamliner passenger jet, the company has outsourced design and innovation for several major sections of the plane in an effort to significantly cut cost and hopefully decrease go-to-market time. In turn, these suppliers maintain aggressive research and development programs to assure that they will retain their differential advantage.

From a leadership perspective, one firm in an alliance will "captain the ship." Typically, it is the organization having the closest relationship with the end customer or consumer. A notable exception is the manufacturing and distribution of Disney products. The products are manufactured with Disney license and are distributed in a number of different marketing channels under auspices by the Disney organization. While Disney does little of the manufacturing, distribution, or retail work, it maintains benevolent but autocratic leadership of the overall process.

Enterprise Extension

The most advanced state of collaboration is enterprise extension. While still rare in the supply chain lexicon, extended enterprise and its potential were first popularized in a *Business Week* article entitled "The Hollow Corporation."[3] The hollow corporation was portrayed as one in which a parent or senior enterprise owns significant patents, intellectual rights, and copyrights but not much else. In essence, the hollow corporation was positioned as a holding enterprise that financed proprietary research and development, acquired property and intellectual rights, and licensed other organizations to manufacture and market its holdings. Thus, the hollow corporation was visualized as owning extensive property rights but not as being involved in day-to-day operations.

The extended enterprise consists of many independent and specialized businesses working together to perform all functionality required for a successful distributive arrangement. The extended enterprise is not bound by legal contracts or formal agreements. It consists of independent business organizations developing highly collaborative working arrangements built on trust and specialization. In part, the relationship models discussed earlier have resulted in constant jettisoning of nonessential or noncore functionality. The result is that many companies are dependent on a network of associated

---

[3]   Norman Jones, "The Hollow Corporation," *Business Week*, March 3, 1986.

suppliers to perform functionality necessary to sustain operations. Such collaborative firms are, in essence, participants in communities of firms. From an operational perspective, these firms are committed to internal efficiency and externally, as a group, to integrated supply chain performance and customer satisfaction.

This form of the responsive supply chain business model is just beginning to emerge on the business landscape. Because of trust, participating firms are willing to share proprietary information concerning business plans and strategic initiatives. Most twentieth-century supply chains consist of independent decision makers each with different objectives. In contrast, the emerging twenty-first-century edition is a global collaborative supply chain built on open information network architecture. Thus, while lacking formal organization structure, the collaborative relationship exhibits acknowledged dependency and shares both strategic and operational information while operating with a shared governance and leadership structure. Many foresee the ability of this collaborative model to consistently meet consumer expectations as potentially greater than today's mass-merchant business. Time will tell just how powerful such collaborative models will become. Thus, true collaboration has the potential to redefine supply chain structure and take operational success to a new level. It is important to learn more about this collaborative model, which we call demand-driven supply chain collaboration.

Demand-Driven Supply Chain Collaboration

The combination of a growing willingness to collaborate supported by Web-based connectivity has expanded the capability of a responsive supply chain business model. This focus on demand moves leadership attention among the collaborative enterprises from solely distribution efficiency toward a strategic capability. Demand-driven supply chain collaboration is focused on the fundamental purpose of the arrangement: to meet and exceed consumer expectations.

Effective demand-driven supply chain collaboration requires three components. First is the strategic alignment of organizations and their representatives. Second is a willingness to share a wide range of actions and information traditionally considered to be proprietary. The many types of sharing important to successful collaboration involve real-time strategic and operational information, event visibility, operational rules, and, most important, risk and reward. Last, collaborative firms need to identify and standardize cross-organizational processes. In final analysis, effective demand-driven supply chain collaboration is, to a large extent, about interorganizational communication between firms engaged in "indispensable relationships."[4]

Demand-driven supply chain collaboration is focused on consumption. It is consumer centric in an effort to stimulate top-line revenue growth for all firms engaged. Of additional importance is the goal of eliminating duplication and non-value-adding redundancy in an effort to jointly improve bottom-line profit results. The joint objective is to drive value across the supply chain to affect consumers as a result of synchronization of participating organizations. Orchestration of a demand-driven collaboration requires the development of sustainable cross-enterprise integration and synchronization. Figure 9-2 provides a list of seven essential integration challenges prerequisite to successful cross-enterprise collaboration.

From each participant's perspective, a collaborative supply chain must represent the best alternative for success and long-term proliferation. A shared customer-centric view of the supply chain is crucial if the collaboration seeks success in terms of market growth opportunity.

---

[4]   R.P. Kampstra, J. Ashayeri, and J. L. Gattorna, "Realities of Supply Chain Collaboration" *International Journal of Logistics Management* 17, no. 3 (2006), pp. 312–330.

Figure 9-2   Seven Cross-Enterprise Integration Challenges

- Acknowledged Interdependency
- Leadership Clarity
- Loyalty and Confidentiality
- Rules of Engagement
- Meaningful Metrics
- Risk and Reward Sharing
- Reposition and Termination Agreement

Likewise, it is important to get the people or cultural side of the equation right. In his work *Living Supply Chains*, John Gattorna stresses the important point that "in the end a supply chain isn't driven by networks, assets or technology, but by people."[5] Such people are the boundary representatives of their individual organizations. It is important that such boundary leaders have a strong belief in the fundamental purpose of the collaborative effort.

Figure 9-3 provides a diagram of the continuous process of creating legendary relationships. A "legendary relationship" is considered to be an arrangement that sets the standard of competition in an industry or market. When a firm's management decides to explore supply chain collaboration, the process starts with a shared commitment among all participating firms to jointly seek and achieve an unprecedented level of operational excellence. It is essential that all supply chain participants have a shared willingness to jointly achieve operational excellence. In most situations, this shared willingness translates to the achievement of a sustained level of superior performance. In other words, the joint supply chain initiative is ratcheted to a level of customer-focused performance higher than traditionally experienced.

---

[5]   J. L. Gattorna, *Living Supply Chains* (New York: Financial Times Prentice Hall, 2006).

Figure 9-3   Creating Legendary Relationships

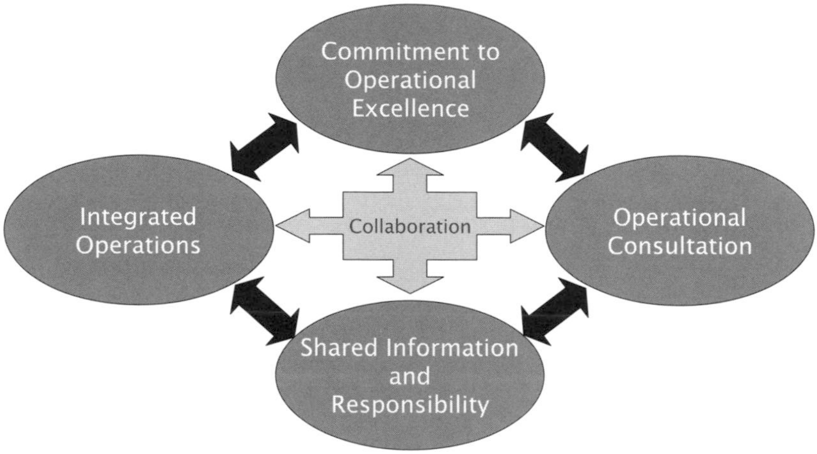

Such ratcheting is reinforced by integrated operations that engage the entire supply chain in continuous replenishment. Such integrative management, as discussed in Chapter Six, now takes on an interorganizational posture. Each firm engaged in the supply chain is focused on performing added activities, concerning which they enjoy a differential advantage. Thus, a combination of basic product companies join together to develop components and technologies essential to create a complex end product. Likewise, other firms in the supply chain perform essential services representing their core competencies. Such integration is supported by supply-chain-wide unbridled information, operational consultation, and shared inventory deployment responsibility.

Achieving a demand-driven supply chain is not easy. The proposed business practice and associated behavior go against most doctrines of how businesses have traditionally gone to market. There is clearly a dark side to such extensive collaboration. Trust can be broken, and the danger of a firm taking advantage of a supplier or customer is always present. Such failure to live up to collaborative expectations may be deliberate or accidental—nevertheless, it is real and can serve to destroy the relational foundations of the collaboration.

Close working relationships open the door for potential complacency. Established suppliers or buyers representing customers in a collaborative supply chain are linked in a dependency relationship. Over time, they may have a tendency to take the relationship for granted. Clearly, many things can go wrong and create dangers to the survival of the collaborative arrangement. However, the upside synergy seems sufficient to justify the risk of exploring the potential of creating legendary relationships.

Collaborating with Customers Who Really Don't Want to Collaborate

For a variety of reasons, many leaders may not be in a mood to collaborate. In fact, while not documented by research, there is a growing feeling that executives not embracing the challenges of digital transformation are also leaders who do not see the benefits of collaborating. Firms that are lagging in supply chain momentum remain deeply committed to win-lose or zero-sum negotiation strategies, contracting and doing business with low-bid suppliers. Is it possible to collaborate with firms that do not want to collaborate? The answer, as always, is yes and no: no in the sense that the highest levels of collaboration, alliances, and enterprise extension are not going to happen if any firm in the proposed arrangement is reluctant to fully embrace the essential prerequisites.

However, lower levels of collaboration can materialize in industry-wide initiatives such as efficient consumer response (ECR), collaborative planning forecasting and replenishment (CPFR), continuous replenishment (CR), vendor-managed inventory (VMI), information sharing made possible by voluntary industry communication standards (VICS), and other initiatives aimed at encouraging successful cross-enterprise collaboration. However, until these traditional or currently dominant firms seek the full benefits of broad-based collaboration, their success will fall short of alliances or extended enterprises.

Ralph Drayer, a former P&G executive and one of the architects of the famous Wal-Mart and P&G legendary relationship, summed the challenge as follows. "The model for creating value has changed. Today companies have highly desegregated value chains, where the majority of operational efficiencies and revenue enhancement opportunities can only come from greater visibility, integration and synchronization among companies in a value network. Collaboration outside the physical walls of an enterprise is the new arena for value creation."

An example of a pioneering effort of collaboration of joint company practices included Becton Dickinson and Company (BD), Baxter Healthcare, and hospitals that in the mid-1990s shared patient usage and individual company inventories of medical supplies. This collaboration was possible because of a shared information system capable of maintaining financial accountability to each other for overall inventory investments and associated costs. As part of this end-to-end supply chain arrangement, joint margins and patient service goals were created and managed. Financial results were dispensed periodically, including recognition and transfer of profit between parties based on agreed integrated service contracts. This early collaboration was achieved without the benefit of Web-based technology. Collaboration is about more than technology. However, information technology has greatly expanded the range of available opportunities.

Part Four
Endurance

Supply Chain Sustainability

O nce change is under way, the guiding light becomes continuous improvement. While it is not difficult to institute change,
it is difficult to maintain both the enthusiasm and the enterprise
energy required to sustain the initiative. Similar to bad habits among
individuals is the tendency of firms to fall back on old or more comfortable ways of doing things once the pressure to change subsides.
Supply chain sustainability, stage four of successful transformation, is
all about the challenges of maintaining momentum. Past experience
indicates that transformations have a tendency to lose momentum
and, in many cases, fail altogether soon after the spotlight fades.

   Two chapters are devoted to endurance challenges, Chapter
Ten, "Relational Leadership," and Chapter Eleven, "Measurement
and Motivation." In Chapter Ten, the leadership model for the

twenty-first century is discussed in terms of lean and flat organizational structures driven by ubiquitous information. Flat organizations require empowerment of frontline workers in order to gain and maintain operational continuity. Today's leaders, accustomed to complex organizations and layers of bureaucratic management, have a lot to learn to be effective in an information-empowered responsive supply chain business model. This challenge is magnified by the need to establish and maintain successful collaboration between the many different firms participating in the supply chain.

In Chapter Eleven, the fundamentally important topics of measurement and motivation are addressed. The typical complexity of a twenty-first-century enterprise makes the tasks of meaningful measurement and motivation some of the most difficult leadership challenges. Measurement and motivation are discussed together because they are interrelated in resolving both the financial resources and the human resources required in the global digital economy.

The final chapter provides a short look to the future. The title "2025 and Beyond" is a look beyond the initial shock of the Information Revolution to the futuristic ways and means of supply chain commerce. The premise of this final chapter is founded in the belief that the Information Age will be ushered into best practice far faster than was true in the Industrial Revolution. It appears reasonable to speculate that information technology, as a driver of change, will begin to plateau by 2050. In short, Moore's law will become history. By 2050 and beyond, the future of continued operational improvement is likely to rest with nanotechnology and the potential dawning of some elementary forms of molecular decomposition. Thus, just as the Agricultural Age was superseded by the Industrial Age and the Information Age superseded the Industrial Age, the world will begin to transcend beyond the Information Age toward what may become known as the "Global Genome Age." This may begin to occur as soon as the fifth decade of the twenty-first century.

To close on the challenges of today's reality, a postscript titled "Initial Steps toward the New Information-Driven Frontier" concludes the book. This postscript addresses many of the potential issues related to day-to-day business operations while simultaneously leading a response-based supply chain transformation. A single appendix discusses supply chain fundamentals. The purpose of this brief appendix is to offer an introductory discussion of the day-to-day work performed in a typical supply chain for readers new to the discipline.

Chapter Ten
Relational Leadership

> *"One way to think about leadership is to consider a jazz band. Jazz bandleaders must choose the music, the right musicians and perform in public. But the effect of the performance depends on so many things; the environment, the volunteers playing in the band and the need for everybody to perform as individuals and as a group."* [1]
>
> —Max Dupree

A critical dimension of digital transformation is the leadership challenge of developing and sustaining organizational momentum. Unlike most other topics, a course on how to reinvent a business is not found in the curricula of most business schools. Digitizing is the ultimate challenge in change management. It affects all organizational levels and relationships of the extended enterprise. Supply chain change does not occur at an office or a plant. It occurs in every place a firm engages in business transactions. Likewise, transformation is not limited to a specific level or unit of an organization. Supply chain transformation involves every aspect of an organization's work blueprint and affects all employee levels, all suppliers, and all customers.

A typical transformation starts with leaders defining and creating a credible supply chain vision for the enterprise—the composite of

---

[1] Max Dupree, Chairman, Herman Miller, Inc.

activities, competencies, business relationships, and goals that when combined and implemented will result in sustainable competitive advantage. Such visioning must be framed within a believable action plan that continues to provide reassurance and tangible proof that the transformation is and remains on track. Because the mission is best described as a journey across time, it will likely require multiple course corrections—but not a change in the target destination. This type of long-term mission is easier to comprehend by analogy to the January 2006 launch of the multiyear planet Pluto exploratory mission. It will not be possible to determine the exact success of the Pluto mission until 25 or more years following the launch date.

Leading a transformation involves a total examination and focusing of all aspects of an enterprise, from the most basic element of work to its most far-reaching synergistic achievement. In a digitally extended enterprise, the words "integrated," "holistic," "connected," and "focused" become essential operating virtues. To successfully accomplish transformation goals, creative thought needs to be given to the traditional roles played by leaders, managers, and followers and how they are likely to change in the future.

Leaders: Changing Perspectives

The roles of leaders, followers, and managers have, throughout the years, been performed by most employees as they navigated their business careers. To illustrate the relative importance of these three roles and the differences among them, let's start with a typical entry-level employee. In entry-level positions, a large percentage of time is spent following disciplined routines and performing predictable work tasks essential to creating value. A substantially smaller proportion of the time of early career employees is spent in managing. Managerial responsibility of a typical entry-level employee might involve deployment of resources, systems, and processes. Likewise, a small amount of an entry-level employee's time is actually involved in leading. Such leadership is most typically by example, or what is often called "silent leadership." Entry-level and early career employees, as a result of their attitudes and actions, influence others to accomplish organizational objectives. This triad of traditional roles continues throughout most careers. However, the traditional balance between leading, managing, and following changes across a career as a result of emerging information technology in at least two significant ways.

First, the increasing availability of information shared among employees at all levels of an organization, as well as across the collaborative supply chain, means that more employees are positioned and sufficiently informed to make timely decisions. Whereas the traditional command-and-control organization structure of business allowed sufficient time for information to transcend the managerial hierarchy, the lean and agile organizations of twenty-first-century enterprises do not. Organizations are increasingly becoming flatter, and authority to act is more and more being delegated to empowered frontline employees.

Second, the basic flattening of the traditional command-and-control organization structure is further accentuated by the globalization of supply chain operations. With information moving at lightening-like speeds, the competitive nature of business will increasingly require on-the-spot decisions. As noted earlier, nearly 95 percent of the work of the supply chain takes place outside the vision of supervision. To achieve the level of performance necessary to gain and maintain leading-edge status, organizations of tomorrow will increasingly require frontline employee empowerment.

In the traditional perspective of a command-and-control organization, employees were viewed as becoming leaders only if and when they were promoted to higher-level jobs in the organization structure. In flat organizations, this perspective of decision-making leadership is being redefined. Figure 10-1 illustrates a hypothetical distribution of time between leading, managing, and following projected across a successful employee's career path.

An entry-level position is viewed as involving approximately 70 percent following, 20 percent managing, and 10 percent leading. While the distribution of time shifts across time, what may be surprising to the reader is the distribution of senior executive time. While the percentage of leadership increases and the amount of time devoted to following decreases, a significant amount of senior executive time, as much as 20 percent, still is devoted to following. The fact of the matter is that everyone has a boss!

The time distributions illustrated are based on a small sample of individual executive time assessments. In a broader-based analysis, these distributions may slightly alter. However, the key point is

Figure 10-1   Time Allocation Across a Successful Career

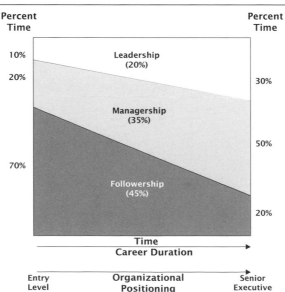

that as a result of distributed information, the engagement of all employees in a twenty-first-century organization is different from that in the past. This recognition of increasingly greater involvement of entry-level and frontline employees in critical leadership roles is one of the primary forces driving modified early career paths for entry-level college graduates.

Previously, the traditional new employee career path was assignment to a single entry-level job until performance merited promotion. The new perspective is a rotational entry-level period. In rotation, new employees typically are assigned three- to six-month durations in frontline jobs across a range of different organizational positions. Thus, an entry-level employee may start in purchasing and progressively move to logistics, manufacturing, and customer facing responsibilities over a two- to three year period. Ideally, rotational candidates will be assigned to each area for sufficient time to accomplish quantifiable results. Such rotation increases exposure to both internal and external constituents and increases the potential of future leaders to better understand cross-functional and integrative management challenges. It also provides the persons involved an opportunity to build an informal relational network among cross-function colleagues.

Before speculation concerning future role definitions and organizational responsibilities required to accommodate a responsive supply chain, it is useful to examine in more depth some learnings of the nineteenth and twentieth centuries for their continued applicability and context. In the following sections, we discuss leaders, followers, and managers.

Leadership

While leadership is a subject heavily studied and documented, the actual word "leadership" is a relatively recent addition to the English language.[2] As a concept, "leadership" did not gain wide-based attention until the late nineteenth century. Before its adoption as an important dimension of business, most attention was directed to the act and the characteristics of the individual leaders. A Google search resulted in excess of 166 million sources of leadership material and 24 million leadership definitions. It seems that most everyone has at least one definition of leadership! Within this repository of information, it is important to define what we mean by twenty-first-century leadership.

Leadership concepts in the early nineteenth century emerged as the Industrial Age matured. Leadership thinking started as a theory of genetics; you had to be born with it. Some retain that belief today. One major perspective on leadership was based on how an individual related and reacted to particular challenges and variables confronted in business practice. This school of thought became identified as leadership contingency theory. As leadership practices were documented, a generalized theory evolved that was based on observing styles and actions of individual decision makers when faced with varied situations.

During the twentieth century, the interaction of leaders with followers generated three different theories concerning the origin and nature of leadership. Behavioral theory identified leadership as a learned behavior developed during a career. Participative theory identified the need for great leaders to build upon experience by learning from the actions of leader models. Finally, the transactional theory of leadership identified the need to take into account the role of supervisors, organization, and group performance. A more contemporary theory of leadership is based on the experience of positive relational reinforcement. This theory focuses on the connectivity

---

[2] Curtis L. Brungardt, *The New Face of Leadership: Implications for Higher Education: Leadership Studies* (Fort Haya State University, 1998).

formed between leaders and followers and their shared experiences related to successful motivation and inspiration.[3]

In combination, these theories do not completely define leadership. They do identify attributes building a more complete definition of leadership working within the human environment. Our perspective is that the typologies are appropriately viewed as a panorama of different lens capturing interpretations of a great picture of leadership, none totally complete but all revealing something new. If we could integrate all the pictures as one and propel the result into motion, our perspective of the leadership model would evolve as a composite of ability, behavior, unique style, and charisma, continuously growing based on the "interaction experience" among leaders, managers, and followers. In final analysis, leadership is not the accomplishment of a single person. The process of leadership is best explained and defined as a "collaborative endeavor" among organizational and supply chain participants. The essence of leadership is not the leader but an influential relationship among leaders, managers, and followers working together for the collective good as an integrated working team.

This perspective that we call "relational leadership" is characterized by collaboration, power sharing, and empowerment. Additionally, it is based on research defining successful leadership within the supply chain resulting from the orchestration of five abilities. They are the ability to identify customer requirements (discovery), identify and quantify competitive capabilities (measurement), understand the firm's competencies and limitations (assessment), quantify the dynamics between requirements and capabilities (visioning), and develop and lead action plan implementation (inspiration and motivation).[4]

Relational leadership reflects the emergence and demands of a global digital economy. While planning is essential, it is important to

---

[3] Kendra Van Wagner, *Leadership Theories* (About, Inc., 2007).

[4] Bowersox, Closs, and Stank, op. cit., 1999.

understand that today's supply chains operate in real time, globally, 24 hours a day, seven days a week. Some strategic, many tactical, and most operational decisions are, and will increasingly need to be, made much faster and much lower in the organization. In earlier chapters, discussions on the associated challenges of integrated management, real-time responsiveness, networks, and collaboration called for a new form of leadership. Responsive supply chain leadership is not just work at the top of the organization; it involves work and responsibility shared throughout the organization. The challenge is to enable relational leadership distributed throughout the organization and across the supply chain. It calls for new ways of learning and thinking. It calls for situational adaptive organizational structures. Finally, it calls for constant change, collaboration, and sustainability of mission.

Relational leadership, such as group leadership and coleadership models, will be a necessity for success in the twenty-first century. Within each of these models, leaders are viewed as providing direction across an extended supply chain organization. This leadership is based on real-time information, timing, and arranging the collaborative supply chain structure best capable of providing the needed expertise to act. While, to some, this may seem to be a radical new convention, group leadership has been in business and music for some time, and coleadership has been practiced as far back as the ancient Romans.

Developing new leadership skills throughout learning-capable organizations shifts the burden of leadership from one to many, as teams and whole companies are empowered with responsibility for caring for and taking preemptive action concerning company well-being.[5] In a world where the information needed to drive organizational success is continuous, the timing of decisions also needs to be

---

5   Sarita Chawla and John Renesch, eds., *Learning Organizations* (Portland: Productivity Press, 1995).

accelerated. This response calls for shared leadership to fully achieve the desired outcomes.

In addition, living in a time of shared leadership calls for new ways of thinking. As a contributing leader in the twenty-first century, one needs to master many schools of thought and practice in order to be able to integrate different disciplines. It's also not sufficient that a leader understand these new collaborative practices. Leaders need to communicate integrated thoughts to others: team members, associates, suppliers, and trading partners. In the global digital economy, there will be both traditional problems to resolve and new phenomena to observe, uncover, clarify, and exploit. Additionally, as mentioned earlier, relational leadership magnifies the need for unfiltered awareness and unwavering appreciation for differences among the people, teams, and organizations involved in daily work. Last, but clearly not least, leadership thinking must be appreciative of the global environment and all that implies.

Followership

Followership is a concept more contemporary than leadership. Throughout history, much of what has been written about followership was not uplifting, engaging, or inspiring. A proper assessment would be that the followership literature has been passive and submissive, essentially describing crowd mentality. One is left in wonderment concerning how, during the golden years of the Industrial Revolution, a followership perspective failed to develop. There is never leadership without followership. In fact, one of the classic descriptions of leadership offered by Peter Drucker was "the only definition of a leader is someone who has followers."[6]

---

6   Peter Drucker, *The Leader of the Future*. The Drucker Foundation Future Series, eds. Frances Hesselbein, Marshall Goldsmith, and Richard Beckhard, 1996, foreword, p. xii.

One cannot be a leader without a least one follower. If each role is important, one wonders why it was not inspiring to talk about or be considered a valued follower. Maybe the reason was because defining leadership originally focused on what one person did, as opposed to what the organization achieved by working together or with the supply chain as a result of collaboration. Maybe this neglect resulted because the term "followership" was perceived as having negative connotations. But, over time, authors began to research and write about followership with central themes that continue to repeat themselves: honesty and courage. While more positive, these are still a pretty narrow set of traits when viewed from the perspective of developing future leaders. As noted earlier, freshly minted college graduates spend most of their time during the beginning years of their careers performing in a follower capacity. At all levels of development, most employees spend a significant part of their business careers following.

Just as the criteria for effective leadership have changed over time, so have concepts of followership. As leaders are learning, the increased speed at which they must identify and understand business developments offers little opportunity for analysis and planning. To exploit opportunity, leaders must learn to delegate power and implement shared leadership. Leadership no longer resides solely at the top of an organization or at specified sublevels of the organization. It is shared with followers throughout the organization.

Thus, following is no longer viewed as the act of passively waiting for instructions. Rather, following requires active participation in decision making on behalf of senior leadership. Being an effective follower within a distributed leadership practice model requires unique skill. Effective followers need to know how to demonstrate respect for senior leadership, learn to appreciate different approaches to achieve targeted outcomes, be proactive, and foster sufficient support to allow other followers to achieve desired outcomes. It means jumping in and out of the followership role continually as the needs and leadership actions of teams and individual team members present themselves.

In the twenty-first century, information visibility allows all leaders and followers to continually know a great deal more about what is happening across the entire supply chain. As a result of such visibility, faster decisions and directions are required to remain competitive. Fortunately, followership is now getting more attention in academic research. Leading business schools have started to create university-level courses defining the role of followership, what it involves, and why it matters. Likewise, progressive organizations are increasingly casting a new image by calling followers "business associates." The knowledge in this important area will continue to expand and become more robust as a result of continued academic research and interest within the business world.

Managership

Given the preceding discussion on leaders and followers, one might rightly ask, is there a role for managers in the twenty-first century? In many ways, leaders and followers are also managers. The role of management in the modern corporation is the development of administrative processes and controls to assure enterprise continuity and integrity. Thus, management is the stewardship process of directing and maintaining a firm's social, financial, and legal compliance. The job of managing a global enterprise is a resource-intensive and time-consuming responsibility. This is an area where information technology has made a major impact. All leaders and followers have some degree of managerial responsibility.

In Chapter Three, we introduced the responsive supply chain business model as requiring continuous redefinition of strategy and tactics. This continuous redefinition means that senior leadership must continually reexamine the organizational framework. Some current organizational challenges were discussed in Chapter Six, "Integrative Management." The focal question becomes one of whether traditional concepts of management have relevancy in twenty-first-century organizations. A partial answer is found in briefly examining the origins of the managerial process.

Traditional organization models focused attention on the single/functional worker's or department's performance. Management as a concept developed in the late nineteenth and early twentieth centuries. The theories of Frederick Taylor's *Scientific Management* (1911) and Peter Drucker's *Concept of the Corporation* (1946) helped frame the management models of the industrial world. Management was often described by Drucker as the organ of institutions that converts a mob into an organization and human efforts into performance. Historical management models assumed a bureaucratic shape dominated by functional departments and able to achieve an unprecedented level of corporate efficiency.

Changing systems of management and related business process developed into a respected field of business process analysis. However, the concepts and skills were for a slower world, a world in which communication between distant parties was expensive and took from days to hours to complete. This pace of information connectivity set the tempo for effective management. The authors recall elapsed periods of several weeks before the detailed sales history of distant markets became generally available. Effective inventory control in such information-void operations resulted in local warehouses and excessive commitment to forward-positioned inventories.

The 1980s were the adolescent time for developing managerial thought concerning how to incorporate information technology into improved practice. Through the 20 years that followed, the sharing of work across business silos expanded. It was during this time that leaders realized they needed a senior management team. It became increasingly clear that a single CEO was not adequate to guide a global enterprise. The senior leadership job required too many different temperaments and just embraced too much work. Organizations began to discover that senior leaders needed an executive team to support the CEO. Drucker said, "The proper analogy for the top management job is the small chamber ensemble, the string quartet, in which each player is equal even though there is always a 'leader.'"[7]

As the tempo of information connectivity increased, the middle management role started to become less relevant. Activities within companies became increasingly shared. Middle-level managers, often referred to as knowledge workers, had to increasingly collaborate with people over whom they had no direct line of control. Global business required middle-level managers to work directly with other managers located in different geographical areas. Senior managers began to ask middle managers to increasingly create, maintain, and run emerging business systems.

Much of the expanded role described above was not traditionally viewed as the role of a middle-level manager. With these changes, it was becoming more difficult to distinguish between middle and senior management responsibility. Additionally, expanding social and fiduciary responsibilities increasingly required senior managers to devote more time to activities affecting the future of their enterprise, society, and the environment in which they operated. Changes ranging from the direct workforce to senior organization were some of the greatest challenges of senior management. Senior managers needed to

---

[7]   Peter Drucker, *Managing in a Time of Great Change* (New York, Penquin, 1995), p. 79.

change functions, relationships, and responsibilities, now and for the foreseeable future. All the great teaching about the knowledge-based organization was rapidly becoming obsolete. Traditional concepts of management, during the last decades of the twentieth century, were increasingly moving into a time of great change.

Leading Change

Business organizations have been traditionally structured round a model very similar to that of a baseball team. That is, players with very different skills each play a position. Basically, each player operates in his or her own space independently on the field but in a manner good for the team. This structured organizational model in business has reached its limitation. The Japanese were the first to initiate organizational abandonment. They redefined the prevailing organizational model and, as a result, their global competitive positioning. Their revised collaborative work model required many painful years to put into full practice. The perfection of their manufacturing model delivered superior new car designs faster and for a lower cost than anything U.S. car manufacturers have been able to match. In 2007, Toyota became the world's and the United States' largest-selling brand of automobiles.

Event monitoring and information sharing throughout the supply chain are providing end-to-end connectivity and knowledge sharing. Business leaders need to develop and operate organizational models capable of functioning in a mode where change is continuous. These organizational leaders, managers, and followers must continuously search the horizon to identify the challenges and opportunities emerging from change. The challenge is to continuously determine what the totality of an organization needs to do differently and to ascertain what is happening within the environment, among competitors, and concerning consumer connectivity. It is a compelling overall organizational responsibility that must be shared by leaders, managers, and followers. But, change means disruption.

Adapting an organizational structure to accommodate new requirements is the most difficult learning conceivable. Identifying what is new is the easy part. The difficulty comes in abandonment of old concepts and practices. Organizations must unlearn skills and valued crafts acquired over the years that have become obsolete. Leaders, managers, and followers must change lifetime habits and treasured human relationships—a very unpleasant experience. In an important sense, it is also viewed as a growing leadership responsibility to improve the communities in which associates work, live, and sell. This is heavy lifting for an individual, a team, a company, and, increasingly, an entire supply chain.

The time spent and the methods required for achieving the desired leader, manager, and follower roles must, by the very nature of the new and challenging technology environment, be different than in the past. Organizations of the future should position change management as an organized discipline supporting managership, leadership, and followership. The process of changing should become a renewable skill used to assure sustainability.

Leading change is the continuous process of aligning an organization with the requirements of its marketplace and doing it more responsively and effectively than competition. What, then, are the candidates for change in a global digital economy? The answer is everything!

Leadership, managership, and followership models must be able to support numerous and rapidly changing decision points. All attempts to improve supply chain performance outcomes must be focused on meeting or exceeding ever-changing customer expectations. They must leverage functional and cross-functional skills of all enterprise associates and the untapped talent of sales and supplier trading partners. The new digital world's speed and awareness call into question traditional, functionally based organizations that operate in sequential steps and with siloed structures. Digitizing requires thinking with process-related end goals in mind. Leaders need to step back and think about how to anticipate the future state of consumers whose interests and minds they want to capture. It is essential to crystallize what attributes are most important to customers and then keep coming back to them for a fresh look time after time.

With the freshest observations in hand, think about architecting, recognizing, and operating organizations that tomorrow might better support achieving consumer sustainability. We believe that future organizations are likely to follow a more horizontally integrated model pivoted to the key cross-organizational strategic processes discussed in Chapter Six. If we believe that the digitized real-time, 24-hour-a-day, seven-day-a-week work world will develop exponentially, a processed-based organizational orientation with distributed relational leadership will be essential. This commitment to process excellence will complement internal organization and externally support connectivity with suppliers and customers. The result will be an end-to-end responsive supply chain business model focused on the sustainability of a loyal customer base.

Moving Forward

While information technology alone is not sufficient to change the nature of leadership, it will continue to drive development and define achievable outcomes for the next several decades. As noted as early as Chapter Two, today's ERP design and implementation are not adequate to satisfy emerging operational requirements. While technology here-today and new developments on the horizon are more than adequate, the application of such technology to assist in managing critical business processes is not sufficiently comprehensive. What is needed is continued development and implementation of highly decentralized decision support systems. The technology applications of the future need to enhance leadership ability to implement increasingly complex operational process-based business models. These models must address cross-functional integration within individual enterprises as well as interorganizational functionality between firms across the supply chain. While communication technology and information are available to support such operationally based imperatives, the lack of strategic modeling development restrains or prohibits cross-functional implementation. While this is all changing, those responsible for transformation must be sure that technology application deployment enhances and complements the leadership and operational needs of emerging end-to-end supply chain processes.

This vision also calls into focus the need for continued development of leadership models to support decentralized or frontline decision making. These new leadership models must be effective in collaborative cultures and within horizontally structured real-time organizations. It also calls into focus the need to build relationships and collaborative business models with new structures focused on customers, leveraged value across the supply chain, and shared risk and rewards. Thomas W. Malone, author of *The Future of Work*, codirector of MIT's "Inventing the Organizations of the 21st Century" initiative, has theorized how technology will change the shape of organizations and leadership behavior. In his work, he speculates how the growing challenges of digitization will affect the structure and role of future organization leaders. Malone makes a case that the most effective structure will be a networked organization model capable of coordinating and cultivating increasingly more flexible real-time decision making at all levels throughout the organization.[8] From our perspective, this vision extends the leaders-follower-manager discussion from the individual organization to the end-to-end supply chain.

Leadership in the future must be prepared to support a consumer-satisfaction-driven organization that executes and adapts competitively on the basis of real-time information. Leaders must be able to fuse the best structure, behavior, process, and decision making to have the ever-changing breakthrough capability necessary to compete. This means developing an organization that is more centralized because of digitization while at the same time more decentralized than ever before in its decision-making process. Digitization, distributed leadership, and follower empowerment will equate to a future organization functioning more like a whole organism than independent extremities.

Senior leadership needs to adopt the essential characteristics of an end-to-end responsive supply chain business model. This model needs to empower change management principles, not traditional functional or command-and-control organizational principles. In concert with other value creation strategies, supply chain integration is essential to organize, lead, sense, and respond to ever-changing customers.

In the rapidly emerging world, functional excellence, to the extent relevant, will at best be a prerequisite for success. All who succeed will have organizations that are functionally excellent. Essential functionalism is achieved by a combination of internal competencies and assorted outsourced arrangements. The primary focus of twenty-first-century leadership will be end-to-end processes. Organizations will need to be structured and operationally pivoted on interorga-

---

[8]   Thomas Malone, *The Future of Work* (Cambridge, MA: Harvard University Press, 2003).

nizational mega-process collaboration. Thus, all eight of the core processes identified and discussed in Chapter Six will need to be increasingly extended beyond the individual enterprise, across the entire end-to-end supply chain.

Having an aligned customer focus strategy combined with a value generating end-to-end supply chain will be essential to achieve fundamental, or basic, business goals. The leadership challenge in the twenty-first-century organization will be to enable relevant technology, to continually develop new approaches, to immediately adjust to sensed reality, and to develop operational solutions to avoid bottlenecks and product, service, or time problems. The organization of the future will represent a perpetual collaborative renaissance of network- and team-based thinking, decisions, and actions, organized around processes laser focused on value delivery to customers.

History has shown over and over that it is more difficult to change leadership behavior than it is to change business process. Changing the leadership process and the business process together in order to meet the growing challenges of a digital global economy requires transformation in the mental models and perspectives of the entire leadership team. Transformation from the mental perceptions of a traditional functional command-and-control leadership model to one propelled by consumer-satisfaction-driven leadership—using a process-based responsive supply chain business model—is not an easy transformation in most organizations.

In most twentieth-century companies, executives and employees embrace a framework of guiding assumptions concerning customers, products, distributive channels, and competitors without question. It is on these assumptions that they base decisions, actions, and behavior. The longer the prevailing business theory works, the more it pervades the organization. The fact of the matter is that traditional principles of management have worked for the entire Industrial Age.

The reality of the matter is that most of these traditional principles will not work in the Information Age.

The design of an organization needs to include processes and subprocesses fundamental to supply chain operating principles. The leadership model should be focused on linking all major business processes, each supported by needed functional expertise, within a company and across supplier and customer organizations. Such cohesion and high performance are essential for satisfying consumer demand. End-to-end supply chain visibility, an important enabler to customer satisfaction and a driver of company performance, must be omnipresent in order to support consumer satisfaction.

The twenty-first-century organizational architecture will increasingly be designed around processes that simultaneously integrate essential functions. The new organization model will operate in a sense-and-response business world, one driven by information and real-time needs. The ability to continually navigate through constant change exemplifies how different the work solutions need to be when communications are instantaneous and facts are available in real time. Future organization will continually need to assess which activities should be performed internally and which should be outsourced. Outsourced shared services, such as logistics, information technology, finance, and human resource services, managed as generic but highly skilled processes, centers, and/or separate divisions or service companies, are just some examples of the changes already taking place in many companies. Clearly, working in the twenty-first-century organization will not be business as usual. The emerging world is becoming increasingly demanding, and the once very straightforward challenges of supply chain management will become more and more complex.

Thus, we foresee great and far-reaching organization and leadership challenges as we move deeper into the global digital economy. The traditional profile of leadership must be redesigned and modified to meet the challenges of the twenty-first century. The organizations of tomorrow will be increasingly horizontal and much flatter from top to bottom. Employees will need to be empowered at all levels of the organization to act decisively and provide essential leadership. All great effort forward will be carried on the backs of overall organizational wisdom, persistence, tenacity, and the ability to collaborate and change. The challenges of leadership are further placed in the context of the twenty-first century with a review of measurement and motivation in the next chapter. Measurement and motivation play major roles in knowing how good a firm can be and how far and how quickly its leadership can move the organization toward increased competitiveness and leading-edge performance.

Chapter Eleven

Measurement and Motivation

". . . most business executives thirst for useful information even while they are drowning in data. Those responsible for creating the fire hydrants that spew data may not know which pieces of information truly are useful. As a result, valuable performance indicators can be buried like needles in a haystack."[1]

—Kenneth B. Ackerman

ew topics gain the attention of senior leadership faster than a discussion of how to measure and motivate an organization. The complexity of a typical twenty-first-century enterprise makes the task of meaningful measurement and motivation one of the most difficult leadership challenges. We decided to discuss these two topics jointly because they are interrelated in resolving both the financial and the human resource challenges facing most organizations.

Motivation of employees generally builds on two fundamental concepts. First is the pride of achievement and personal growth. Employees, from the front lines to the executive suite, take a great deal of pride in being part of a successful enterprise that is concerned with employee development. Most employees like the recognition of performing their assigned responsibilities and achieving specific business objectives at a level generally acknowledged as leading edge.

---

[1] Kenneth B. Ackerman, *Warehousing Forum* 22, no. 8, July 2007.

The motivating drive of pride has been proven over and over by incentive programs based on achievement and recognition, instead of only financial compensation. Acknowledgement of being the leader, being part of a high-performance leading-edge team, or being the very best has proven to be a greater incentive to stimulate extra performance than pay alone. Additionally, independent of level in an organization, experiencing the opportunities for new learning by participating in on-the-job projects, new special assignments, or more formal training and education programs demonstrates the value senior leadership places on development. Thus, motivation and recognition are clearly linked.

The second fundamental concept is pay for performance. All employee evaluation systems are based on the measurement of performance as it relates to company goals or expectations. In all job structures, actual day-in and day-out compensation is based on the quality and quantity of work performed by an individual. Today, in job situations from manager level upward, overall compensation is generally a combination of base salary, cash bonus, and varied forms of company stock, depending on level of department, business unit, or overall enterprise achievement. Such incentive pay structures typically are based on achieving and exceeding both individual objectives and a measurable contribution toward achieving the overall business plan. Some forward-thinking firms, in the case of more senior leadership, have started to give incentives to individuals and teams by granting performance-based stock options and restricted stock that vests on the basis of the enterprise achieving strategic goals continuously over a three-year, or longer, period. All of the above examples illustrate the evolution of compensation programs designed to motivate the behavior of teams and individuals to help achieve enterprise goals.

Thus, from both a pride and a performance motivation perspective, the ability to lead an organization rests on meaningful measurement. Without meaningful and believable measurement, it becomes a difficult task to achieve the level of performance required to catapult and sustain organizational performance. These basic facts and the overall importance of organizational motivation are important to keep in mind as we address the complex subject of metrics.

In a business culture characterized as having rapidly evolving performance expectations, the strategic business plan serves to establish operational direction and specify overall performance goals. The yearly business plan drives performance as business units and individuals seek to achieve their assigned financial and operating objectives. These objectives are the foundations for operating goals or targets driving both organizational and individual performance. While simple to describe, the actual challenges related to rewarding performance based on achieving and exceeding planned expectations are among the most difficult tasks of senior leadership. Implementing compensation systems that support the sustained achievement of firms financially and operationally over multiple years is still not a common practice. Additionally, recent practices regarding executive compensation not directly correlated to enterprise or shareholder profit represent some of the most controversial dimensions of contemporary corporate leadership.

In chapters past, we have discussed many of the challenges related to leading collaboration among organizations. Some of the most important challenges within and among organizations are related to leading supply chain collaborative initiatives. In a supply chain, many different organizations are engaged both within themselves and with other firms. Collectively, they perform a vast array of work required to achieve the collective goals of all participating firms. As noted earlier, firms participating in a supply chain are voluntarily linked in joint operations, driven by the belief that their individual business goals will be easier to achieve. However, our earlier discussions highlighted that across functional areas of a company, there can be multiple conflicts of interest, goals, and reward systems. When these varied conflicts are reviewed collectively, they may not support the overall mission and goals of a firm. Additionally, such inconsistencies within a firm have, in all likelihood, not been reviewed or discussed with supply chain partners. These collaborating partners, however, are supporting the supply chain in a joint effort to achieve success in selling their products. Not all members of the supply chain have typically reviewed overall missions and goals for consistency or conflict. The collaborative efforts needed to achieve a high-performance responsive supply chain may be relatively simple or very complex in terms of organizational missions and structure. Even if simple, the task of integrating objectives, goals, individual firm reward systems, and any methods to link legally separate enterprise goals and rewards has happened among only a handful of collaborating companies.

Of course, all this collaborative effort has to be measured and motivated, similar to the operations within each individual firm. Thus, issues of motivation and measurement become even more complex as we become concerned with overall supply chain performance. A first step toward developing a meaningful system is reviewing some of the fundamental guidelines of successful measurement.

Measurement Guidelines

Good metrics are essential because they drive behavior and decision making. The challenge is to identify which metrics will provide information necessary to support the operational decision process as well as achieve meaningful managerial oversight. The typical problem in any situation is the abundance of activities to potentially measure. The key is to focus on a few metrics that really matter. How many represent a few?

No magic rule exists concerning how many metrics to use. As a general rule, most firms use far too many metrics and run the risk of measurement overlap and duplication, leading to potential confusion. The key is to first determine what practices or actions really drive operational success. The role a metric plays in the management process is educating leaders and workers of the verifiable status of an event. This requires measuring and providing necessary information to undertake corrective action. The key is for senior- and middle-level leaders to understand that metrics exist to change behavior and drive performance according to or beyond a plan. While of course there are end-of-year and end-of-period metrics that are important for financial reporting, these "end-of" numbers in final analysis are the accumulated results of day-in and day-out work first reported as performance metrics.

A maximum of five to eight key metrics is typically adequate to provide a diagnostic framework. The selected metrics should be simple in their structure and capable of being easily understood throughout the organization and, as appropriate, across the supply chain. The metrics, once selected, should be referred to as key performance indicators (KPIs) for the department, division, or enterprise and should be directly related to measuring high-level performance. On the basis of measured status, any KPI should be capable of being diagnostically exploded into several supportive measures that provide greater detail concerning work performance. In fact, one of the fundamental purposes of a performance metric is to drive "root cause analysis" of forces driving the reported performance. When a performance metric indicates unexpected performance, high or low, managers must be able to "drill down" to identify the cause of the variance in order to take corrective action and prevent replication. An effective measurement system should be closed looped in the sense that detection leads to corrective or preventative action and understanding to help resolve and prevent situations reported as having less than or greater than anticipated results. Corrective action is normally appropriate when performance varies in either direction of the plan. Thus, implied in any metric and associated activity is a standard of planned performance.

The managerial perspective driving effective measurement and motivation is that of enabling a process capable of cutting through the extreme complexity of a modern business to isolate KPIs. Of particular interest are KPIs reporting variance to plan or anticipated operational results. Following discovery, the measurement system should facilitate inquiry into the cause of the performance discrepancy and provide the necessary information to undertake corrective action. Thus, a performance measurement system should be closed looped in the sense that it drives performance to plan.

Cross-Functional Enterprise Performance

The ultimate choice of the few KPIs needs to result from the examination of what leadership attention will drive the behavior and the expected results of the department, division, or enterprise involved. As discussed earlier when reviewing integrative management, we suggested that the focus of KPIs should encapsulate the integrated process's purpose and activities of the firm and its resources. One way to distill a firm's activities into a few key indicators is to examine activity by performance centers, namely, financial stewardship, customer relationship management, operational management, and human resource management. Each of these centers encapsulates cross-functional activity having and delivering performance impact both within and outside the firm.

Financial Stewardship

Publicly traded firms have a requirement to report their financial results to the public, shareholders, and stakeholders every quarter. That reporting process and its content are a "less than perfect" assessment of what business results took place over the past quarter and comparisons with the same period the prior year. There is an increasing amount of resistance to trying to measure a complex multinational firm's operations on a quarter-to-quarter basis. However, how a firm operates daily and weekly to produce profitable growth largely produces "end of critical time results" that determine how the company will be valued by its current and future stakeholders. Thus, selected financial metrics need to be a part of the final KPIs. There are a number of methods of providing financial results. Most are helpful in getting a better understanding of overall financial performance. However, all have shortfalls in either information used or ease of accessibility. Two commonly used financial measures are the DuPont model and economic value added (EVA). They can both be successfully used at multiple levels of an organization to measure and monitor department, division, or company progress.

The DuPont financial analysis model, while not new, continues to be widely used. Figure 11-1 presents a version of the model invented in 1914 by Donaldson Brown. Brown was an electrical engineer assigned to the Treasury Department of DuPont Chemical. Later, he was assigned to General Motors after DuPont Chemical bought a significant percentage of GM. His assignment was to untangle the finances of GM for Alfred Sloan, who was then chairman of the company. The original model quantified a firm's return on assets by highlighting the measurement of:

- Effectiveness with assets used to produce revenue
- Investment in working capital needed for operations
- Investment in long-term revenue producing assets.

Figure 11-1   Modified Dupont Financial Model

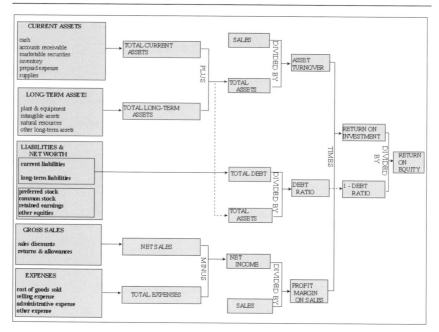

The essence of the DuPont model is the integrated display of a firm's income statement and balance sheet. The model has been modified to solve for return on equity, thereby bringing it closer to providing KPI alignment with shareholder concerns. Both versions of the model have a number of shortcomings, including not being linked to the cost of capital, the time value of money, or long- or short-term measurement.

Stern Stewart & Company, in the late 1990s, developed a financial performance measure called economic valued added (EVA).

EVA equals net operating profit after taxes minus the sum of capital minus the cost of capital. EVA has the advantage of being conceptually simple and easy to explain to managers throughout an organization. It can also be used to measure an overall collaborative supply chain.

A more recently developed performance metric to measure a firm's integrated supply chain performance in cash-to-cash conversion.

Cash-to-Cash

The cash to cash measure is designed to track performance related to liquidity. The focal question is "How fast are we turning a dollar of cash spent for raw materials and inventory into a dollar of revenue?" Several traditional metrics are combined to determine this important measure of elapse time to convert purchases into customer sales. A firm's cash-to-cash performance is calculated by adding its days of inventory to its days of outstanding accounts receivable and subtracting the days of outstanding accounts payable. Each component of the cash cycle is briefly discussed.

Customer payment cycles (accounts receivable) are closely linked to pricing policies. One of the longest-standing discounts is a deduction on invoice if payment is completed within a specified time. An example is 2% 10, Net 30, which has been the standard payment term in the package grocery products industry for decades. This simply means that if the invoice is fully paid within 10 days, the seller is entitled to deduct 2 percent off the total invoice as originally issued. One of the main objectives of supply chain collaboration has been for manufacturers and customers to jointly develop integrated operations to position products on retail shelves faster. The ideal arrangement would be operational collaboration capable of achieving final consumer purchase within a few days of delivery to the retail store.

Under this arrangement, cash flow would create value greater than the 2 percent discount. Of course, any such arrangement would require a high level of network connectivity between supply chain partners.

Internal conversion of materials and components into final products represents one of the most advanced processes within business organizations. The impact of lean and six-sigma initiatives combined with just-in-time delivery has significantly reduced raw material and work-in-process (WIP) inventories. These improvements have resulted in greater responsiveness. It comes back to the transition from push to pull, the main theme of this book. While the so-called back end of manufacturing can be significantly improved by following the initiatives noted above, the end result is limited to gains in inventory efficiency and not too much else. The key is maintaining manufacturing efficiencies while simultaneously reducing forward levels of speculative inventory. While most firms can't fully convert operations to become a build-to-order enterprise, technologies and processes devoted to postponement and customization are rapidly being introduced across industries. The goal is to reduce assets committed to finished inventory—one of the single largest components of most balance sheets. This transformation among leading firms is the number-one producer of improved cash-to-cash performance.

The final component of cash-to-cash is accounts payable. This is the area where a great many senior managers make a critical trade-off capable of becoming highly disruptive. The process goes something like the following. First, suppliers are required to earn business by use of a bidding process. These bids generally contain operational provisions designed to help the bid-granting firm implement new manufacturing processes such as lean, just in time, or six sigma, and in many cases, they require suppliers to hold dedicated or consignment inventories of ready-to-ship parts and components.

The final part of the relationship is payment terms. The manufacturers want extended payment terms, and the suppliers, faced with the need to perform significantly increased functionality, want invoices paid faster. Many manufacturing firms have driven their cash-to-cash cycles down by putting pressure on their suppliers for longer account payable time. While this tactic can appear to improve performance in the short run, the stories of supplier bankruptcy and refusal to continue doing business are not hard to find. Simply stated, manufacturers have had to learn that they can't have it both ways.

Cash-to-cash is an important metric that is relatively easy to track using standard business financial and accounting records. What is less easy to isolate are off-balance-sheet interorganizational affects that occur between firms linked in a supply chain arrangement. Some firms take great pride in pushing their cash-to-cash performance into negative numbers. While the goal is admirable, the long-term proof of performance is in supply chain sustainability. This gets very close to the challenges related to sharing benefits as well as risk.

Customer Relationship Management

Of equal importance with the measurements to ensure financial success and viability are metrics supporting customers. These KPIs tend to center around how satisfied customers are with the product purchased and consumed. One such important metric is demand responsiveness.

The general concern of demand responsiveness is identifying how well a firm's operations are meeting specific customer requirements. The fundamental unit of demand responsiveness is measurement of plan accuracy. Most firms have significant difficulty developing accurate operational plans, so it has become common practice to develop a sales and operations planning (S&OP) process. The S&OP process quantifies all known information concerning future operating periods into a time-phased statement of expectations by the company, its departments, and its supply chain partners. This provides a time-sequenced picture of future expectations based on all available information presented in sync with the overall business plan. Once again, as discussed earlier, the primary objective is to develop a "single" highly visible plan and report one version of results to be shared by all. It is becoming increasingly common for customers and suppliers to contribute information to the planning process and to share in finalizing and tracking the plan. The more formal and operationally linked the collaborative supply chain participants are, the more likely there will be a shared S&OP process.

Another common point of interest is forecast actualization. Understanding that forecasting is far from being a science, participants in a metric support system should be able to offer continuous tracking of demand forecast accuracy. It is important that forecast errors be quantified to improve accuracy in future planning periods. The balance of operating statistics capable of diagnostic review could range across various areas of plan adherence. For example, tracking manufacturing schedule actualization will help determine whether manufacturing is performing to the schedule established during the S&OP process. Other metrics could focus on material supplier performance to plan, order processing, and logistics system responsiveness.

In today's world, the location of a firm's organization and suppliers performing concept to design, design to production, and production to retail may be scattered throughout the globe in order to access world-class talent pools, material or manufacturing supply, or other economic factors. Supply chain length has continued to affect a firm's ability to respond quickly to changes in demand. Managing time to market measurably determines how reliable a firm's performance is and how fast it can radically change. Examples of associated metrics include measuring adherence to time and action calendaring of concept to design or design to production, production-to-retail availability, and replenishment cycle time. Technology is continually shortening each of these pathways by providing new media to conduct the necessary steps of business. Metrics of time adherence and process innovation help maintain customer satisfaction and much more. Virtual meetings and showrooms and reengineered production processes economically capable of producing store-ready products are but some examples of innovation transforming supply chain time-to-market paradigms and metrics.

Operational Management

The first place any firm needs to look to improve its supply chain is itself. From the beginning of supply chain operations to the final product sale, many complex functional activities can be misaligned and poorly performed. It is important, however, to create not functional KPIs but rather process KPIs that cover the full effort of an organization to complete a major process or subprocess. Below, we'll discuss two metrics that are excellent candidates to be included in the short list of KPIs, namely, perfect order and total cost to service.

Perfect Order

Metrics related to perfect order achievement may be among the most difficult for a traditional organization to continuously quantify and monitor. To fully measure perfect order execution requires feedback concerning customer experience. However, once the appropriate information leading to continuous perfect order measurement is formatted and tracked, it is likely to turn out to be among the most important KPIs. At the highest level, the incident of perfect order should be tracked across the enterprise. Such high-level performance is not operationally easy to attain and is even more difficult to maintain. However, the primary value proposition driving digital transformation rests on commitment to continuous improvement toward the goal of perfect order execution.

The key is identifying causal factors leading to less than perfect order execution. Actual performance related to standards can be tracked for each element of the order-to-delivery process. Any order falling short of expected performance will result in a less than perfect order. The important point is documentation of why the order didn't meet expectations. Critical information should be identified and isolated to guide corrective action. The key is to track down and identify factors causing substandard performance and to follow up with corrective action. Such corrective action may often require operational or inventory stock policy change, replacement of a transportation carrier, or modification of existing operational standards. If a senior leadership team truly decides to pursue perfect order execution, it must be dedicated to continuously identifying root cause and resolving problems one at a time. No matter how large or complex a business is, in final analysis, operational excellence boils down to individual orders, individual customers, and individual delivery events.

Total Cost-to-Serve

Determination of the total cost-to-serve is not easy, given the complexity of modern corporate accounting. At the root of the matter is the determination of whether a specific customer, order, or individual product (SKU) is profitable. Two traditional practices, averaging and aggregation, hinder our ability to specifically measure the profitability of individual transactions using standard accounting documents. The focus of total cost-to-serve metrics is to better manage supply chain direct costs.

Direct costs are expenditures related to performing the work associated with servicing a specific customer's order. The objective is to assign cost related to order management, warehousing, inventory, transportation, delivery, and all value-added services to the revenue generated by each specific order. It is also desirable to assign costs related to returned merchandise and, when possible, reverse logistics expenditures. While the cost to manufacture may be the same for all units of a specific product, all of the above-noted variable costs of distribution will be different. It is these variable costs that determine the relative profitability or loss of different orders and different customers. In a normal accounting system, these costs get aggregated into functional and departmental cost statements. However, before roll up, specific costs are available and can be assigned on an order-by-order basis. The result is a clear measure of contribution to indirect and overhead costs generated by doing business with a specific customer or group of customers.

Total cost to serve measures the direct contribution across an aggregation of customers. The aggregations can be by any cut of segments, down to the individual customer. The drill down, or diagnostic, process allows specific inquiry concerning the detail associated with individual customers. This drill down provides the basis for undertaking a detailed analysis of the profitability of specific customers. In Chapter Four, the importance of dealing with customer specifics, as opposed to averages, was stressed as an important step toward understanding what is required to meet and exceed customers' expectations. Total cost-to-serve metrics provide the financial structure to make meaningful customer-related decisions. It is an understanding of direct customer profitability that provides the information for making sound customer accommodation decisions.

Some experienced managers reading about the benefits of total cost-to-serve information may believe, on the basis of their past experiences, that generating this type of specific customer-related information may not be practical. While they may desire to know customers' intimate information, the amount of detail involved may appear overwhelming. Keep in mind that every bit of the necessary detail is known at the time a customer order is processed and serviced. Developing a database of supply-chain-related specifics is both attainable and affordable, given the capacity of current information technology. The real problem is learning how to managerially digest the meaning of specific account information and how to implement corrective action. These are but some of the challenges involved in managing a responsive enterprise.

Human Resource Management

Supply chain business models at their core are gated by the talent and skills of being able to create vision, develop plans, set inspirational objectives in motion, and execute to achieve the desired results. We previously discussed the multitude of human demographics both in age groups and in diversity. Each has different interests and expectations about how its professional role will evolve. Acquiring, keeping, and growing the needed talent and skills for groups with diverse populations and ethnicities have become matters to be managed and measured with depth and seriousness.

Talent management, then, should be one of the most critical areas any firm develops. Creating KPIs to help develop and maintain a high-performance organization capable of leading both current operations and a transformation is a critical leadership responsibility. Talent assessment should be one of the first metrics in building or maintaining the required resources to meet tomorrow's required challenges. Figure 11-2 illustrates key attributes to be assessed to help identify associate development needs. Attribute assessment and measurement are essential for leadership development.

Figure 11-2   Key Talent Attributes

- Functional Competency
- Challenge Status Quo
- Insightful Analyzer
- Lead Change and Innovation
- Customer Orientation/Bias
- Broad Business Experience

- Coaching Skills
- Vision Ability
- Drive Execution
- Network Skills
- Sense of Urgency
- Foster Teamwork

Attribute assessment should be done periodically with all current associates, as well as with new hires. Simple statistical KPIs such as internal versus external position fill rates and the percentage depth of position bench strength tell a lot about the health of an organization and its internal talent processes.

In order to keep highly talented associates, individual development programs must be real and embraced by all involved while supporting the strategy of the business. Programs, whether formal education or project based, should produce a return on investment for the individual and the company. Measuring the amount of money, time, and subsequent achievements is a way to assess development performance. Development management is increasingly considered a key component of performance feedback for recognition of a current responsibility and to quantify necessary steps toward fulfilling a larger or different assignment. Statistics on internal promotions and those selected for transfer to another part of the organization can be meaningful gauges of the health of an organization. Finally, simple metrics such as percentage change in people by management layer and/or function might help to provide the needed insight to human resources critical to maintaining current capabilities and accomplishing new challenges.

Much of what has been discussed above was presented from a leadership perspective. Equally important for a company is measuring associate satisfaction. As discussed earlier, job satisfaction, the job giving the individual the feeling of personal accomplishment, is an area of needed understanding that goes beyond typical talent management. This area of analysis expands to associates' personal assessments that can color and influence individuals' appreciation of their employer. Besides the formal policies and procedures of a firm, associates themselves should measure how they value their leadership and how well their leadership manages change and work effectiveness. It is also important to assess work/life balance and whether inclusive or parochial thinking is pervasive in their work and in their leaders. Finally, employees do care about what and how they are paid, the benefits they are offered, and how well both are administered. All of the above can be measured by a many-to-one electronic survey system.

Human resource management represents critical activities essential to supply chain performance. The characteristics of an organization and industry will determine which KPIs should be used to support and measure human resource health.

Creating a Dashboard

The sustainable challenge of integrated performance measurement is the creation of a set of cross-functional performance measures that capture day-to-day operational functioning. In essence, these performance measures should be established to capture critical and interrelated information concerning the eight universal supply chain processes discussed in Chapter Six dealing with integrative management. The purpose is to monitor daily operations and provide early warning of performance discrepancies. Current best practice is to develop a performance measurement hierarchy containing a limited number of performance items to be monitored. This small number of measures is often formulated into a continuous reporting format referred to as a dashboard.

The term "dashboard" has many different applications across firms. The concept is quite simple and graphic. The dashboard is a presentation of key performance statistics in a format readily allowing leadership to access information on how day-to-day operations are tracking. The term "dashboard" comes from the arrangement of gauges in an automobile to display speed and distance and monitor operating status. The idea is to present, at a glance, a comprehensive picture of current operational performance. The dashboard provides a graphic snapshot of just how well a company is performing at any given time. Others may prefer a series of snap reports or other methods of presenting key metric performance.

The basic ideas behind continuous reporting are twofold. First and foremost, the dashboard provides one version of the truth concerning the status of operations to be viewed by all employees of the enterprise. Thus, the age-old practice of shaping the numbers to tell or not to tell a story is eliminated. Second, the high visibility of a continuous reporting mechanism focuses a great deal of creditability concerning the senior leadership's commitment to operational excellence. The only road to continuous improvement is through continuous visibility.

To illustrate, assume that a firm has decided to track five key performance metrics on a continuous basis: demand responsiveness, time-related performance, perfect order performance, cash-to-cash, and total cost-to-serve. Figure 11-3 illustrates a dashboard containing five performance gauges. Each gauge is driven by a composite of measures meaningful to the specific performance metrics selected by the leadership of the firm or supply chain collaboration.

Figure 11-3   Example Performance Dashboard

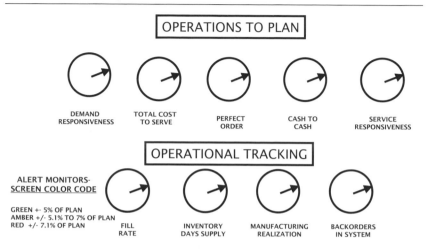

In developing the displayed information, several different individual metrics are typically combined to arrive at the specific measures reported. In terms of updating, the gauges could report from real time (continuous) to short-interval batch updates (hourly, daily, or weekly), depending on the management philosophy of the firm. Many firms are color coding to identify and highlight deficiencies. For example, "green status" indicates normal or within performance tolerance, "amber status" indicates that performance is deteriorating or trending below plan or expected performance, and, finally, "red status" indicates the need for immediate action. The information technology of the twenty-first century is not the limiting factor concerning either compiling or reporting updates across all participating in the network. The decision variable is the speed of the firm's decision process.

Proprietary Collaborative Arrangements

The discussion thus far has focused on overall measurement of business performance within a single firm. In an increasing number of supply chain situations, two or more large firms become highly collaborative in planning and conducting their day-to-day operations. These firms acknowledge dependency and seek to jointly leverage their combined operating capabilities. One of the earliest collaborative business relationships, noted previously, is the highly publicized alliance between Wal-Mart and P&G. Another long-standing alliance is the working relationship between Sears and Whirlpool. While most other arrangements have not gained as much publicity, almost all successful organizations have and are continuing to establish ongoing operational integration with key customers and suppliers. The point of interest is how such mature relationships establish joint goals and measure performance. How do these collaborative firms measure their combined performance, provide reward and recognition, and invest in their human assets to make the process work? Clearly, all of the measures discussed above are applicable when it comes to managing extended supply chain arrangements. In addition, some unique or business-specific metrics may be developed.

To some degree, the point of emphasis in a collaborative arrangement shifts from evaluating specific order performance to tracking overall business activity. Because each key account-operational arrangement is unique, the configuration of metrics developed and tracked should also be different. Thus, each collaboration justifies its own unique dashboard. Likewise, the metrics selected to track each performance category should be different. However, an essential point is the willingness of collaborative partners to share operational and strategic planning and execution information. It is essential that all key players in the collaboration be able to observe identical information at the same time.

A common practice is to appoint account-specific cross-functional teams to interface with large customers. These cross-functional teams consist of members representing all key functions from each company responsible for some facet of successfully conducting business with each other. These customer relationship teams are typically armed with aggregated information concerning performance of the business relationship. The dashboard concept provides a specific cut of performance information directly focused on a detailed view of their specific collaboration. Thus, for example, sales by specific delivery destination can be isolated and diagnostically evaluated. Overall analysis could drive to a detail level concerning a specific order, destination, or territory. Simply put, fact-based management requires facts.

Open-Architecture Collaboration

The challenges of meaningful measurement become significantly more complex when the focus is on open-network collaborative supply chain arrangement. As we noted in previous chapters, a collaborative network may have many different members who individually have significantly different degrees of loyalty, commitment, and involvement in any specific arrangement. In fact, most who participate in any specific collaborative arrangement are likely to be simultaneously engaged in other supply chain arrangements, some of which are directly competitive. Open-architecture collaboration requires the overcoming of many traditional hurdles existing in today's business paradigm.

When reduced to the transaction level, the anatomy of a complex collaborative network becomes relatively easy to define and quantify.

The fact that firms are linked in a many-to-many networked arrangement adds one more level of complexity to the measurement process. The dilemma faced today in collectively taking full advance of an open-architecture network is not unlike the dilemma poised in the early stages of the Internet or in the creation and maintenance of the Linux systems operating language, which has been, from the beginning, free to all potential users. A new business social order was established around both of these technologies. This social order allows new capabilities to exist while maintaining much of everyone's best interests.

Admittedly, at this early stage of development, we know precious little about creating the necessary social order as well as measuring the functional benefits or the integrated performance synergism in an open-network-based supply chain. In Part Three, the chapters defining catapulting raised the bar concerning attainable performance building on real-time responsiveness, network leveraging, and collaboration. These concepts are comparatively easy to measure with respect to overall business and management of customer-specific supply chain arrangements. The difficulty comes in calibration and measurement of performance in open-architecture collaborations. Is an aggregation of transaction- and account-specific collaboration adequate for successful responsive supply chain management? Most students of the topic are of the opinion that failure to push operating models into the challenges of open collaborative arrangements will result in significant missed opportunities.

One approach to open collaborative measurement is to develop a new framework to calibrate just how well the arrangement is performing. To this end, the performance diamond offers a framework for aggregation.

The Performance Diamond

The challenge starts from the perspective that performance within an open-network collaboration moves beyond the specific relationships of both the transactional and the proprietary collaborative models for conducting business. Naturally, there must be a customer base from which the open collaboration seeks to attract revenue. The concept of an open architecture means that at times, new functionality is absorbed into the collaboration while at other times, it is spun out on the basis of operational and strategic need. This implies the idea that leadership is at work.

To illustrate, a firm having leadership status may decide to participate in a transportation network or an open auction to accomplish operating objectives for a limited time. This participation could be followed by periods of nonactivity. The degree of participation is determined by leadership perception of the potential benefits.

To aggregate data at a level above an individual firm for cross-functional and customer-specific structured collaborations, it is important to develop a big-picture performance perspective. Figure 11-4 presents the performance diamond. The performance diamond framework provides a linkage between firms engaged in a collaborative supply chain. The framework provides a common ground to align collaborative goals, objectives, resources, results, and rewards to achieve supply chain synchronization. An open-architecture supply chain seeks to bring all participating firms into operational synchronization. Synchronization requires balancing four main capabilities: reliability, responsiveness, resource minimization, and redundancy. These four capabilities must be configured to reflect the aggregated performance of all firms engaged in the supply chain collaboration. Thus, they are viewed as being synergistic.

Figure 11-4   Responsive Supply Chain Performance Diamond

Reliability reflects the important quality of maintaining the specified level of supply chain performance over time. If a supply change is reliable, firms participating in the process begin to count on others to perform their assigned roles as specified. High reliability with boundaries results in stable operating patterns that facilitate economy of scale in operations and logistics. Perhaps most of all, reliable performance allows all involved in the supply chain to maintain lower inventories, namely, smaller, or no, safety stocks.

Responsiveness relates to a supply chain's agility to meet and exceed when confronted with unanticipated operational demands. A simple example is consumers positively responding in an unprecedented way to a new or improved product or environmental circumstance (storm, hurricane, flood, drought, etc.). In the next section, we will talk about unplanned disruptions to supply chain performance.

How collaborative supply chain performance reacts to disruptions is a significant measure of its inherent responsiveness. This capability can be designed into how a collaborative arrangement performs.

Resource minimization is concerned with the deployment of human and financial resources. One potential of a networked operating arrangement is gaining synergistic resource benefits. It follows that collaborative arrangements should build on specialization, wherein each participating firm undertakes those aspects of work that it is most qualified to perform. At the end of the day, this synergism is the primary force driving collaboration. It is also a journey shared among supply chain partners, as both the product creation and distribution processes continue to be reinvented as a result of technology, economics, or changing consumer taste.

Finally, redundancy is viewed as the capability of maintaining a specified level of performance across time. Supply chains must be flexible with respect to operational requirements. When disruptions occur, it is important that they return to scale rapidly with the least amount of operation disruption possible. Vivid examples of this took place after September 11, 2001, when some companies were able to restart their business model within days while other firms took months to come back to "normal" operations.

All aspects of the performance diamond are hard to measure. In fact, there may not be metrics capable of gauging multifirm performance in open-network collaboration. The fact that no universal or easy-to-generate metrics exist does not negate the fact that the inherent processes need to be managed. Likewise, the fact that end-to-end supply chain processes involve the work of many different organizations does not negate the need to develop measurements. Individual firms can, on the basis of what we discussed earlier, establish a few KPIs to help them more successfully transform to a responsive supply chain business model.

In conclusion, while it is uncomfortable not to be able to point to best practices that can be rapidly duplicated, working in unstructured situations is the essence of leadership. If open collaboration creates sustainable value, tomorrow's leaders will learn how to implement, measure, and motivate the desired performance.

Supply Chain Disruption and Resiliency

Supply chains have always been subject to disruptions. When such disruptions are not caused by nature, they are caused by people. The fact is that no one likes disruptions. However, since the events of 9-11, the word "disruption" has taken on new meaning. More and more, the responsive supply chain business model is becoming a global event. Most firms are linked to many different parts of the world in the daily performance of supply chain work. It is clear that globalization increases risk. Supply chains are longer and involve many more touch points from inception to completion. Each new linkage and associated touch point introduce the potential for unplanned events.

Supply chain managers have long confronted various forms of disruption. Fires, tornados, floods, snow, hurricanes, strikes, capacity, and so forth are the traditional disruptions requiring work-around during day-to-day supply chain management. New areas of concern, such as sabotage and terrorist intrusion, have the potential to be far more disruptive than natural events and demand both risk assessment and mitigation strategies.

Risk assessment and prevention have become important parts of the work of supply chain management. The probability of disruption requires a predetermined recovery plan. Likewise, the potential magnitude of the event is significant. In the daily operation of a supply chain, there are surprises. Surprises such as bad weather or local traffic disruption happen often and require a minimum amount of recovery planning. However, today's supply chain also must plan for catastrophic surprises. Such surprises are unsuspected events resulting in major disruption of the transportation and information infrastructures.

Terrorism, while a significant threat to supply chain continuity, represents only one form of a potential catastrophic event capable of affecting supply chain operations. Other issues of significant concern in risk assessment are contamination of food and water supplies, SARS, Asian bird flu, and any other form of potential life-threatening disruption. Planning for recovery from unidentified disruptive events is not an easy task.

The security of Web-based architecture and system software is another significant pillar in maintaining a responsive supply chain business model. Maintaining a reliable and available network capable of immediate recovery requires protocols and oversight beyond those of any individual, firm, industry, or country. The emergence of the global digital economy has started to reveal how important Web security is to commerce and government operations throughout the world. World leaders have begun the process of creating unilateral Web security and capacity for the planet's best interest. This journey has only begun.

The potential of disruption requires magnified preventative measures designed to contain possible expansion or continuation of a disruption. It also requires new collaboration between businesses and governments around the world. All companies today, if they want to maintain a fast and reliable international supply chain, must work closely with customs and border patrol agencies of all governments to ensure adherence to ever-changing rules for transport, inspection, and product release throughout the global supply chain. Business must have preplanned alternatives for routing air, ocean, or domestic shipments. In a world of more uncertainty, ensuring that your products' quality is unaltered as they move through the supply chain has now become a new basic requirement.

Supply chains today and in the future must be ready to respond to suspicious product alerts and support, when necessary, the secure reacquisition and disposition of altered dangerous products. Additionally, global supply chain human resources, which are normally very inclusive populations, must continue to be made aware of the legitimate differences of cultures. Only then can a global multiethic supply chain team positively embrace all that can be accomplished by reliable performance in times of uncertainty. First and last, the human resources deployed around the world supporting a global supply chain are a company's greatest assets. The human assets need protection and the resources necessary to continually monitor their safety, including plans to bring them home or to safety whenever they are in harm's way. Supply chain disruption today has become much more than worrying about closing ports and borders. The way people and governments react to disruptions can create significant magnification of the original disruption for a substantial time. Supply chain capacity lost today cannot ever be recovered tomorrow. Speaking about tomorrow, we now turn to the final chapter, "2025 and Beyond."

Chapter Twelve

2025 and Beyond

> *"We arranged a civilization in which most critical elements profoundly depend on science and technology."*[1]
>
> —Dr. Carl Sagan

At 7:46 Tuesday morning October 17, 2006, the population of the United States reached 300 million. Accompanying the announcement was a projection that the U.S. population would increase to 400 million by 2041—just 35 years into the future. This rapid rate of projected growth is mind boggling when viewed in the context of the traditional growth rate experienced in the United States. However, when viewed in a global perspective, the numbers pale in comparison to the balance of the world. China alone is projected to have in excess of 1.4 billion consumers by the year 2010, of which more than 660 million will be between the ages of 20 and 50.[2] By 2010, China and the United States combined will have in excess of one billion consumers! Adding in the balance of the projected world population means that between 7.5 and 8.3 billion consumers will be living on the planet Earth by 2025![3]

Given the clogged supply chain arteries of today's global economy, it appears obvious that massive change will be needed to sustain today's standard of living, notwithstanding the challenges of meeting

---

[1]   Dr. Carl Sagan, Astronomer, Astrobiologist, and Science Popularizer.

[2]   http://www.iiasa.ac.at/Research/luc/ChinaFood/data/pop/pop-1.htm, October 4, 2006.

[3]   *Mapping the Future of World Population* (Washington, DC: Population Action International, 2007).

the needs of the world's impoverished. In this final chapter, our attention is directed to a discussion of global sustainability and why it is becoming increasingly important to stop pushing and start pulling our supply chains.

Most all of the preceding chapters have been devoted to challenges related to the transformation of individual enterprises in highly developed economies. While digitizing the typical twentieth-century enterprise to take advantage of Information Age technology requires massive transformation, the challenges of individual firms are miniscule in comparison to those faced by developing nations and regions of the world. While full discussion of such pervasive global challenges is truly the subject of another book, some of the issues must be on today's and tomorrow's leadership agendas. To better frame the overall challenge, the first part of this chapter is devoted to an introductory discussion of growing global complexity. In a connected global digital economy, characterized by all pervasive high-speed optic-fiber broadband communications, even the most improvised people will harbor growing expectations that viable alternatives exist to poverty and disease. The growing discontent of the world will not tolerate continuation of the status quo.

The chapter concludes with a discussion of seven potential dimensions of radical change. Meeting and exceeding these challenges could make a significant difference in future supply chain performance. Solutions to six of the seven challenges and their related benefits appear to be at least partially attainable between now and 2025. The final impact area may not occur in our lifetimes, or, for that matter, it may never occur—or it might occur far faster than one dares speculate. The point of speculating on future events as a closing statement emphasizes that digital transformation is just the next step forward, not the final destination.

Growing Global Complexity

In 1992, M. Mitchell Waldrop introduced to many readers a newly emerging science in his book entitled *Complexity*.[4] Complexity was positioned as the emerging science found "at the edge of order and chaos." For those of us who were schooled in the equilibrium theories of classical economics and who have spent a career in the reality of defining and implementing the emerging principles of responsive supply chain management, setting aside notions of optimization was a welcome relief. The fact of the matter is that despite a common practice of using the word "optimize" to explain partial solutions to almost all complex problems, few, if any, involved in supply chain management have ever optimized anything!

Take, for example, the classic facility network design problem wherein a firm is seeking to determine how many distribution warehouses to use to serve its domestic market, where to locate them, what assortment of inventory to place in each facility, and which customers to service from each location. The answers derived from mathematical models and simulation processes are far closer to representing best guesses to these complex design problems, not true optimizations. Most knowledgeable supply chain leaders are far more committed to achieving continuous improvement, but they can become carried away by the thought that such a complex and dynamic problem can, in fact, be optimized. However, more so than ever, the use of advanced computer models is increasing as supply chain leaders seek to sort out improved operational arrangements. The correct perspective is to acknowledge that the growing complexity of global supply chain planning requires the deployment of all available tools or models capable of helping formulate and implement a cohesive strategy. However, these tools, at best, represent aids to and not substitutes for leadership.

---

4   M. Mitchell Waldrop, *Complexity* (New York: Simon & Schuster, 1992).

The supply chain leadership challenges of the twenty-first century are and will become increasingly complex. It is interesting to note that a growing number of papers published by the Santa Fe Institute are devoted to better understanding the inherent complexity resulting from advanced information, technology, and the network effect, discussed in Chapter Eight, as affecting a wide range of interdisciplinary subjects. It seems that networks and complexities are affecting most all disciplines.

However, the sheer increase in complexity anticipated for twenty-first-century supply chains is much broader than that driven by technology. As noted earlier, by 2025, the world is projected to have between 7.5 and 8.3 billion inhabitants. These humans will demand and deserve a quality of life better than that of their predecessors. Meeting such quality-of-life dreams will, to a significant degree, depend on supply chain performance. The many people of the world will desire, even demand, that they be enabled to participate in the health and hygiene that cure sickness and perpetuate life. Achieving that desire for a healthy life will depend on supply chain execution. For economic growth, the people of the world will have to engage in global commerce and be able to use their talents and natural resources to achieve the benefits of industrial specialization. Achieving such specialization will depend on supply chain execution. In short, while many other forces will be at work in the year 2025, some of the most extensive impacts and important solutions will rest on developing and perfecting supply chain solutions capable of meeting the challenges and overcoming the impact of growing global complexity.

Independent of issues related to the population of the world, challenges need to be resolved concerning capacity, risk, security, energy, architecture, infrastructure, environment, and seemingly every other dimension of day-to-day supply chain operations. Despite significant advancements in technology, the work of supply chain remains a tedious process dominated by human labor. While seasons, from fall to summer, and traditional holidays will continue to shape the magnitude of demand preferences and, to a significant degree, structure supply, most of the associated supply chain work will still require lead time to plan, execute, and administer. As one looks ahead, no easy solution is apparent for resolving the challenges of growing supply chain complexity. Each day will have 24 hours and each year 365 days. What will change is the sheer magnitude of supply chain work that needs to be successfully accomplished each and every day. To retain and improve supply chain performance, business and governments will jointly need to navigate radical change.

Seven Dimensions of Radical Change

As this book comes to a close, the year 2025 is but 17 years away. As suggested earlier, there is growing evidence that the impact of the Information Age will play out much faster than either the agriculture or the industrialization counterparts did. Thus, assuming that our impact assessment is correct, where will we stand in 2025? What progress will be made? What seemingly small and not so small problems will be resolved? What challenges are likely to linger, and which are likely to become showstoppers? Perhaps more important, what are the most likely dimensions of radical but achievable change? While many candidates came to mind, seven dimensions were selected for discussion. In six of these areas, we feel that substantial and sustainable improvement can be instituted and achieved by 2025 or before. They are (1) talent and resource swapping, (2) knowledge-dependant process automation, (3) extreme postponement, (4) transportation reinvention, (5) green, and (6) alternative fuels. The seventh area, nanogenome supply chain technology, offers a less clear picture of what might become reality.

Some areas on our list of seven should be slam dunks to implement once they become corporate priorities and industry-wide initiatives. Others ideas are currently in implementation infancy and will require substantial groundwork and planning before measurable progress will materialize. The potential of nanogenome supply chain technology may not occur for decades to come—if ever. In achieving the first three initiatives, industry leadership will require little or no governmental approval or support. The final four will require continued government leadership at a local, a national, and, for some initiatives, a global level. One thing seems for sure: commercial enterprise in general, and supply chain operations in particular, will not be business as usual as we proceed deeper into the twenty-first century.

Talent and Resource Swapping

At one point earlier in our discussion, we talked about how IBM was building a global human resource database detailing talent across its massive workforce. The idea of sharing talent is clearly not a revolutionary concept. When we discuss these innovative actions on the part of specific firms, they seem both logical and practical. However, one hears numerous reasons why such swapping is a difficult sell in most human resource departments. People belong to departments that have serious functional work to perform. Most managers feel that if they have talent to "lend," they will be viewed as overstaffed and wasteful. And, after all, "We have real work to do in our own department!" For a variety of reasons, fully comprehending "talent swapping" is not a common practice. IBM, UPS, Siemens, and selected other global enterprises are breaking new ground with their revolutionary human resource swapping approaches.

However, the emerging question is why should such swapping initiatives be limited to talent *within* specific firms? In addition, why is swapping limited to human resources? Why not trucks, warehouses, vessel container reservations, aircraft cargo bookings—in short, any type of scarce or disposable resource?

To make the proposition clear, most of us have experienced short-term talent swaps when a supplier or customer temporarily assigns a person to help in a specific initiative. In a similar vein, some collaborative processes between firms, such as vendor-managed inventory (VMI), collaborative planning, forecasting, and replenishment (CPFR), and some customer relationship management (CRM) initiatives, actually call for employees of one firm to work in residence for extended time at another firm's facilities. While all such arrangements are noteworthy, they are not what we have in mind when addressing the potential of resource swapping.

Resource swapping is all about increasing capacity utilization. How many of us own boats, airplanes, lake cabins, vacation condos, or other tangible assets that sit with little or no use for extended periods of time? Most businesses experience the same type of idle capacity on critical items of machinery, buildings, and transportation equipment. The concept of resource swapping is similar to the management of time-shared vacation property. Clearly, time sharing is not a new concept. Farmers have long-standing practices of shared utilization of harvesters, combines, trucks, and other expensive agricultural equipment. What is new is that the information technology and applications are now available to make widespread resource swapping among business operations easy and practical.

In fact, the entire notion of 3PL companies is built on a shared resource model. The 3PL invests in a building, work force, and specialized material handling and, in many situations, provides transportation capacity. The 3PL then sells integrated functionality to firms in need of such services. In fact, at several points in our discussion, we have talked about the growing practice of these firms to make a profitable business out of performing value-added services (VASs) for their customers.

Even more to point is the growing number of 4PLs, often called nonasset service providers because they typically do not own supply chain assets but rather coordinate the use of a combination of 3PL facilities and transportation equipment. The typical 4PL provides the technology resources required to facilitate the flow of goods and services using shared resources. These 4PL operations are analogous to a supply chain orchestra leader. They provide the service of coordination, traffic management, and selected VASs, such as freight bill auditing and payment, without becoming physically involved in performing actual work required in the supply chain operational process. Numerous truck rental fleets, such as Penske, Ryder, and U-Haul, make equipment and even drivers available when excess transportation capacity is needed. In the construction industry, extremely expensive machinery, such as earthmovers, can be rented on an as-needed basis.

No legislation or expensive infrastructure is necessary to establish Web-based information networks to facilitate resource swapping. On-demand exchanges currently provide the framework necessary to facilitate such swapping. The only thing stopping widespread proliferation of resource swapping is the leadership to make it happen and a wake-up call for financial and human resource executives. In fact, the situation is very analogous to the way business leaders viewed reverse logistics just a few short years ago. It was not until a few academic and industry leaders created widespread awareness of the fact that reverse logistics was a value-adding process that business leaders embraced the challenges to make such processes a reality. Today, a few short years later, we have a professional organization dedicated to research and development of reverse logistics and several 3PLs that specialize in performing reverse logistics VASs. In a similar manner, organized talent and resource swapping will become widespread supply chain activities sooner rather than later.

Knowledge-Dependant Process Automation

At various times in the past chapters, we have talked about the potential to automate repetitive processes. Of course, the fundamental premise of automation is that the work involved is repetitive and standardized. In the later days of the Industrial Revolution, the idea was to replace human labor with machines whenever the routinization of the process could be quantified. From the first process machine to advanced robotics, the underlying concept of automation has remained unchanged.

In the Information Age, we have a new dimension to add to the equation; digitization has added the element of "knowledge" to the equation. Working with advanced numeric concepts, we can quantify a wide range of behaviors and outcomes into automation logic. Logic that structures variance and corrective action based on cause-and-effect experience can be developed and programmed into the decision process to increase flexibility and help achieve a broader range or more variable performance. Again, most of this digital advancement is based on well-tested logic. The newest is the application of information-directed automation to processes occurring between two or more firms engaged in supply chain operations.

In Chapter Eight, considerable time was devoted to potential automation or elimination of the traditional order-to-delivery process. At that time, our point was to stress the fact that repetitive processes based on transaction information exchange could be eliminated if participants would share strategic information and establish operating agreements. Sharing sales information within the frame-work or parameters of a business collaboration or promotional plan contains all the information needed to undertake repetitive inventory replenishment. Thus, traditional replenishment orders could be elim-inated, and therefore no errors could occur during order processing. While delivery would still be required in this illustration, the concept of a perfect order, an idea of extreme popularity in today's business environment, would cease to exist—namely because there would not be any orders! What would exist is a high level of consumer satisfac-tion. In final analysis, what else really matters?

The fundamental question is to what degree an intelligent inter-organizational information system can be deployed to handle highly routinized processes. Early evidence suggests that the opportunity is far greater than one might expect. A careful analysis of the routine or highly repetitive information exchanges between two collabo-rating enterprises may in fact disclose that such messaging may be representative of a majority of their interorganizational information exchanges. We may be rapidly moving to the point when routine transaction and information exchanges can be automated much in the same way we automated the drill press of yesterday.

Extreme Postponement

In Chapter Seven, the seminal concept of postponement was dis-cussed. At the core of a firm, increasing responsiveness is the strategy of developing ways to achieve last-minute customer accommodation. Any form of postponement requires that customers agree to some delay during the purchase process. Delay time is required to accom-modate product customization and delivery, which are necessary to precisely meet exacting customer specifications. In the illustration of mixing paint, the delay was only a few minutes. In fact, services soon developed to allow professional painters to call in requirements to suppliers and pick up customized paint at a specified time. For the typical retail customer, the time required to mix paint was consumed by browsing and shopping for painting accessories.

The key to expanding postponement is to better understand the dynamic of customer waiting. Regardless of the specifics of the postponement strategy, the customer must be willing to wait some period of time for the product to be customized. The waiting period could be a few minutes or hours, as accessories are added to a car, or several weeks, maybe months, while a customized car is built to order.

The benefits of being able to postpone rest on the ability to provide customers with products that exactly meet their expectations. Beyond this all-important capability to meet customer expectations is a broad series of operational economies. Most important is the reduction in speculative inventory throughout the supply chain resulting from customization. Little, if any, totally finished inventories would be required in anticipation of customer purchase. Thus, all costs associated with distribution and maintenance of speculative inventories can be significantly reduced. The economies resulting from the ability to postpone extend across the supply chain to all stages of the distribution process. If nothing is done until an order is in hand, then a firm has implemented the ultimate pull strategy.

Many may equate the pull strategy, when it is based on compliance to a customer request, as a variation of the traditional make-to-order manufacturing strategy. Actually, two fundamental things are different in supply chain postponement arrangements. First, the activity to customize to exacting customer specification can occur at any location across the supply chain and not necessarily at a manufacturing plant. Second, the postponement activities are not limited to the basic product being distributed. Postponement can include addition or elimination of features, accessories, supplemental products, and even customization services.

"Extreme postponement" is a term we use to take traditional customization to the next level of complexity. To illustrate, assume that appliances such as dishwashers or dryers could be customized in a consumer's home. The process could go something like the following. A consumer orders a specific model of a dishwasher from the local store. The appliance delivery person comes to the consumer's home to install. However, what the installer is actually doing is taking a standard, universal, or base model of a generic "dishwasher" and then, during installation, activating the appropriate electronics to create the desired functionality. The final step in customization is the addition of a front panel that appropriately modifies the dishwasher appearance to match kitchen decorative décor.

In the dishwasher example, the consumer is given exactly what he or she wants in terms of style, functionality, and appearance. Thus, from the consumer's perspective, no additional delay has been introduced to the buying, delivery, or installation process. In fact, the instant availability of a variety of dishwashers has increased the range of consumer choices, with all models having equal in-stock availability. From the retailers' perspectives, they are stocking parts or kits, not multiple dishwashers in inventory. The basic dishwasher frames are all essentially the same. What is different is the desired functionality and appearance. From the manufacturers' perspective, the resulting simplicity, reduction in overall value-added inventory and vulnerability to forecast error, and elimination of the need to build specific models in anticipation of future sale all combine to reduce risk and improve efficiency. In fact, the institutionalization of postponement across the supply chain dramatically improves overall EERS value performance for all participants, including the consumer. Recall from Chapter Four that winning performance is based on the simultaneous achievement of effectiveness, efficiency, relevancy, and sustainability.

Extreme postponement is about the design and implementation of strategies that achieve all the associated economies attainable by reducing speculation to near zero while simultaneously maintaining or reducing traditional customer order-to-delivery wait time. Development and implementation of extreme postponement arrangements may be among the most promising ways to achieve dramatic supply chain improvement. The limit to creating and implementing extreme postponement seems to be leadership imagination and that old bugaboo, namely, resistance to change.

The next three areas of essential change are unique because private sector leadership alone can't successfully resolve their associated challenges. Each involves significant public sector policy, investment, and participation. However, failure to achieve all three will serve to place serious limits on global growth and may create far-reaching negative consequences. In any event, failure to achieve closure on these challenges will cause significant stagnation in private-sector supply chain performance. Each area of concern represents a topic worthy of a separate book. Therefore, our discussion is restricted to a brief look at the supply chain consequences if these challenges are not resolved. The need for resolution is sufficiently important to rank these issues among the top seven future concerns.

Transportation Infrastructure Reinvention

The last comprehensive investment in U.S. transportation infrastructure was the National Highway program, initiated under the Eisenhower Administration. This ambitious program was officially launched by the National Interstate and Defense Highways Act of

1956, which, as amended, outlined the planned development of more than 46,000 miles of interstate freeways. However, the original plan as expanded has yet to be fully constructed. A significant cause of this failure to complete the original plan has been the high annual maintenance and repair cost. Maintaining expressways and associated bridges is costly business.

However, not maintaining expressways and bridges is a far more potentially tragic and costly proposition. On August 1, 2007, the world became painfully aware of the potential danger to human life, as well as significant disruption in commercial and daily activity, when reinvestment is not made in transport infrastructure. The collapse of the Highway I-35W bridge in Minneapolis and the subsequent public awareness that more than 13 percent of all bridges in the United States were to a significant degree structurally deficient sufficiently drive home the point! While failure to complete and expand the original interstate highway construction plan is one dimension of the story, the more important aspect is the need to continuously tackle the challenges of safety, maintenance, mobility, and congestion. More specific is the challenge to determine ways and means to resolve the growing congestion, avoid stagnation, and simultaneously maintain safety in the movement of people and freight. It is important to note that the infrastructure challenge is not limited to the United States. In some emerging countries, the challenge is to develop an initial transportation infrastructure. In most developed nations of the world, the issue is reinvention and expansion. The United States is used to illustrate the overall infrastructure challenge.

This challenge is clearly at the core of maintaining meaningful supply chain operations. Simply put, it is time once again to reinvent our national transportation infrastructure. A few comments concerning each mode of transportation will help scope the enormity of the issues at stake.

Truck transportation is the backbone of the distributive network. Most everything must move by truck for at least part of its journey to market. In 2006, 78.6 percent of the total U.S. transportation expenditure was for truck transportation.[5] In 2005, the U.S. highway network carried 77 percent of the tons and 92 percent of the value of U.S. freight.[6] Most freight shipment origins and destinations occur in highly populated areas where automobile and other passenger movement is also intense. Some congestion problems can be resolved by scheduling. For example, early-morning and nighttime deliveries can reduce the need to move trucks during commuter rush hours. Nine cities that are competing for $1.1 billion in federal aid to fight congestion have proposed variable tolls based on traffic volume. Several others are designating HOT lanes with variable tolls for controlling traffic flow and vehicle occupancy during selected hours. Some cities such as New York are considering city entry fees to reduce congestion. It is clear that the problem is much larger than freight delivery.

Another dimension of the growing problem is the intensity of trucks moving between metropolitan areas on interstate and other public highways. A major potential improvement in capacity would be to allow truck trains consisting of multiple trailers to be moved with a single power unit. Safety concerns have limited most highways to double-bottoms, which involves the hauling of a maximum of two trailers that when combined do not exceed a specified overall length. It is becoming increasingly clear that the only solution capable of achieving the desired movement flexibility is the construction of at

---

[5]   Rosalyn Wilson, 18th Annual State of Logistics Report: "The New Face of Logistics." CSCMP, June 6, 2007, National Press Club, Washington, DC.

[6]   Issues related to U.S. national transportation infrastructure are elaborated in detail in a special report prepared for the National Surface Transportation Policy and Revenue Study Commission of the U.S. Congress by AASHTO "Transportation: Invest in Our Future," Washington, DC, 2007.

least a number of "truck-only highways" for movement of freight between and around major metropolitan areas. In short, it's time to go back to the drawing boards to reinvent, and then finance and construct, the appropriate infrastructure to allow the motor system to work to its full capability.

Another past due alternative to achieve more intercity movement capacity is to reinvent the railroads. Once the backbone of our economy, the rail infrastructure has been allowed, with a handful of minor exceptions, to deteriorate since World War II. Despite significant reinvestment in improvement and maintenance of existing track, the fact of the matter is that a great deal of the rail lanes do not go where freight now and in the future will have to move and often are restricted to slow orders concerning freight movement during specific times of the year. To increase safety, a slow order limits the speed a train can move while passing through highly congested or populated areas. This is in contrast to high-speed rail services available in Japan and throughout Europe. In terms of infrastructure, most U.S. rail tunnels are too narrow or do not have sufficient overhead clearance to allow passage of double-wide or triple-stack containers. Key corridors to move fright rapidly from seaports to main areas of manufacturing and consumption are limited. Terminals are inadequate to facilitate rapid interchange of trailers on flatcars or containers to relieve highway congestion.

Rail has great potential to help meet our twenty-first-century needs to move people and freight. However, to meet the challenge, massive investment and reinvention will be required. Just one project, the Heartland Corridor, is estimated to require a $96-million investment to raise tunnel clearances to allow double-stack containers to move from the Hampton Roads area of Virginia to Columbus and beyond. The challenges of reinventing the rail system to facilitate intermodal movement, considered by most to be at best a short-term fix, are enabled by the "Safe, Accountable, Flexible Efficient Transportation Equity Act: A Legacy for Users," enacted in 2005. Called the SAFETEA LU Act, just the name indicates the challenges involved in railroad-related reinvention.

Ports and their related congestion represent another weak link in the transportation infrastructure. Significant freight movement bottlenecks are a potential threat in every season of high-volume movement. A major problem in all ports is the loading and unloading of containers. Ships, the most expensive component in the high-seas cargo equation, are often required to wait offshore for dock availability. Once at dock, many ships confront unplanned delays as a result of slow container loading and unloading. Highway and rail congestion are also significant factors causing delays in surface movement into, out of, and beyond port facilities. New and faster container transfer methods hold the potential for future improvement. For example, the use of magnetic lifts holds the promise to load or unload a container in half the time required using current material handling devices. However, the question remains: Will all such advancements be sufficient to resolve today's congestion problems, let alone accommodate the increased cargo movements projected for the future? Probably not. Many feel that a significant part of the answer is to design bigger and faster container ships. For example, Maersk Lines recently commissioned the *Emma Maersk*, a container ship capable of carrying 15,000 20-foot containers between China and the United States at a speed four days faster than that of traditional container ships.

A specific problem in Great Lakes shipping is the water level. In key ports and locks connecting major sections of the lakes, water is at the lowest level since the mid-1920s. In 2006, Great Lakes shipping vessels were reported to be operating light loaded, at a capacity of less than 80 percent, due to insufficient waterway dredging.[7] Such failure to maintain essential right of way is just one example of how infrastructure neglect affects all methods of transportation.

Similar assessments are valid concerning the challenges faced by pipeline and air cargo movements. Each face infrastructure and equipment challenges. Worldwide transportation capacity has confronted increased challenges related to risk and potential terrorism since 9/11. Maintaining security is and will continue to be a continuous part of future transportation management. Both those involved in providing transportation services and those responsible for managing corporate transportation are fully aware that, at any given time, their equipment can be commandeered by terrorists to be used as delivery systems for weapons of mass destruction. In total, the challenges faced by industry and government in maintaining, let alone improving, the systems' capabilities are near overwhelming! This, however, is a challenge we must meet on a global basis. Similar problems exist in either reinvention or initial construction of transportation infrastructure in Europe, Asia, and South America.

Green

Equally important challenges relate to the many environmental issues facing business in general and global supply chain operations in particular. Energy utilization issues are addressed in the next section. Here, the subjects are emissions and overall unfavorable environmental impact. Awareness concerning the importance of protecting our planet from a variety of disruptive factors is at an all-time high. On 7/7/07, Live Earth coordinated "The Concert for a Climate in Crisis." The concert, parts of which were performed on all seven continents, was aimed at creating global awareness of the "green crisis."

---

[7] Wilson, op. cit.

Many different firms have announced commitments to improve their environmental impacts. For example, Cadbury Schweppes recently announced an environmental strategy designed to transform key processes to minimize the use of energy, packaging, and water, in response to challenges related to climate change.[8]

The question of carbon emissions has been the subject of growing global concern. The Kyoto Protocol, a 1997 United Nations agreement between 169 countries, introduced the concept of "carbon credits." Carbon credits represent incentives for countries and companies to reduce emissions of greenhouse gases. The basic idea is to offer companies ideally positioned to reduce carbon emissions incentives to actually initiate reduction programs. For successful reduction, they are awarded carbon credits that can be traded on an international basis at prevailing market prices. Such incentive and exchange programs clearly have direct impact concerning supply chain strategies of the future.

The fact of the matter is that in the supply chain space, considerable attention has been directed to reducing the impact of emissions. The introduction of ultra-low-sulfur diesel (ULSD) fuel is a step toward further reducing engine emissions. Because 94 percent of all goods shipped by truck, train, boat, and barge use diesel fuel, the impact could be significant. To get a feel of the cost of reinventing our supply chain system, the annual expenditure to convert to ULSD to meet EPA regulations is estimated at $8 billion.[9] While operating costs may increase as much as 2 to 5 cents per gallon, the impact is a dramatic improvement in emissions quality. For example, the U.S. trucking industry estimates that truck emissions by 2010, when in full compliance with ERP standards, will be cleaner than their fresh-air intakes when operating in selected metropolitan areas.

[8]   Brad Kenney, "Cadbury Schweppes Announces Absolute Commitment to Climate Action," *Industry Week*, July 16, 2007.

[9]   *Logistics Today*, October 2006, p. 14.

Of course, the entire issue of environmental impact is much larger than that of emissions. All responsible industry leaders have a growing awareness of the importance of environmental improvement. Most agree that responsible industry collaboration with government, not government alone, offers the only meaningful way to turn the tide in favor of environmental improvement. The minimum goal for all socially responsible firms must be overall commitment to a policy of zero environmental impact. The point of discussion here is to stress that a positive environmental impact and improvement program must be high on the agenda of twenty-first-century supply chain leadership

Alternative Fuels

The age of fossil fuel is over—the funeral will be expensive! The initial steps toward achieving positive environmental impact and global independence from oil and petroleum-based products are under way. Alternative fuels mean anything capable of powering commercial and consumer needs other than gasoline and diesel. The list of alternative fuels is long, namely, ethanol, methanol, natural gas, propane, hydrogen, electricity, biodiesel, and biomass. To date, the long-tern answer concerning which fuel will most effectively and efficiently meet our future needs is not clear.

Part of the current answer is found in the increased use of biomass products to create heat and energy and to power vehicles. While biomass, such as ethanol and biodiesel, holds great potential, it does not provide the complete answer. Fuels created from agricultural and animal products have the combined advantages of diverse supply and reduced greenhouse gases or emissions, and they foster agricultural economic development. McDonald's Corporation has announced plans to convert its British delivery fleet to run on its own recycled cooking oil. The U.S. Postal Service is extensively experimenting with alternative-fuel delivery vehicles. While encouraging, biomass-based fuels remain an expensive alternative.

In the automotive sector, hybrids are making their way into dealer showrooms. Hybrids that combine traditional fuels and electrification have been surprisingly well accepted by consumers. General Motors claims to have produced more than one million flex-fuel vehicles capable of using what are called P-series fuels. P-series fuel blends traditional petroleum and biomass products. Each of these initiatives is contributing to moving the industrial world closer to fossil based energy independence.

However, most involved in the freight side of the equation are betting on the development of hydrogen-based fuels as the long-term answer to energy independence. BMW has manufactured and is currently consumer testing an H-7-series sedan that operates on liquid hydrogen. Ford has announced the planned commercialization of a hydrogen-power vehicle by 2012. The main problem with hydrogen is the logistical complexity of making fuel conveniently available throughout the nation. In any event, one of the most significant unanswered questions for the future is by what and when the supply chain will be liberated from the "ball and chain" of fossil fuels. Our ability to avoid economic stagnation rests on the answer to these fundamental questions.

Truly, the combined challenges related to infrastructure, environmental impact, and energy combine to form a dark cloud over the future of essential supply chain services. Within the chapters of this book, we have addressed the challenges of digital transformation initiatives to harness available technology and catapult individual firms to the position of industry leadership. Such leadership success depends on the simultaneous resolution of significant constraints. In earlier chapters, we talked about the growing responsibility of senior leaders to be involved in issues beyond those typically found in day-to-day operations. The need has never been greater for responsible business leadership involvement in social and government issues. However, there may be at least one more massive change in our future.

Nanogenome Supply Chain Technology

To our knowledge, the term "nanogenome supply chain technology" is invented here. However, we have lived sufficiently long to realize that seldom is anything ever really new. The derivation of the term comes from three separate disciplines. The "nano" is taken from the emerging field of physics in which elements are reduced to a scale smaller than one micrometer. Clearly, the many implications of "nano" measurement represent a disruptive technology of the future. In fact, the APEC Center for Technology Foresight offers the following assessment:

> If nanotechnology is going to revolutionize manufacturing, health care, energy supply, communications and probably defense, then it will transform labor and the workplace, the medical system, the transportation and power infrastructures and the military. None of this will be changed without significant disruption.

Of course, our interest here is about the impact on the transportation infrastructure and supply chain responsiveness. The second part of the term, "genome," comes from the field of medical science. Perhaps the story is best told in Matt Ridley's national bestseller first published in 1999.[10] It is the story of mapping the human gene structure and the development of a human blueprint or, as stated by

---

[10]   Matt Ridley, *Genome: The Autobiography of a Species in 23 Chapters.* (New York: HarperCollins, 1999).

Ridley, "You can now download from the Internet the near-complete instructions for how to build and run a human body."[11]

The third term, "supply chain technology," hopefully has been fully described in the many pages of this book. The three terms together, "nanogenome supply chain technology," offer one view of the future. Well—where is this all going?

The popular science-fiction series *Star Trek* may have said it all in the famous quote "Beam me up, Scotty! There is no intelligent life here." Does our future hold the possibility of actually transmitting physical matter from one location to another? It was only a few years ago when Federal Express sponsored "Zap Mail." This revolutionary new service was designed to commercialize the ability to transmit documents from one physical location to another.[12] While truly revolutionary at that time, what FedEx overlooked was the rapid commercialization and adoption of fax machines by individuals. What one day appeared as a near miracle, transmitting a document in minutes, became a household reality almost overnight. The world rapidly adopted new technology capable of serving as a printer, copier, document scanner, and fax transmission device. Today, we find it common practice to electronically distribute documents, films, and all forms of music.

On November 13, 2006, *Fortune* published a mind-stretching article discussing the research of Dr. Neil Gershenfeld. Greshenfeld is the director of MIT's Center for Bits and Atoms (CBA). The title of the article, "A Factory of One's Own," refers to a machine called a "personal fabricator." What is in fact being discussed is desktop manufacturing, a personal computer with the ability to "cut, score, etch, and sew." And, here is the bottom line: "Want a new dining

---

[11] Ibid., p. 1

[12] The service called "Zap Mail" was introduced by Federal Express in 1984 and discontinued two years later. .

room chair? You'll design it on a PC and press PRINT, and your personal fabricator will create it for you right before your eyes. Just make sure tray No. 2 has enough wood."[13] Will this really be part of the story of the supply chain of the future? We assume, given our current limitations, that the wood for tray No. 2 will still need to be moved to the desired location by a conventional transportation method such as a truck. But, one is left to ponder whether that will always be the case. Gershenfeld's perception is that one does not need home manufacturing for what you can get at Wal-Mart, limiting the personal fabricator to "products that make you unique." We wonder, however, whether *not* shopping at Wal-Mart might make you unique.

However, when we link two concepts, namely, nano and genome, and then add supply chain technology, one might wonder why it may not be in our future to actually transmit physical products from one geographical location to another. A new and revolutionary sixth mode of transportation, when combined with information technology, gives birth to nanogenome supply chain technology. While a sixth transportation mode may not be in our short-term or maybe never in our future, it is becoming increasingly clear that nanomaterials offer a promising way to manufacture smaller and denser products. Product miniaturization offers unprecedented opportunity to reduce transportation cost by more efficient utilization of carrier cubic capacity. The primary drivers of transportation cost are product value, weight, cube, and density. Only time will tell just how nanotechnology will affect daily supply chain practice.

Across different disciplines, some have speculated that the Information Age will rapidly morph into what might be called the Nanotechnological Age. One of the authors recalls a dinner with a prominent materials researcher, who described a revolutionary

---

[13]   Jeffrey M O'Brien, *Fortune*, November 13, 2006, p. 138.

reduction process having the potential to reduce biomass to compressed gas in the farm field. This new biomass reduction process held the potential to radically change the currently accepted best practice for manufacturing biofuel. At least two good things would happen if biomass could be compressed to gas in the farm field. First, the transport of several trucks of materials on crowded highways to the refinery could be reduced to one tanker. Second, the waste by-product remains available for use as fertilizer on the farm, thereby eliminating the need to transport fertilizer. Our position concerning nanogenome supply chain technology is "never say never."

Concluding Statement

Our interpretation of the responsive supply chain business model story has now been told as we see it unfolding to date. Hopefully, you agree it is well past the time to stop pushing and start pulling your supply chain. Most of what has been written is in fact supported by decades of history. Other parts of the book represent our shared speculation concerning events most likely to happen. In some cases, events discussed are likely or not so likely to occur as we move deeper into the new millennium. The startling observation is just how little the fundamental purpose of supply chain work has changed over the decades—even centuries. However, how we work in the supply chain has changed dramatically to capitalize on discovery, invention, information technology, and, most of all, leadership. This change will accelerate.

New techniques have been invented and new processes implemented. While progress has been noteworthy, ever-growing demand has served to neutralize the widespread impact of advancements. Looking back, at times, we appear to have, at best, just held our own in the race between growing global demand and satisfactory supply.

Of course, such a conclusion is not true. We have made substantial progress, resulting in the highest standard of living some of the world's populations have ever known. The critical or focal words in the above statement emphasizing the future challenge are "some of the world's populations." Now, the entire world stands at a crossroad. The technology of the Information Age is at our command. The question is will the emerging leaders of twenty-first-century commerce and industry be able to harness and implement this responsive, or pull, potential?

Initial Steps Towards the New Information-Driven Frontier

> *"Man's mind, once stretched by a new idea, never regains its original dimensions."*
>
> —Oliver Wendell Holmes

The thoughts and recommendations presented in this book call for business leaders to radically rethink their traditional business model in order to enable continual competitive superiority in the twenty-first century. Each of the six imperatives of the responsive supply chain business model serves to challenge the paradigms of the traditional anticipatory methods of conducting business. The traditional model has outlived its time. The traditional model was built on the pillars of the Industrial Revolution. However, given the capabilities of the emerging Information Age, the traditional model is becoming ineffective, losing its relevancy, and becoming increasingly difficult to sustain.

The challenge for you, the reader, is to fully recognize that you are living in the reality of an increasingly synchronized world. While transformation is critical, you can't walk away from current operational responsibilities that are essential for continued survival. Your challenge is to maintain profitable business operations while simultaneously investing time and energy toward leading a transformation initiative. Modern business enterprises are complex. Any effort to redesign and implement a new structure with new capabilities typically requires years of business model transition. But, we hope that by now you have become convinced that the rapidly emerging digital world requires changing many practices, behaviors, structures, and purposes to excel in the future. The process of reinventing a twentieth-century business enterprise is not an easy task.

Change leadership can be described as the continuous process of aligning an organization with its marketplace and doing it more responsively and effectively than competitors. As you began reading this postscript, you are committing yourself to becoming, if you were not already, a change leader. You are becoming increasingly curious about how you might turn some of these thoughts into reality within your own work environment. Before we proceed to discuss initial steps toward the new frontier, it is appropriate to spend a few minutes reflecting on the nature of change.

Change can be, and many times is, a very disruptive force to you and to all you affect. Harry Levinson, Ph.D., a world-respected clinical professor emeritus of psychology in the Department of Psychiatry at Harvard Business School and founder of the Levinson Institute, once said, "All change is loss, all loss must be mourned and psychological contracts must be continuously renegotiated."[1] Our joint experiences generally support these thoughts. To have a high potential of success in carrying out any large-scale change, there are six generally accepted conditions that foster change and permit it to occur. All parties involved must acknowledge and comply with these six conditions in order to achieve successful change.

The first condition is for all involved to fully understand and accept the fundamental need to change. The change initiative must

---

[1]   Harry Levinson, "Easing the Pain of Personal Loss," *Harvard Business Review*, September–October, 1972, pp. 80–88.

be widely viewed as a burning platform. If, for example, any of what we have written about created a fire in your soul, that was good, but it would normally not be sufficient for you to initiate a new journey and direction. You must develop and communicate a clear vision to all involved concerning where you want to take the organization and why it is essential to undertake the journey. Significant and sustainable change must be viewed as essential.

Second, one must clearly delineate where the company, division, or department currently is and what specific things must change. Situational analysis leading to an action agenda is often difficult. But, it must be specific. Many of the processes or capabilities that must be changed are likely to be viewed by many individuals involved as not being broken. In short, a leader must often change activities that appear to be functioning well. Without the knowledge necessary to vision a new and better order of affairs, why would anyone listen to you or want to follow you?

Third, when you understand the desired changes, you and others must be reasonably satisfied that the attainable benefits will outweigh the costs and difficulties of making the change. While we strongly believe that the benefits of digital transformation are real, you need to talk to the points of change with impact facts based on your specific business situation, not generalities. Normally, a cost-benefit assessment quantifies opportunities identified during visioning and situational analysis.

After you have completed the first three conditions and the desire for change has been established, the fourth step is to develop an implementation plan to define how to get from today's situation to tomorrow's vision. A journey of this magnitude must define what needs to be accomplished by whom and when. Like any long-term journey, the change plan must continually access what is happening and must adjust. The fundamental challenge is to stay focused on the original vision. We describe this as analogous to sailing a ship to a specified destination. The vision of getting to a specific destination should not change. However, wind, rain, and water current may call for periodic change in the ship's course or more "tacking" to maintain heading toward the original destination.

Fifth, in order to achieve the change initiative goals while periodically revising the implementation plan for unknown anomalies, a comprehensive measurement system is required. Measurement is difficult but essential to sustain the support and commitment necessary to complete a transformation. Transformations often burn out because they become difficult to measure and communicate progress. There is a natural tendency for organizations to revert to more comfortable traditional practices when the change initiative faces resistance or becomes operationally difficult. It is essential to be able to articulate progress in order to maintain change momentum.

Finally, in order to create and reinforce desired changes, a comprehensive reward and recognition system needs to exist that complements the efforts required and recognizes all performance. One of the most common derailers of change is not focusing goals and rewards on meeting key milestones toward achieving the end vision. To sustain change initiatives, it is fundamentally important to administer rewards based on achievement as broadly as possible throughout the organization. Driving integrated horizontal or cross-functional management is not easy. People at all levels of the organization need to be recognized. In the case of supply chain operations, this means that all involved, from the shipping and receiving docks to the boardroom, need to be acknowledged. It is also important to keep reward systems simple so that everyone can easily understand them.

To illustrate, initially at Colgate-Palmolive, functions and divisions each had individual goals. Despite achieving individual goals, the company received less than satisfactory reports on its customer service. One year, the chairman decided to simply change the goals and rewards for everyone in the company. All executives were assigned a revised objective that represented 25 percent of their combined bonus compensation. Unless the revised service goal was achieved for all of the top-50 customers, compensation would not be paid. The result was analogous to taking down the Berlin Wall. Service improvements started to happen after a number of weeks, and the company continued toward achieving the new goal within months. The example illustrates the importance of picking performance indicators that drive desired change.

Figure P-1 below lists these critical six "must-have" conditions essential to drive change in any organization. In total, they should be viewed as prerequisites for successful change. These conditions set the stage for much more transformation work to follow. The conditions should be viewed as supportive guideposts to help keep a change leader fully understood, accepted, informed, engaged, and,

Figure P-1   Six Essential Conditions for Leading Meaningful Change

- Want or need to make a change
- Have a vision of where we would like to be
- Be reasonably satisfied that the benefits will be greater than the costs and difficulties of making the change
- Have a means of moving from where we are to where we would like to be, i.e., an implementation plan
- Have a measurement monitoring system to assure that we are staying on course
- Adjust reward and recognition systems to reinforce desired change

most of all, followed. We would not suggest taking any major steps toward the new frontier without having plans to establish and maintain these six conditions.

The six essential conditions for achieving meaningful change can be positioned in the context of a change leadership model. Figure P-2 presents a diagram of such a model. It is important to understand that the leadership change model is a repetitive process that requires continuous renewal while the transformation process is playing out. For example, metrics that reflect meaningful measurement at one point in the change process may lose relevancy at another point.

Figure P-2   Leadership Change Model

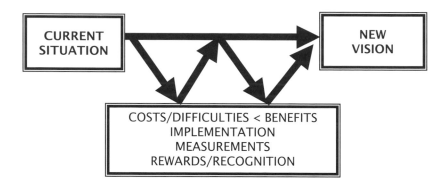

As we stated earlier in the book, all knowledge concerning transformation needs to be internalized into the specifics of your business today and in the future in order to have relevancy. A less provocative approach but one that we think is valuable for evaluating the need for a digital transformation in your business might be to imagine yourself as a new senior executive brought into your company to lead a transformation. An alternative would be to view yourself as a senior member of a consulting firm hired to assist in a transformation. This should not be too hard to imagine. It is happening daily throughout the world for one reason or another, be it an unhappy board, an interested hedge fund, or a potential acquisition. In either of these roles, a few fundamental steps would be required, starting with a series of assessments.

Most assessments start with a review of the financial condition of the company and a basic understanding of the sustainable marketability of the company's products and/or services. You may want to start the process by finding out whether the company is making and will continue to make an appropriate growth return for its shareholders. Additionally, you may want to examine both your and your competition's product offerings, market size, and growth potential and who owns what percent of market share across all relevant sales channels. The above information, while basic, is very important and normally essential to framing transformation of existing business operations. For the following discussion, let's assume that we are not radically changing the products sold or our existing sales channels.

Let's begin our assessment with the most important participant in this troika, the customer. At earlier stages in this book, we differentiated between consumers and customers who we do business with throughout the supply chain. All represent important decision-making constituents in implementing a responsive supply chain business model. On the basis of the business you are doing today and whatever long-term planning that has been done, do you really know who your customers are, what they really want or need, and how well they are being serviced and engaged? If your customers are not the ultimate consumers of your product, do you fully understand your firm's contribution to satisfying consumers and whether you could enhance consumer value, sales, or consumption by improving existing services or developing new services? To illustrate, in the retail grocery industry, companies should set their consumer performance metrics on portions delivered, not cases, ounces, or pounds of products sold. Their competitive analysis should be based on consumer "share of stomach" because they know their competition is not just comparable products but alternative products distributed in alternative distribution channels. In the fashion apparel industry, competitive analysis should be based on consumer "share of dresser drawer or closet" because, again, the competition for consumer apparel purchases goes far beyond your obvious competitors. While such metrics are hard to identify and implement, they focus on the basic value proposition your firm has to offer and who will be the true competition over time.

Thinking about how a transformation should begin and end around consumers is always a correct place to start the development of a new value proposition. The consumers' perspective, their expectations concerning products, services, and experiences, is the fundamental force that drives sales and profit. What this book asks you to think about is how connected you are to your consumers today. What do you comprehensively know about their demographics? Do you know what is important to keep their loyalty? Are you satisfying the most important market segments? What would they describe as legendary about your overall product and service offering? How have you initially, and where necessary over the longer term, satisfied them?

A traditional business model, and how it is managed, is typically based on a historical perspective and commitment to practices created many years ago. Such positioning is most often based on one perspective and related premises made by one or a limited number of founders or leaders of that time concerning what consumers originally wanted or needed. On the basis of all these initial assumptions, every effort was made at start-up to deliver a unique assortment of products and services. This initial strategy worked or your firm would not have survived and would not be facing the need to transform today. However, twenty-first-century consumers are different. Likewise, the best business model to excel is also different.

In the global digital economy, consumers can be expected to know much more about your company, your products, your services, and, most important, those of others with which you directly and indirectly compete. In some fashion-focused firms, executives describe their mantra as striving to know the customers like they know their best friends. You might want to think about what level of consumer understanding is essential for you to successfully compete in the twenty-first century. To illustrate, take the desire of consumers to listen to music. They never asked for a single vinyl record, any type of tape player, CD player, or iPod, or even the iPhone. They simply had a desire to listen to music. Is this a contemporary example of making a series of the best buggy whips? Consumers have always wanted to listen to music of their choosing as conveniently as possible. Do you think the original market leaders in this industry really understood that this was what the consumers really wanted? Or, did they simply apply the technology of the day without a fundamental understanding of the true consumer motivation? Our point is simply that twenty-first-century digital technology is changing the game.

Today's consumer is an active and engaged participant in the economic equation we call business. With today's technology, consumers are empowered to quickly engage or disengage with your business and what you offer, help put you into another business, or vote you out of business by rejecting your value proposition. With technology and more information-intensive lifestyles, consumers are valuing their time much differently and hence valuing products and services and sustained company follow-through much differently. In today's world, consumers can shop online for products as basic as groceries. They can comparatively shop different grocers' advertisements and can arrange for pickup at a specified time or arrange home delivery. In fact, an increasing number of consumers are reporting that a primary driver of increased online shopping for consumer big-box products is the ability to negotiate or "haggle" price without the face-to-face intimidation of a salesperson.[2] With rapid changes in technology, consumers are also fast-track-engaging new technology at an unprecedented speed. One of the first steps you should take after concluding this book is to find out how much you really know about your consumers' needs and wants and how well you are meeting their rapidly changing expectations.

In today's business climate, it is becoming increasingly common for senior leaders to spend time working the frontline jobs that are critical to the business success. DiVita, Disney, Continental Airlines, Sysco, and Amazon are among firms requiring members of their senior leadership teams to spend time performing frontline jobs that are essential to their business success.[3] While getting a frontline view of the business is not entirely new to successful leadership, today's consumer connectivity is making such understanding a prerequisite for successful transformation.

Another continual drumbeat of this book has been technology, teams, and the availability and flow of information. It has been a drumbeat because technology continues to disruptively change individual and team behaviors within our organization, across the supply chain, and with and by consumers, all at relatively lightning speed. The fundamental point is that few involved have conscious thought of what is really happening and how they should be repositioning their firms, given a very radically changing paradigm. To illustrate, what is your firm's impact assessment concerning widespread availability of WiMAX technology?

---

[2] Cheryl Lu-Lien Tan, "Haggling 2.0," *Wall Street Journal*, June 24, 2007, p. 1.

[3] Joan S. Lubin, "Top Brass Try Life in the Trenches," *Wall Street Journal*, June 25, 2007, p. B1.

In a more general sense, many individuals, depending on how old they are and when they were first introduced to information technology, have an entirely different perspective on its actual impact. Baby boomers, a core group of today's consumers and business leaders, have been catapulted from telexes to having to continuously respond to beeping smart cell phones and buzzing Blackberries. These new real-time communication devices are capable of transmitting messages, advertisements, presentations, and near-instantaneous statuses of activities. Their world has changed from information exchange in days and hours to global connectivity within seconds.

On the other hand, it is important to keep firmly in mind the fact that younger generations have moved well beyond baby boomers when it comes to using technology. They are more competent with technology, use it more in all facets of their lives, and have developed user dexterity not likely ever to be replicated by baby boomers. The younger generation has, by the age of six, developed eye/hand dexterity to exploit technology both in play and in new potential careers. For example, young kids today have all the physical dexterity, albeit not the maturity and knowledge, needed by surgeons using modern medical technology to perform many laparoscopic procedures. This dexterity is the result of mastering computer games before they could walk. What levels of new mental and physical skills will they have achieved as they enter their college years?

The broad availability of information creates many opportunities as well as many challenges. Who within an organization should get all this information? Is your firm organized to best use the information and make better and timelier decisions to change your direction and velocity and ultimately enhance consumer takeaway, satisfaction, and consumption? Are you best organized to support essential processes? The fundamental challenge is to transform today's seemingly best practices in order to implement a responsive supply chain business model.

We believe that the pathway to meeting this challenge rests with a leadership plan that encapsulates the alignment, process, and content of ideas consistent with the focus of this book. We presented the stages of transformation as awareness, ratcheting, catapulting, and endurance. These four phases describe the challenges anyone interested in forging a new pathway to a responsive supply chain should consider. Within ratcheting and catapulting, we identified six imperatives essential to achieving industry leadership.

Understanding the full potential of what the Technology Age is bringing to the twenty-first century will require a much more in-depth analysis of your business specifics when compared with the generalities presented here. It would probably be a good idea to immerse yourself in some of the latest discoveries and applications supported by technology that are fundamentally changing the way people will work, relax, communicate, remain healthy, and so on. Much of the knowledge of this potential is all around us. However, we often fail to take the time to observe and reflect on its possible impact on our business.

Recent examples in the medical field include the emerging ability to grow organs from a person's own DNA. On the basis of research at Lake Forrest University, growth of bladders has been accomplished, and these new organs have successfully replaced diseased organs in selected patients. Research concerning replicating other organs is now in process. Some in the scientific world appear on the brink of creating a synthetic microbe to replicate artificial life.[4] With all this technology and application, it would seem that we could use such unfolding capability to get the responsive supply chain business model right.

---

[4] John Carey, "On the Brink of Artificial Life," *Business Week*, June 25, 2007, p. 40.

A few years ago at another university research effort, a professor and student became the conduit for electronic information transfer between two computers.[5] The technology breakthrough was that the two computers were not connected by either cable or radio frequency. The professor and the student each had a computer cable connected to a chip imbedded in the heel of their shoe, and the electronic connection was completed as they shook hands. This story is both interesting and relevant. One of the new potential health care products that sprung from that invention was a bedsheet capable of continuously reporting a patient's temperature. The temperature was recorded as the sheet made contact with the patient. A related product was a device, the size of a wristwatch, capable of dispensing insulin through an absorption patch at a flow rate based on patient sugar level monitoring. A substantial list of potential new product concepts was developed on the basis of this one technology discovery. The point is to develop awareness of what Information Age technology, combined with a natural curiosity, can do to help a leader vision change. Supported by frameworks such as the responsive supply chain business model, leaders can go a long way to vision how their organizations could be ratcheted to a new and more competitive place in the twenty-first century.

Technology is an enabler. Taken alone, technology is rarely sufficient to make a real difference. Aligning technology with present and potential products and services as well as the process flow and capabilities of business operations is where it can have a pervasive impact on all outcomes of a firm. It presents the opportunity for leveraging incremental change into significant impact. The impact could be new products, new economics for commercial value, new processes, or new capabilities. Implementing a responsive supply chain business model enabled by technology has been the focal point of interest

---

[5] Confidential Business R&D report.

of the authors and this book. The ratcheting we see needed is in three areas. We spoke first to connectivity with consumers because it is the essence of why businesses are in business. The consumer is the one person who makes a business's efforts have meaning. Making the world's best widget is a hobby until someone purchases it at a price sufficient to provide a sustainable economic return. While the above observation may be much too basic or obvious, complacency serves to make work today and its purpose become a bureaucracy. Bureaucratic organizations seem to flounder and lose direction without connectivity to consumers, who really make all wheels turn. The ratcheting we are calling for is leveraging more comprehensive consumer understanding and remaining vigilant to that relationship for success. Assessing whether you sufficiently understand your customer should be a simple capability to exploit.

How we do our work to achieve a sale to a satisfied consumer can be as important as what we sell. We asked for focus on operational excellence and development of integrated horizontal organizations. Horizontal organizations and integrative management, discussed earlier in the book, seek to utilize real-time information to produce immediate action throughout the supply chain. The logic of both of these emerging concepts is based on here-today information technology capabilities and irrefutable discoveries expected in the next few years. But, do you, as a change leader, have the emotional will to honestly step into the twenty-first century and accept the reality concerning how your firm is formally organized, how you carry out work, and how you are goaled and rewarded? And, do any or all of these aspects of today's enterprise need to be rethought and redeveloped?

The situation you face is no different from the type leaders faced early on in the Industrial Revolution and enhanced throughout the twentieth century. The key is to take full advantage of human talent and technology that is more than ready to be enabled. The evolution of technology is now at a speed where organizational deployment should be reviewed at no more than 18-month intervals for relevancy and effectiveness. Maybe it is time for your company's 18-month checkup!

The concept of catapulting is one of moving overall performance to a higher level of achievement by building on awareness and ratcheting. Catapulting is about leveraging people, knowledge, processes, value propositions, and the general environment. One of the required pillars of any successful change is leadership. We talk about the changing model of leadership in the twenty-first century. With ubiquitous information, relational and distributed leadership may be the only way to operate in a real-time connected world. Any meaningful analysis should start with you. As you read the chapter on relational leadership, did you agree with its message, and, if the answer is yes, did you feel that it reflected who you are or who you might like to be? The theorem of the shadow of the leader is that your actions, not your words, are what people follow. Starting to transform yourself so that your actions demonstrate the attributes and characteristics of a relational leader will generate much more organizational impact than trying to verbally convince others to change. Your leadership behavior should demonstrate the culture you want embraced within your immediate team and hopefully throughout the entire company. Culture is a foundation for new insights capable of influencing others' behaviors and habits. New habits and behaviors can create the paradigm shift you are looking for to enable a responsive supply chain business model. Your new leadership practice model should be in place as you look to implement it within your own leadership team. Your personal behavior will help other peers or key management better understand the value available to the entire organization.

In Part Three, we talked about developing real-time responsiveness, leveraging many-to-many networks, and learning how to effectively collaborate. The potential to catapult to a new level of integration builds on capabilities fundamental to ratcheting and serves as the foundation for moving a firm to global industry leadership.

Once transformation is achieved, a digital enterprise has learned that it is a continuous challenge requiring renewal. UPS is well recognized in the logistics service provider industry as a firm that has successfully completed multiple transformations. The journey from a limited-scope U.S.-based department store delivery service to a global provider of a full range of logistic services involved many different transformations. However, despite past success, emerging technology capabilities are once again driving a far-reaching UPS transformation. From global package delivery, UPS is leveraging to become an "all supply chain services provider" for its customers: in essence, a one-stop shopping service for transportation, logistics, and all forms of responsive value-added services. To achieve this end, UPS has spent more than $1 billion on technology each year for more than a decade. The UPS current transformation goal is to provide customers a seamless full-service global product movement and value adding service individualized to each specific customer. The end goal is a one-to-one global relationship meeting all supply chain operational needs of its enterprise customers. The fact that UPS has developed and implemented an information network capable of identifying the exact location of every piece of freight at all times is one of the technology capabilities that enables such a far-reaching reinvention of a currently successful business enterprise.

Unfortunately, as stated at the start of this postscript, change is appropriately viewed as loss for all concerned, even if it is needed for all the best reasons. While few of us like to see things that used to work changed, such transformation is essential for survival. The pace of technology is pushing in all areas whether we like it or not. The traditional notion of change was to stay functionally excellent. Existing organizational models bring with them comfort, trust, and historical performance expectations. New models will ultimately result in similar comfort levels, but their adoption requires developing new and refreshed psychological contracts that fit today's and tomorrow's digital worlds. As you take steps toward the new frontier, you may want to understand the implied psychological contracts you and your teams have with the people you support every day as well as the teams that support you. How well are the performance expectations of both groups known, measured, shared, rewarded, and recognized? Is any of this in writing? Do supply chain partners know each other's roles and how they jointly help achieve sustainable consumer satisfaction? Are these enterprise goals aligned with the customer's goals? Have you, regardless of functional domain, thought through how to achieve stated results with the highest effectiveness, efficiency, relevancy, and sustainability (EERS)? What changes would you recommend as you complete the EERS assessment to better operate tomorrow? Again, this is the time for radical and forthright thinking and discussion. What could be the final implementation model remains several steps away.

Throughout the book, we have introduced and illustrated how a twenty-first-century company has to step away from today's best practices and historical solutions. The Web-based Information Age is enabling radical capabilities and, with them, even more radical expectations. The discussion introduced the potential of leveraged networks where many-to-many ubiquitous information is available to all and can be used in real-time, or almost real-time, instances, radically changing both expectations and available options for near-real-time response. These capabilities raise the bar concerning expected outcomes. These expectations do not result from applying more effort but rather from applying effort differently, being able to make better selections from among more available choices. The challenge is to achieve the benefits of six-sigma lean performance across the supply chain because of the new "network" of information availability and accessibility. All the above provide new degrees of freedom for achieving and maintaining operational excellence. The fundamental key is leadership that can see the new resources available and is willing to apply them differently, in some cases by different teams with different skills, decision making, accountability, and rewards.

Do you dare to "open the kimono" to others inside your company and its trading partners, thereby allowing your combined teams to analytically dream how the world could be and how you jointly could perform better in it? Such trust was rare in twentieth-century organizations. Can you see how a better solution could improve attainable outcomes in terms of consumer satisfaction? Does the information gathered and earlier conversations concerning leveraged networks providing real-time responses between trading partners ratchet up expected operational excellence? Do you see that providing more choices through harnessed flexibility, agility, capacity at more competitive costs, and faster time to market results in real value for your consumer?

While the above series of questions and related discussions might sound more like a flight of stairs versus a step toward the new frontier, significant results can be achieved a step at a time. As noted repeatedly, a transformation is, in reality, a continuous journey. Experience has shown that such fundamental change requires new bonds of trust and extensive understanding concerning how culture needs to be both humanly exercised and humanly enhanced. All of the above constitutes a multiyear "fitness" program. The challenge is to get started today, with the promise and a growing understanding of facts necessary to achieve increasingly improved performance and higher customer sustainability tomorrow! The creation and maintenance of a responsive supply chain business model could be thought of as the outcome of many good decisions taken within and across companies. This discussion has focused almost entirely on what you could start to think about and take action on in your organization today to start moving you, your team, and maybe your company into the new frontier of the twenty-first century. We hope it sparks possibilities and pathways to initiate whatever changes you need to make in yourself to stimulate your team to begin to develop an initial definition and implementation plan to take the first steps toward a responsive supply chain business model.

Whether you are running the company, a division, or a department really makes little or no difference. All areas of a business must adapt to digital transformation and all it will affect over time. Armed with the six essential conditions for achieving meaningful change (Figure P-1), you and your team can initiate and sustain the transformation journey. You will also be better prepared to extend your thinking to your key trading partners who support you and the customers you serve.

John F. Kennedy once said, "Change is the law of life. And those who look only to the past or present are certain to miss the future." We hope that this book provided you with the sparks to think more openly about your future and the direction and steps to start that journey.

Appendix
Supply Chain Fundamentals

A formal definition of supply chain management is "when a firm's management implements a strategic initiative to align suppliers and distributors into collaborative relationships to gain and sustain competitive advantage."[1] Thus, supply chain is a collaborative operating strategy. It follows that two otherwise competitive firms can be expected to design and implement significantly different supply chain functionality and unique structural arrangements to achieve their operational goal of gaining and retaining competitive advantage. The creativity of supply chain management is found in the design and implementation of a distinctive strategy.

In one sense, the concept of a supply chain is relatively easy to illustrate by use of a linear structural diagram. Figure A-1, on the following page, structures a set of relationships being managed by a hypothetical manufacturing firm, stretching from the source of raw materials and concluding at the destination of product/service consumers.

This diagram was originally developed to describe the structure and scope of the Supply Chain Management Program at Michigan State University. The overall supply chain is illustrated by a set of business relations extending from a firm's supply base to its consumers.

The three primary supply chain participants are illustrated in a linear manner. Across a supply chain, enterprises are linked by two

---

[1] Bowersox, Closs, and Cooper, op. cit., p. 4.

flows, or dynamic processes, namely, information exchange and logistics. These two flows are multidirectional in the sense that they move both forward and backward across the supply chain. In the case of information exchange, such multidirectional flow reflects the willing exchange of information between collaborating firms, ranging from transactional status to strategic content. The logistics flow is also multidirectional, reflecting both forward and reverse physical asset movement. In total, the model presents a comprehensive picture of the collaborative framework of a responsive supply chain business model. However, it fails to capture the scope, complexity, or dynamics involved in a global digital economy.

Figure A-1   Supply Chain Diagram

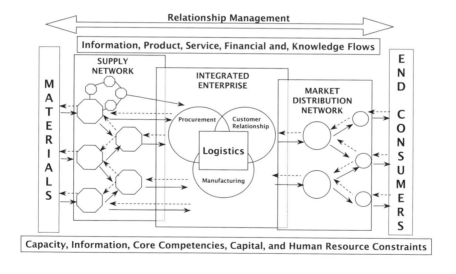

A real-world version of a supply chain is immediately complicated by the fact that multiple customers and suppliers are simultaneously engaged with many different firms and often even with competitors. One dimension of supply chain management is a commitment to integrate with each customer in a unique manner that creates as much value as possible for participating parties. The shear magnitude of engagements across a large number of customers and a vast range of suppliers requires deep understanding and a multiplicity of different integrative relationships. In other words, the supply chain can be viewed as a complex network of relationships between firms that are also typically engaged with competitors. It follows that no two firms will have even remotely similar supply chain structures. To state this reality differently, no supply chains are ever identical. While each firm may typically do business with similar customers, each supply chain has unique and distinctive DNA.

A second concern with linear, or graphic, models is a failure to adequately illustrate the unlimited range of potential supply chain engagements. No two-dimensional diagram can capture or illustrate the depth and complexity of a many-faceted networked. Information technology is increasing the potential connectivity of firms linked in supply chain arrangements.

The hallmark of supply chain operations is the integration of four traditional functional areas of operational specialization into a single customer-orientated value creation process. A closer look at the range of options available in each of the operational areas of the supply chain illustrates why no two firms, although they may compete in the same industry, will have identical supply chain structures or strategies. Each operational area is briefly discussed.

Customer Relationship Management

The tipping point of any supply chain is the interface with customers. The moment of truth occurs when a potential customer becomes an actual customer. Expectations are set, and those firms party to the transaction assume new responsibilities. For decades, the customer interface was exemplified by the personal relationship of a salesperson with the customer. This traditional one-to-one interface placed a great deal of importance on personal relationships, as opposed to business relationships. During the decades of limited information technology and relatively small customers, such reliance on the "personal factor" was understandable. However, during the last decades of the twentieth century, the selling environment radically changed. Large retailers gained unprecedented power by virtue of consumer loyalty to their store networks. Retailing giants, such as Lowe's, Target, Publix, and Kroger, are representative of the changing retail space. Large-scale retailers are masters at distributing merchandise efficiently to their retail stores or outlets. In addition, most retailers have developed and perfected methods for consumers to shop using Web-based technology supported by unique last-mile delivery systems. For example, Federated Department Stores recently constructed two new distribution centers to process consumer direct sales. Sam's Club maintains customer connectivity using Web-based technology for merchandise ordering with store pickup at appointed times. Consumers are provided exacting information concerning merchandise arrival and expedited pickup.

Suppliers are able to simultaneously flourish in such innovative direct, as well as volume-orientated, retail environments by having strong product brands and supply chain competency. They are committed to working with their retail partners in a highly collaborative manner that requires coordination of every facet of their business operations. Suddenly, almost overnight, the "sales hero" has disappeared, having been replaced by customer relationship management teams. The goal of such teams is improved promotional coordination and operational customer alignment.

Alignment is the process of integrating a firm's expectations and operations with those of its key customers. Operational alignment typically occurs at a customer's distribution center or, in some situations, at the retail store. For example, if a retailer such as Meijer plans to replenish its retail stores via a cross-dock operation, the alignment expectation for a supplier, such as Kellogg's, is precise performance of expected logistical operations. The Meijer expectation is that a trailer loaded with a desired inventory assortment and quantity will be delivered to the specified dock at the precise time for inventory sortation and combination with other suppliers' merchandise into an outbound trailer for shipment to specific retail stores. The business justification and reasoning driving the need for such operational precision is elaborated later when discussing logistical operations. At this point, it is important to understand that the relationship between the retailer, Meijer, and the manufacturer, Kellogg's, is built on precise expectations jointly developed and agreed to by each firm's management during collaborative planning. Working together, both firms have developed a shared vision of operational expectations.

Such expectations, of course, are much broader than purely the logistical transfer of freight. The entire customer relationship experience is multifaceted and encompasses all aspects of a collaborative business arrangement. In other words, a set of unique expectations exists between the managers, who represent the customer, and those who represent suppliers. Such expectations cover the full range of business variables, spanning from product content and packaging specification to promotion, price, and terms of sale. Such terms of sale include unique delivery expectations, promotional activities, and timing, payment terms, and postsales support, including repair, warranty, and, if and when required, reverse logistics.

Such holistic business arrangements require extensive collaboration between the management teams of both the retailer and the supplier. Integrative teams of specialists on both sides of the transaction jointly create and manage the relationship. In this context, the retailer (customer) and the manufacturer or wholesaler (supplier) are, in combination, best viewed as a collaborative team. To address all aspects of such an extended relationship, it is not unusual for both sides of the transaction to be represented by a cross-functional team consisting of marketing, logistics, manufacturing, finance, and whatever other specialists are deemed helpful to facilitating seamless operations. A business-to-business collaborative process has replaced what was once a price-dominated transactional structure.

Clearly, not all customers are of equal importance. One of the basic pillars of the marketing revolution of the post–World War II era was that individual customers desire a unique set of products and related services. While this is clearly true for individuals, it is also true for retailers and industrial buyers. In terms of profit potential, doing business as a key supplier to a major automotive company will most likely be more lucrative than servicing a small retailer that sells in the aftermarket. Regardless of where a firm fits in the competitive structure, it is a basic fact that not all customers offer equal profit opportunity. It follows that the specific details of the business arrangement between a supplier and different customers should each be significantly different.

Herein we find one of the most puzzling facets of business operations. More often than one might dare to believe true, firms, in their day-to-day operations, have extreme difficulty in customizing their services to meet the expectations of specific customers. While logic dictates that different customers will place different value on different dimensions of service, a typical practice among manufacturers and wholesalers is to adopt a "one-size-fits-all" approach when it comes to customizing their distribution operations and services. The result is that a firm's one-size-fits-all service will typically overservice some customers while underservicing others. Some customers receive from suppliers costly to perform value-added services on which they place little or no value. For example, when a firm plans to receive merchandise for cross-dock processing, the arrival of pallets or slip sheets containing neatly stacked and shrink-wrapped merchandise provides no value. In fact, the shrink-wrap will have to be removed and the material cleared from the working area before the merchandise cross-docking process can be performed. On the other hand, shrink-wrapping could represent a feature of major importance to a different customer who is using a warehouse-based distribution process. In short, the value of a service is in the eyes of the recipient. The challenge in a responsive supply chain business model is to master the art of matching services provided to exact customer expectations. Some customers' expectations may be more than a supplier is willing to accommodate. For example, many food retailers want manufacturers to provide inner packs within master cartons to facilitate handling of slow-moving products in less than full case quantities. For manufacturers who have highly automated factory processes such accommodation may be costly to perform. Each request needs to be fully evaluated from the perspective of both parties in the relationship. The ideal result is agreement to a precise business arrangement that eliminates either over or under servicing customers.

A cornerstone of customer relationship management is segmentation. Understanding that all customers are not created equal—and then doing something about it—is at the heart of strategy. A firm engaged in marketing should be viewed as having a portfolio of competencies. The exact mixture of these competencies important to customers will vary depending upon the type of business and the operational role of each firm in the supply chain. For example, the competencies of a retailer, manufacturer, and third-party logistics service firm are all different. Likewise, the competencies enjoyed by different retailers, manufacturers, and logistics service companies are vastly different. The goal of customer relationship management is to define, dimension, and operationalize how collaborative engagements are structured and implemented. Such important collaboration requires a much larger representation of management than typically found solely in sales or marketing.

Manufacturing

Manufacturing represents work that results in tangible value, such as a product, material, component, or service. During the manufacturing process, raw materials are forged, fitted, cooked, and otherwise processed into unique and useful products. Some products are for immediate consumption. Other products, such as tires, wheels, and so forth, are components or parts that later will be assembled into finished goods as the overall manufacturing mission is completed. The lessons learned from the Industrial Revolution remain firmly entrenched throughout contemporary society as a result of the culture and best practice that dominated the twentieth century. However, for better or worse, the twentieth century is gone. Today's manufacturing competency and expectations are focused on responsiveness, postponement, customization, and agility. Traditional operating concerns related to the scale and scope economies of manufacturing are being augmented with flexibility and changeover speed. Once honored like the "holy grail" of manufacturing, the principles of mass manufacturing are being rewritten by the emerging technologies of flexibility. While manufacturing productivity is achieving record outputs, fewer workers in the industrialized economies are employed in manufacturing. Today, explosive growth in manufacturing is occurring throughout the world. Twenty-first-century manufacturing is increasingly becoming global.

The traditional perception is that manufacturing is a process that takes place in a factory and is characterized by employees who work on assembly lines or on a shop floor. In a broader context, manufacturing can be viewed as any process that creates form value. In other words, anything that creates an assortment of products or components that increases customer value is appropriately a form of manufacturing. In this context, retailers complete a manufacturing process when they create an assortment of related products for consumer purchase. Likewise, warehouse product selection results in a precise assortment of merchandise to meet a specific customer's expectation. In this sense, one could say that the warehouse order selection process is the manufacturing of a unique assortment of products and quantities. In fact, many warehouses are designed to perform a wide variety of value-added services (VASs) in an effort to customize their product assortments and features to exact customer specifications. One could argue that manufacturing is a significant part of any activity that creates unique value. In this context, insurance companies, advertising agencies, and even traveling ice shows are engaged in the value creation process. In the twenty-first century, managers are beginning to understand that the form or physical characteristics of a value creation process occur at many different locations and in many different formats throughout the supply chain. Manufacturing strategies require more in-depth understanding.

Over the years, three traditional manufacturing strategies have been perfected. They are (1) make to plan (MTP), (2) make to order (MTO), and (3) assemble to order (ATO). The traditional difference among the three is the length of time required to complete a cycle of work and the degree of product customization to meet customer expectations.

The traditional manufacturing process developed and perfected over decades, following and implementing the lessons learned from the Industrial Revolution, was MTP. The goal of a MTP strategy was to achieve the lowest cost of manufacturing by creating a process capable of achieving and maintaining maximum economy of scale. The plan specified what and when specific products would be manufactured. In order to capture lowest cost of manufacturing or assembly, the plan was designed to achieve economy of scale. When a manufacturing process achieves scale, product output is accomplished at the lowest possible total cost of manufacturing or assembly. Thus, MTP typically builds inventory in anticipation of future sale.

The MTP process typically starts with a forecast of product requirements. Once forecasted requirements are dimensioned in terms of time, place, and quantity, a master production schedule (MPS) is created. The MPS serves to identify what is to be manufactured and when it will happen. On the basis of the MPS, a bill, or schedule, of materials (BOM) is created that specifies what components and materials will be needed when and where to accomplish the planned manufacturing. The BOM is created for hand off to purchasing. Simply put, the MTP manufacturing process seeks the most economical use of constrained and limited manufacturing capacity. Naturally, the MTP process is dominated by planned capacity utilization and is therefore not typically flexible. The process seeks maximum value by achieving the lowest total cost of manufacturing. The risk related to MTP is that it typically creates inventory in anticipation of future sale. The MTP process can be only as good as the forecast—and forecasts traditionally have not been very accurate. However, the cost advantage of manufacturing at scale is viewed in MTP as providing sufficient economies to offset the costs associated with maintaining inventory.

The MTO manufacturing strategy is at the opposite end of the process continuum. As compared with building to forecast, MTO as a strategy waits until an order is in hand and then completes the manufacturing process to exacting customer specification. Most MTO manufacturers maintain a stock of commonly used materials and parts in anticipation of customer orders. The maintenance of material and parts inventory reduces the manufacturing response time once a customer order is received. Several different variations of MTO exist. At one extreme, when a product is highly customized, it may be necessary to complete engineering drawings and develop new and unique solutions before the actual manufacturing can commence. At the other extreme, a specific order customization may be limited to cosmetic features such as accessory selection or color combinations. The good news concerning MTO is that finished inventory is eliminated. The bad news of MTO is longer waiting or lead time for customer availability and potential loss of manufacturing economy of scale.

ATO combines features of both MTP and MTO. When an ATO manufacturing strategy is followed, key components of finished products are manufactured in anticipation of future assembly into products commonly purchased by customers. Anticipatory component manufacturing creates the flexibility to rapidly shift final assembly activity to accommodate specific customer requirements. While ATO reduces risk related to final product inventory, it involves substantial risk in terms of speculative procurement of materials and advanced manufacturing of key components.

The primary differences among the three traditional manufacturing processes are time and risk. Proponents of each strategy place different degrees of importance on how fast a customer can be serviced with standard versus customized products. For decades, consumer durable industries such as automotive and appliances have debated the relative cost, benefit, and risk of a MTO versus a MTP strategy. The time difference of a consumer purchasing a car from stock versus customizing a to-order car can involve several months of waiting for delivery. The best-in-class firms have trouble sustaining the construction and delivery of a customized car in much less than a month. The resolution of manufacturing strategy lies at the root of current deep purchase incentives to buy cars already in stock at dealers or within the supply chain. Information technology, however, is shifting manufacturing strategy.

Emphasis in contemporary manufacturing planning is focused on three main initiatives. The first, lean manufacturing, focuses on new techniques to reduce all costs associated with the manufacturing process. Modeled initially after the Toyota manufacturing system, lean seeks to reduce waste in materials and labor to a minimum by arranging how the work process is planned and executed. Lean manufacturing challenges the traditional commitment to linear manufacturing by placing a premium on balanced resource deployment.

The second major thrust in contemporary manufacturing is adoption of a six-sigma mentality. For decades, emphasis has focused on total manufacturing quality in an effort to reduce waste created by reworks and product lot rejections. The rigor of six sigma is that errors in process must be reduced to a near-zero level. The actual concept of "sigma" is a statistical measure that identifies the probability of, or the frequency of, a specific outcome occurring, given a wide range of outcome experiences. At the six-sigma level of achievement, the error rate would be 3.4 defects per million, or 99.99966 percent perfect. Needless to say, few fully achieve six-sigma excellence. The significant point is the shift in mentality involved. In place of accepting a given high error rate, a six-sigma-based quality initiative is focused on continuous improvement.

A third contemporary goal in world-class manufacturing is flexibility. Extensive analysis is undertaken when planning a manufacturing strategy to identify a profitable balance between scale of effort and speed of customer accommodation. Of course, the answer to identifying the proper or best balance is unique to each individual company and its specific customer supply chain engagements. The concept of flexible manufacturing introduces scope economy as a consideration in manufacturing planning and design. The operative questions become those of how fast a specific manufacturing process can be switched or changed to a different process and what the associated loss in scale economy will be. Inherent in flexible manufacturing is the concept of modularity. In manufacturing design, modular assembly units that can accomplish varied processes in different sequences become the key to flexibility. Thus, flexible manufacturing rests on two fundamental attributes. The first attribute is speed of changeover from one manufacturing process to another. The second attribute is the scope of capability of a specific process to accomplish multiple, but variable, work tasks.

Manufacturing has been among the most important business capabilities for more than 100 years. As such, the doctrines of manufacturing have been perfected to the point that they have become aligned with accepted principles of finance and cost accounting. Most firms can measure manufacturing efficiency to the fraction of a cent and are very sensitive to small variations of actual cost and operations to plan. However, this functional strength is also manufacturing's Achilles' heal. The broader doctrines of the responsive supply chain business model are focused on the total cost to serve a customer. Manufacturing cost is only one part of the total cost equation. The total cost of product delivery to customers is often significantly larger than the total manufacturing cost.

Procurement

In the broadest context, often referred to as supply management, procurement is concerned with the total spend of an enterprise to support business operations. Total spend consists of all direct and indirect purchase of products and services. The actual work of purchasing consists of the "organization and alignment of a supply base to assure continuous business operations supported by achieving lowest total cost of materials, supplies and service ownership or engagement."[2] Most firms have a substantial annual spend. How that spend is managed is key to gaining and maintaining competitive superiority. In many ways, the operating missions and responsibilities of procurement and customer relationship management (CRM) are analogous. They both focus on managing collaborative relationships. Some go as far as calling the procurement efforts of business the process of supplier relationship management (SRM). Whereas CRM seeks improved results by collaboratively working with customers, SRM seeks the same synergic results with suppliers. It is clear that the traditional notion of buying at the lowest price is significantly expanded in sophistication and strategic importance in the responsive supply chain business model. Least cost procurement has been sophisticated into value management in modern business. The development of an effective procurement organization requires an in-depth understanding of the strategic importance of procurement, a process for rapidly completing make versus buy analysis, and a sustainable process of value management. Each is briefly discussed.

A simplistic description of strategic purchasing is the process of buying at the lowest total landed cost. While such low-cost procurement is and always will be important, it is only one facet of strategic

---

[2]   Robert Monczka, Robert Trent, and Robert Handfield, *Purchasing and Supply Management* (Mason, OH: Thomson South Western, 2005).

procurement. The overall responsibility of the supply management mission requires several important initiatives. First and foremost is continuous quality improvement. A final product is seldom better than the composite of its components. The goal is to identify continuous quality improvement while maintaining or reducing component cost. However, cost control and reduction are not limited to the purchase price of a component or part. Operating costs are directly related to procurement lead time in terms of duration and operational consistency. A low-cost component or material supplier that fails to provide dependable delivery, thereby requiring expensive expediting and premium transportation of essential components or materials, falls short of being a total low-cost provider. Likewise, material markets are not always in abundant supply. Procurement organizations must establish the contacts, relationships, and contracts to assure continuity of supply when shortages develop. Finally, organizations traditionally look to their suppliers to identify new technology and opportunities for final product innovation. For example, it is widely acknowledged that most innovations in the automotive and aircraft industries were pioneered by suppliers. Thus, supply management involves much more than simply buying things.

As one might expect, the decision to purchase a component or a service, as opposed to making it or performing it by using a firm's internal personnel and equipment, is a major decision. Some items, such as basic commodities, highly processed composite materials, energy, and so forth, must be purchased from outside sources. Other things traditionally made within an organization have become prime candidates for outsourcing. Surprisingly, such basic activities as data processing, transportation and warehousing, and human resource management, once performed internally by most firms, have become leading outsourced activities. Considerable time and attention have been devoted to the make versus buy decision. Figure A-2 provides a summary of an eight-step process for deciding whether a specific product or service is a candidate to be outsourced. As one can see, the decision to outsource should be well planned and executed. Managing the outsourcing process is typically a supply management responsibility.

Figure A-2   Make Versus Buy: An Eight-Step Process

- Position Product/Service Relative to Core Competency
- Evaluate Suitability for Outsourcing
- Quantify Benefits of Outsourcing
- Evaluate Qualitative Factors
- Access Current and Identify Potential New Suppliers
- Evaluate New Suppliers as Necessary
- Source
- Monitor and Modify

A final responsibility of procurement is sustainable value management. Of course, value has been a significant part of the procurement initiatives discussed thus far. However, as a basic philosophy, value management engages all suppliers of an organization in a collaborative effort to reduce complexity, stimulate innovative product design, and reduce total cost of ownership. Many firms maintain an active supplier council to facilitate collaboration and the exchange of innovative ideas that require cross-enterprise synergy to effectively implement.

Similar to customer relationship management and manufacturing, procurement offers a highly defined body of knowledge. This knowledge has developed and expanded during years of focused attention concerning how value and quality are improved.

Logistics

The fourth area of the responsive supply chain business model is logistics. Similar to the areas discussed above, logistics is a critical operational component of any supply chain. Logistics is defined as the process of moving and positioning inventory to meet customer requirements at the lowest possible total cost.[3] In an operational context, logistics is responsible for timely positioning of raw materials, work in process (WIP), and finished inventory. Thus, the term "customer," in the context used in logistics, means any specified delivery location. For the management of a twenty-first-century enterprise, logistical responsibility equates to positioning, controlling, and directing all types of inventory as it flows in a domestic or global context. Typically included in the logistical structure of such enterprises are the traditional functional areas of order management, transportation, inventory, warehousing, and material handling. These five dimensions of logistical performance are integrated in an operating system and a facility network design. Included within these primary areas are important strategic and tactical matters such as protective packaging, building and material handling design, facility location, and network design, as well as reverse movement related to product warranty, recall, and disposal (commonly called reverse logistics).

Prior to the 1950s, most of the activities included in logistics were managerially dispersed throughout a typical organization in a manner that facilitated integration with the most closely affiliated activity. For example, transportation was typically part of the manufacturing organization. Warehousing was typically split between manufacturing and sales. Warehouses close to plants were considered part of manufacturing. Field or forward warehouses holding finished goods

---

[3]   Bowersox et. al., *Supply Chain Logistics Management*, p. 22.

inventory were typically a part of the sales and marketing organization structure. Inventory belonged to everyone, with the financial organization having a very deep interest. As management gained awareness of the opportunity for cost reduction and improved enterprise-wide performance, such fragmented management gave way to integration of the logistical process. Most firms learned that the lowest cost of transportation typically didn't equate to the least total cost of serving a customer once all associated costs were factored in and fully measured. Senior leadership became acutely aware that the logistics of business was indeed big business.

Figure A-3 provides a relational diagram of a high-level integrated logistics structure. The emphasis is on integrated process management, with two goals in mind: first, the provision of a desired level of timely inventory delivery to both external and internal customers and, second, the consistent achievement of the desired service level at the lowest total cost.

Figure A-3   Logistics Operating Structure

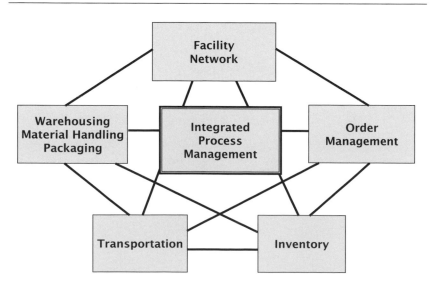

In Chapter One, the fact that 2008 global logistics expenditures are projected to exceed $8 billion was discussed to illustrate just how many resources are being devoted to moving products and materials throughout the world to the right place at the right time. Statistics are not available to fully dimension global logistics cost. However, data are available to detail just what is and has been happening in the United States. Figure A-4 provides a recap of what U.S. business was spending for logistics in 1980, the year that transportation was deregulated. A comparison is presented with the most recent year (2006) for which data are available.

While Figure A-4 presents a variety of interesting comparisons, the alert reader will observe that logistics expenditure in 1980 represented 16.1 percent of GDP. That expenditure was close to what the U.S. population was expending on health care in 1980. Looking to 2006, logistics expenditure was reported as $1.305 trillion, or an

Figure A-4   The Logistics of Business is Big Business

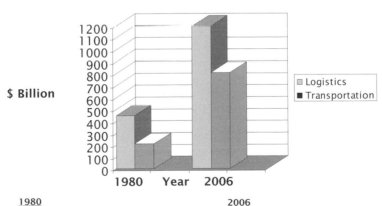

1980
· GDP $2.80 trillion
    –Logistics Cost $451 billion
· 16.1% of GDP
    –Transportation Cost $214 billion
· 47.5% of Logistics Cost

2006
· GDP $13.18 trillion
    –Logistics Cost $1.305 trillion
· 9.9% of GDP
    –Transportation Cost $809 billion
· 61.9% of Logistics Cost

Source: The Council of Supply Chain Management Professionals "18th Annual State of Logistics Report®" June 6, 2007

amount equal to 9.9 percent of GDP.[4] These data make an interesting statement. Health care and logistics expenditures in the United States were about equal in 1980. In 2006, logistics expenditures represented 9.9 percent of GDP, whereas health care costs were estimated to exceed 20 percent of 2006 GDP.

An important comparison presented in Figure A-4 is transportation expenditure as a percent of total logistics cost between 1980 and 2006. In 1980 transportation represented 47.5 percent of each dollar expended on logistics. In 2007, the percent was 61.9. These data serve to illustrate the transformation that has taken place in the management of logistics. Within an environment of increasing efficiency (lower cost as a percent of GDP) the balance of logistics cost has shifted away from inventory toward transportation. This shift reflects the logistical integration progress as cost moved from risky inventory to more flexible and timely transportation. During this time period, new forms of package transportation, such as UPS, FedEx, and DHL, became common participants in corporate logistics.

A few short decades ago, "logistics" was not a mainstream business term. Logistics was reserved for military use and viewed as being concerned with the art and science of supporting troops. During the last four decades of the twentieth century, business turned to logistics because it offered a framework to integrate operational activities directly related to positioning and moving inventory from suppliers, within an enterprise, and to downstream customers. By treating the composite of activities related to logistics in an integrated manner, cost-to-cost and cost-to-service trade-offs could be quantified and better managed.

---

[4]   Wilson, op. cit.

Concluding Statement

Individual discussion of each supply chain operating area runs the danger of positioning them as isolated, siloed, or functional, as compared to orchestrated, parts of an integrated process. In fact, integration across the supply chain, driven by customer and supplier collaboration, represents the operational vortex of the responsive supply chain business model.

Index